ALBERTA
HUNTER

ALBERTA HUNTER

A Celebration in Blues

FRANK C. TAYLOR
with Gerald Cook

McGRAW-HILL BOOK COMPANY

New York   St. Louis   San Francisco
Toronto   Hamburg   Mexico

First McGraw-Hill paperback edition, 1988.

1 2 3 4 5 6 7 8 9 S E M S E M 8 9 0 9 8

ISBN 0-07-063172-7

LIBRARY OF CONGRESS CATALOGING-IN-PUBLICATION DATA

Taylor, Frank C.
    Alberta Hunter : a celebration in blues.
    1. Hunter, Alberta.   2. Singers—United States—
Biography.   I. Cook, Gerald.   II. Title.
ML420.H948T4 1986   784.5'3'00924 [B]   86-21294
ISBN 0-07-063172-7

BOOK DESIGN BY KATHRYN PARISE

ACKNOWLEDGMENTS

Heartfelt thanks to the following people who helped me understand the life and appreciate the joy of Alberta Hunter: Chris Albertson, Robert Altman, Jean Claude Baker, Mae Barnes, Barbara Bordnick, Charlie Bourgeois, Gene Brame, Vinie Burrows, Louis ("Louie the Greek") Calamaras, Dick Campbell, Leonard ("Baby Doo") Caston, Cesar and Sueli Castanho, Dorothy Clark, Eddie Coleman, Marion Cooper, Edward Cornelius, Chris Ellis, Howard Garrison, Stuart A. Goldman, Adelaide Hall, John Hammond, Wyer Handy, Mikie Harris, Johnny Hudgins, Revella Hughes, Delilah Jackson, Eve Jackson, Caterina Jarboro, Max Jones, Barney Josephson, Fred Koester, Bill Krasilovsky, Mae Gaddy Lanier, Rosetta Le Noire, Max Lerner, Mildred Crisp Littles, Mollie Moon, Mrs. Herman E. Moore, Alan Rudolph, Pauline Reed, Maude Russell Rutherford, Sam Sharp, Jr., Bobby Short, Hatcher Story, Francis ("Doll") Thomas, Leslie Thompson, U. S. ("Kid") Thompson, Flo Thornley, Phyllis Utz, Harry Watkins, Ruthie Watts, Margot Webb, Margaret Weeks, Elizabeth Welch, Dorothy West, and Dorothy Mabin Young;

to the dedicated staffs who generously answered all my questions at: the Institute of Jazz Studies at Rutgers University, the Memphis Room of the Memphis Public Library, the American Society of Composers, Authors and Publishers, the American Federation of Musicians, and the New York City Public Library's music and theater collections at Lincoln Center, its Schomburg Center for Research in Black Culture in Harlem, and its telephone reference section;

to Michael Carlisle, my agent, and to Leslie Meredith and Lisa Frost, my editors, for their guidance, enthusiasm, and good taste;

to Gerald Cook for his elegance, talent, mind, and heart;

to my great friend and former wife Dr. Patricia Taylor-Edmisten for her thoughtful comments on the manuscript, and to our son, Damian, my source of inspiration and pride;

to all my friends in the United States and Brazil who told me I should write a book and then put up with me while I did it;

and especially . . .

To Francisca,
who made the corn bread!

Contents

Come on up . . . my castle's rockin' . . .

INTRODUCTION

Gerald Cook called me in October 1983 in São Paulo, where I was working as a journalist. Sue Willis, an actress in New York and a mutual friend, had suggested he look me up in Brazil when he accompanied Alberta Hunter there to perform.

"Mr. Cooky is on the phone," said my lovable housekeeper, Francisca da Silva Santos, who, like all Brazilians, puts a *y* on words ending in *c* and *k* when pronouncing them.

"Mr. Cooky" sounded charming. He was. We became friends right away. My only disappointment with him was that he didn't introduce me immediately to Alberta in spite of the fact I went almost every night to see their show at the 150 Club at the Maksoud Plaza Hotel.

Alberta was terribly frail, and Gerald was simply protecting her health by keeping everyone he could away from her. I sent her flowers and several notes telling her how much I enjoyed her performances. On one of the cards I told her I had followed the advice she gave all her "children" in the audience: "Call your parents." I called my mother in the States about 3:00 A.M. (Alberta's shows didn't start until after midnight!) and said I was calling because Alberta told me to.

"Well, bless her sweet heart," my mother said, once she was over the shock of an overseas call at that hour.

I'd been infatuated with Alberta ever since I'd tried to get out of a blistery snowstorm one night in 1978 in New York by ducking into a little place in Greenwich Village called The Cookery. The place was jammed. A dreadnought of a doorman assured me not one more person would fit in the place.

I paused for a freezing minute and peered through the glass door over his shoulder. A little old lady, clad in a simple blue dress, was preaching a blues song. With one hand she slapped her hip as if it were a tambourine; with the other, her long fingernails lacquered with Elizabeth Arden's Red Door Red, she pecked electrically at the air around her. Every part of her was in motion, from her eyebrows, which punctuated risqué lyrics, to her gold earrings, the size and shape of doughnuts, which dangled and swayed with her sassy beat.

People of all ages in the audience shared an expression of enchantment as they watched Alberta Hunter, a person whose name I had never heard before.

I came back several times and got in with the help of reservations made far in advance. I was entranced. She made me feel happy to be alive. Never did I imagine that I'd get to know intimately the most unforgettable woman and performer I've ever seen in my life.

As it turned out, it was difficult even to meet her. Gerald called one day during their first stay in São Paulo and was noticeably perturbed by Alberta's latest demand. She was in the mood for corn bread, and that meant she wanted it right away. Corn bread wasn't on the menu at their hotel, one of the poshest in South America. In fact, no one there had ever heard of it.

It dawned on me, a southerner who loves corn bread, that I had never seen it in Brazil in all the fourteen years I had lived there. I asked Francisca. She knew everything.

"Of course," she said. "It's called *bolo de fubá*." By that time Gerald had been to my apartment several times and had wisely and warmly praised Francisca's cooking. Even though he and Francisca understood little more than the lovely feelings they each put behind the words of their different languages when talking to each other, they gave each other the Brazilian hug, or *abraço*, and kiss on each cheek each time they met. So any problem Gerald had was Francisca's problem. Also, she had seen Alberta on television and was smitten by Alberta's age, spunkiness, color, and charisma.

Francisca offered to make the corn bread on the condition that she get to deliver it personally to Alberta. Gerald, ever polite and desperate, agreed.

It took twenty-four hours for Francisca to select the right dress to wear, do her hair, and make the corn bread. She made an enormous pan of the stuff and covered it with a starched linen cloth, tucked in at the corners with rosebuds. With her two arms outstretched under the tray, she marched into the luxurious hotel lobby like one of the Magi carrying a gift to the Baby Jesus. I walked behind her respectfully, recognizing that it was she who was getting me in to see Alberta offstage for the first time.

At their meeting Alberta let Francisca hug her, something she allowed no one to do. Francisca cried and praised the Lord that He had put her in Alberta's arms. I translated.

Alberta stashed the corn bread away so that she could have it all to herself. However, she discovered later that it was made with sugar (Brazilian style) rather than with salt (southern style). Thankfully Alberta was always one to appreciate a sincere gesture.

She set me straight, telling me not to call her Miss Hunter. "Call me Alberta, honey. I'm no prima donna." More important, she told Gerald he was to bring me around more often.

I did see Alberta privately a few more times during that tour and during her second one to São Paulo in May 1984. I never tired of going to her performances. She might vary only one or two songs each night, but each show seemed totally fresh.

Alberta obviously throve under the spotlight. The lights of the 150 Club were turned low at the time of her entrance. She came part of the way to the stage in a wheelchair. The few cautious steps she took up to the piano were guarded and braced by Gerald and Cesar Castanho, the Brazilian producer of the show. The audience wondered how she would ever be able to stand up, as she insisted on doing, much less get through an hourlong performance.

But when the spotlight clicked on, Alberta stood strong and bold and ready to do as she promised: "I'm gonna lay it on you." Her metamorphosis was magic. She sang, winked, cackled, giggled, squeaked, wriggled, yelped, and squealed. She was raucous one moment, reverent the next. She rocked, she rolled, she roared, and she romped. At eighty-nine she was having the time of her life, all the more so because her Brazilian audiences turned themselves inside out for her. They had never seen anyone like her.

Wherever she went, Alberta teased the press and public with tidbits of information about her life. From a background of poverty, discrimination, and little formal education, she propelled herself in the 1910s and 1920s to the top of the entertainment world, performing at Chicago's Dreamland Café, on Broadway, at the Drury Lane in London, and in sophisticated cabarets from Cairo to Copenhagen. She wrote at least seventy songs, one of which—"Down Hearted Blues"—made Bessie Smith famous in 1923. She herself was a recording star for decades and traveled the world, entertaining U.S. troops. Then, in the 1950s, unable to find singing jobs and saddened by her mother's death, she lied about her age, "jived" the director of a YWCA training program in Harlem to let her study to be a licensed practical nurse, and went to work for twenty years at Goldwater Hospital in New York City. Alberta was enraged in 1977 when they made her retire at the hospital. They thought she was seventy. In fact, she was eighty-two. Months later she was rediscovered. She went back to singing and became an overnight sensation. She achieved her glory the night she sang at the White House for "her" president, Jimmy Carter.

The story was intriguing, but I knew there had to be a lot of grit between the glamorous lines. I asked Gerald to tell Alberta how much I wanted to write her biography. She must have remembered the corn bread because she said, without hesitation, "C'mon, baby."

I moved back to New York even before the end of her engagement in Brazil and went to work researching the life of this incredible woman. In between her concerts in the United States that summer I sat on the floor of her Roosevelt Island apartment, surrounded by boxes and grocery bags filled with photos, theater programs, correspondence, and scraps of paper she had saved over her long life. With a tape recorder running, she and I chatted for hours on end. We had almost five months together before she died.

She never spoke much about any one event or person, and her speech often had a staccato beat, like her blues songs, usually five to seven words to a line. For instance, when Alberta said how happy she was that neighborhood girls had stolen her childhood boyfriends, she said:

> *Oh, Lord. God is good!*
> *They got the marriage,*
> *And I got the fame.*

Fewer words would do if she wanted to reject an incorrect interpretation of mine of some detail in her life. Then all she said typically was "No, baby," with the *no* stretched out for emphasis.

I was overwhelmed by her memory of places, dates, addresses, and people.

Sometimes, though, I doubted the veracity of her stories, like the one describing the dead man standing up inside the door of a funeral parlor in Memphis at the turn of the century. I chuckled when I found proof, as I often did, in an old book that the dead man (a mummy) was really there, as she said, "deader than a doornail."

At times she knowingly mixed up details of her past simply because she had always done it that way and didn't want to confuse anyone, least of all herself, by changing the story. She simply didn't remember other moments in her life that obviously had little importance to her, like the dates of the few weeks of her only marriage.

The really important facts of her life were in all her boxes and bags. Alberta hadn't saved them because she felt she was worthy of a place in history. She'd saved them simply because she wanted people to believe she had done what she had.

She'd tell me often, "That's the truth. I've got it written down," or "I've got the photos to prove it."

After all, Alberta grew up without much nurturing of her sense of self-worth. There was no daddy to tell her to dream and to believe her dreams would come true. Her mother favored Alberta's older sister; whites made her come to their back doors; her stepfather beat up her mother and despised her; a school principal molested her; uppity, lighter-skinned blacks kept her at a distance. Then, in the early days of her performing, other singers made fun of the way she sang; some people in the record business cheated her of royalties, and American vaudeville theaters denied her top billing. Only by going to Europe in the early decades of this century could she and most black entertainers be treated with respect. In later years the U.S. Army made her eat in kitchens or go without food. By the mid-1950s club owners wouldn't hire her because they thought she was out of style.

It wasn't until her comeback in 1977 that the white press in this country recognized Alberta as the talented performer she had always been. Suddenly it dubbed her "a national treasure."

"Better late than never," said Francis ("Doll") Thomas, electrician at the Lafayette Theater in the 1920s who knew her then. "But it's still sad. A lot happens to a person in sixty years."

A lot happened to Alberta, but it was usually disappointment, not bitterness, that she expressed about it all. The only person she went out of her way to get even with was her sister when they were still kids. The rest of the people who tried to put her down would get theirs. "You reap just what you sow" was a favorite saying of hers.

Alberta held her head high throughout her life. She was proud of her accomplishments, given the obstacles she had to overcome. She was an optimist. And she was a survivor.

She expressed those instincts in one of the last songs she wrote (in 1977), the title song for the film *Remember My Name*:

> *I've been sloughed way down, but*
> *I'll slow drag up again.*
> *When that big day arrives*
> *Remember my name.*

Alberta was determined that this book would also help preserve the memory of the names of many other black entertainers. Even days before she died, when she was very weak, she would suddenly interrupt herself to tell me to write down the name of someone else. "Baby, you have to mention him," she would say.

I asked her why some of their names should appear in a book about her if they weren't close friends of hers. It was because they were entertainers, great ones in her mind, who had shared some of her eighty-nine years of struggle to live dignified lives, onstage and off. Some of those very performers refused to comment on her after her death. I don't think that would have really mattered to her. She would have rationalized that the frustration or difficulties in their lives made them less generous with her than she was with them.

I was even more impressed with Alberta's kindness toward complete strangers, poor people she'd meet on the street or on a bus or read about in the newspaper. She liked helping those less fortunate than herself, but she did it with a low profile, partly to keep from embarrassing those she assisted.

She also wanted to protect her privacy, while she respected the privacy of others. In the front of one of her little notebooks from the 1930s she wrote the following "daily prayer": "Oh, Lord, please help me to keep my nose out of other people's business. Amen!" She took care of keeping others' noses out of her business.

Alberta was very tolerant. She didn't judge others by what they did or by their economic or social status. She did like to be around people who were more educated than she so she could learn from them. But she was also very fond of many of the gangsters, pimps, and prostitutes she'd met in her early days in Chicago. She was always grateful for the help they gave her, and she told them so, even late in her life. What she insisted on before she gave her friendship to people was that they be gentlemen and ladies. She detested coarseness in demeanor and language.

And she had no patience with lazy people or those who had given up on living. Even after breaking her hip and wrist at age eighty-five, she was back up on her feet in record time, saying, "There're plenty of good tunes left in an old violin."

She believed people, no matter what backgrounds, no matter what ages, could do whatever they wanted if they were patient, took their time, worked hard, and believed in themselves. If you followed that recipe, she said, "You can't miss. Look at me. Oh, Lord, have mercy, I sleep like a dog."

Alberta worked hard with me on this book because, as she said, she thought her life would serve as an example and help people who were becoming discouraged.

People of all ages did look to Alberta. Many of them wrote to her, saying they had never written fan letters before but had to tell her that they were lacking courage, motivation, or faith in their lives until they saw or heard her perform.

Weslia Whitfield, a singer formerly with the San Francisco Opera, was one of many. She wrote Alberta saying she was still paralyzed two years after being shot by a youngster. "People want me to come back to singing, but I was afraid," she told Alberta. "Then one day I heard you on KJAZ in San Francisco. Decided 31 was too early to give up—so I'm singing again—thanks to you."

Alberta saved each letter, card, piece of paper, napkin, and handkerchief on which fans wrote her adoring words. Nothing meant more to her than knowing that she had put smiles on their faces and in their lives.

One of those notes, unsigned, speaks for them all: "Alberta Hunter, you've enriched and tantalized and exhilarated me. Thank you for your energy, your vision, and your spirit of life. I will hold you again."

Yes, thank you, Alberta.

P.S. I hope, for their sake and yours, Alberta, that they have the right kind of corn bread in heaven.

CHAPTER ONE

Messing Around and Biding Her Time

The minute the smart-looking horse and buggy started kicking up dirt as it entered High Street everyone on the block of clapboard houses, most of which hovered above rickety piles of brick like sandpipers on their spindly legs, knew that Laura Hunter was about to give birth. The gentleman cracking the reins was Dr. Albert S. J. Burchett, a young physician who had his office on South Main Street, a prosperous address in black Memphis. His high white collar was a pedestal for his elegantly chiseled mulatto face. He appreciated the admiring looks his presence always caused but didn't dally in arriving at 288½, home of Charles E. Hunter.

Hunter was a sleeping car porter, the most prestigious job open to black men in those days outside of the professions. In other words, he had been what was called a goldfish, a good catch, for his twenty-two-year-old wife, Laura. Only the best doctor of their race would do to deliver their second child on this first day of April 1895.

They named the baby Alberta in honor of the good doctor, hoping his prominence would augur well for her future.

By the next afternoon Hunter was packing his grip to go work the night train to Chicago. Miss Laura lingered a bit over the white newspaper, the *Commercial Appeal*. Because they were living with her mother and father, Nancy and Henry Peterson, she had the luxury of resting another day before getting up from bed. The newspaper was the only treat she insisted on every day. It took the place of the schooling she never had.

She read that on the day she gave birth trainloads of spirited Germans went to Friedrichsruhe to celebrate the eightieth birthday of Prince Otto von Bismarck. In Washington, D.C., a sixty-five-year-old man with "gewgaws" all over his coat and hat lugged a heavy bag to the portico of the White House about the time President Grover Cleveland was finishing his coffee. He offered to sell pieces of glass and tin for the current price of gold. A paddy wagon from the local precinct swiftly removed William Lavery along with his commodities.

And six miles north of Magnolia, Mississippi, sixteen-year-old Eugenia Hart slid into the Tangipahoa River and let the weight of her troubled world sink her slight body into the muddy bottom. She scribbled one word on a scrap of paper and stuffed it into the shoes someone found on the riverbank. "Good-by."

The newspaper failed to report that the dogwood was in bloom. That was a common occurrence, as was the birth of Alberta Hunter, just another child born to another black woman on the dusty underside of Memphis, Tennessee.

Although often away from home, Charles Hunter was a good provider for a while. Before each trip he made sure there were ample supplies of rice and beans, sugar and flour piled up in the kitchen so his family would never want for anything while he was gone. That protection ended early, however. Alberta said her father died of pneumonia before she was old enough to remember him. The *City Directory* of Memphis indicates he lived until Alberta was at least five years old but at a different address from hers. His abandoning his wife and two children was good enough reason for Miss Laura to tell her children their father was dead.

Alberta was so frail an infant that she had to be carried around on a little pillow. Her mother later told her that she had had a "stroke of paralysis" when she was very young.

She may have started out weak, but there was never anything dainty about Alberta. As soon as she learned to get up and around on her scrawny legs, she was always a mess. Miss Laura kept their house clean as a pin, but there wasn't anything she could do to keep Alberta neat. She was always so dirty that family and friends called her Pig, a name that stuck to her for the rest of her life like cold grits to a breakfast plate.

La Tosca, her older sister by two years, didn't fare much better. No one knew why she had received that name, much less her nickname, Dump.

La Tosca was tall and beautiful. With her high cheekbones and long nose, she had the best of the Indian features the whole family shared. What most galled kinky-haired Alberta was that her sister had long, straight, shiny black hair, a symbol of beauty for black women in those days. Alberta went to sleep each night praying that she would awaken the next morning to find that her hair, too, had grown long and straight. And each morning, when she found no such thing had happened, she prayed that La Tosca's hair would fall out. What was worse, La Tosca strutted around showing she knew she was more beautiful than Alberta. She treated her kid sister as a nuisance at best.

"She would never give me credit for having any sense," Alberta said bitterly in older age. "But I was too slick for her. That's what she resented."

The greatest injury in Alberta's eyes was that their mother seemed to love La Tosca more, spending much more money on her than on Alberta. "She always kept me well dressed but not as expensively as my sister," Alberta remembered. "She always bought silk stockings for La Tosca and cotton socks for me." From an early age Alberta knew the value of a nickel and knew who was getting what and spending how much on whom.

Many of the clothes the children wore were presents from Misses Emma and Myrtle Taylor, two white sisters who owned a "sporting house" (a bordello) at 122 Gayoso Street, where Miss Laura worked as a maid after her husband had deserted her.

Alberta never heard the first word about what went on inside the place her mama worked, not from Miss Laura anyway. Her mother was very prudish about her daughters' upbringing, seeing the way many young girls gave away their youth to the "sportin' life."

Actually, it was hard to know what Miss Laura was thinking or feeling. She "never mourned anything," said Alberta, not the death of her first child, John, at birth or the disappearance of her first husband. "She wasn't a crybaby type. I guess that's the reason I'm so strong. She'd say if something's gotta be done, let's get it done. Don't feel sorry for yourself or anybody else. I guess that's the reason I'm so cold.

"Am I cold?" Alberta asked, surprised at what she had just revealed about herself.

Miss Laura wasn't the affectionate kind of mama who would put her children to sleep with the hushed sounds of a lullaby. "Nobody ever sang to me at home," Alberta said. "No one took pains with me."

At least Alberta never got a spanking. But she knew when Mama meant business, especially about being in the house at a certain hour. She would come scurrying in at one minute before the appointed hour to avoid certain punishment.

"She just wanted me to be a girl who had respect for herself and respect for other people," Alberta said. " 'Respect yourself, and you can always demand respect from others.' Those were her words."

It was Alberta's grandmother, Nancy Peterson, who did most of the bringing up of her grandchildren. Grandfather Henry Peterson, a bricklayer, known at home as Buss, died when Alberta was still a young girl, but not before leaving her the memory of his being a "buzzard" at the kitchen table. "He used to eat all the good chicken and leave us the feet and the neck," Alberta said. "We couldn't stand him."

Alberta vaguely remembered two cousins, a boy named Arthur and a girl by the name of Kenneth—they pronounced it Kennette—who looked as if she were white and had chestnut brown hair. They were the children of Aunt Fletcher, Miss Laura's half sister, whom everyone called Aunt Mary, and a white judge by the name of Bissel. Aunt Mary was beautiful, very fair in complexion with straight black hair "like a white woman."

Alberta's fondest memories were of another of Aunt Mary's children named Tom. "Tom was a handsome boy. He looked like an

Indian," she said. "But they treated Tom like a dog." He had to sleep on the kitchen floor while the other four children huddled under her grandmother's patchwork quilt on the floor of the only other room in the house, where her grandmother slept.

"I don't think Tom and I were treated as nice as the other children," she said. "That's probably why I wanted to go to the top and stay there."

Then there was Ella Campbell, Aunt Babe, another half sister of her mother's, who was a "stray," according to Alberta. She married a man named Benjamin who was a minister of sorts. "He was a hustler," said Alberta. "Every time they came to stay with us, he'd have us all writing letters: 'Dear Sister in Christ. I am well with the exception of a bad cold. Send me five dollars.'

"And the fools, they'd send him money all the time."

Granny was a special lady to all those children. She knew just what to do if you had an ache or pain. If it was a headache you had, for instance, she'd crumble jimsonweed and peach tree leaves into vinegar, then soak a bandanna in it and put it on your forehead. That potion and her soothing words and touch had you feeling good again in no time.

As is the case with most grandmothers, she was the one dishing out the sweets while Mama was slapping out the discipline. But Granny Peterson was no pushover when it came to external threats to her clan's survival. Alberta remembered when the landlord wanted to raise the rent on Granny's little house from $5 to $5.25 a month.

"It'll never happen," her grandmother said, threatening to move if the owner persisted. "It never did," Alberta said.

Alberta loved Sundays because that was the day her grandmother made macaroni and cheese *and* tomatoes—"Tomatoes that had taste because they were ripened on the vine, not like the ones today that are harder than I am," Alberta said at age eighty-nine.

Granny wouldn't let her family eat chitlins. "They thought that was cheap," Alberta said. "We were always supposed to be big-timey niggers."

Granny bathed Alberta in the round zinc tub in her kitchen. Each time she gave Alberta a scrubbing she touched the three moles on the bottom of her little feet and said, "This child is going to be a wanderer."

"She was right, too," said Alberta decades later, after years of circling the globe. "I've been more places accidentally than most people have been on purpose."

Sunday was one day Alberta was supposed to start off clean because her grandmother would always take her to the Collins Chapel Colored Methodist Episcopal Church at 344 Washington Avenue. Theirs wasn't a religious family. Miss Laura didn't go to church or ever tell her children they had to serve God. There wasn't a Bible in the house, and nobody did any praying before meals or bedtime, not out loud anyway. Granny did tell all the children about God and Mary and Joseph and the Baby Jesus.

As far as Alberta was concerned, Sunday was a social event, a day to put on your hat and act really civilized—for as long as you had on a starched and pretty little dress anyway.

Now, there were churches and there were churches in Memphis. Miss Laura's sister Aunt Harriet Walker went to prayer meetings somewhere else in town where they had "jump-up songs" that inspired those present to stand up and moan and shout. "They'd say, 'Child, Harriet Walker walked those benches today,' meaning that she was shouting and carrying on," said Alberta. "I'm certain it was so she could be seen and talked about. She yelled and screamed and threw her hat away—that kind of stuff."

Alberta was never like that. "Oh, no!" she said.

The Collins Chapel CME Church wasn't like that. Its site at that time was a place where slaves had met in 1842 to receive permission to establish their own church. Until then they had suffered from heat in the summer and cold in the winter in the balcony of the white Wesley Chapel (now the First United Methodist Church). It took seventeen years for the Methodist Episcopal Church to name a pastor for the little group, a white one at that, the Reverend J. T. C. Collins, for whom the church was named.

In spite of its modest origins, the congregation developed into the most refined of the black churches in Memphis. It was the church of the teachers, doctors, lawyers, postal workers—the "socially ambitious"—"where virtues of educating children, paying debts, and buying property were extolled over shouting the loudest on the amens."*

Alberta paid attention to what she heard in that church about social mobility, about finding one's place in heaven, if not also on earth, by and by. She even remembers the theme of one sermon she heard when she was five or six years old and the name of the preacher who gave it, the Reverend Nelson Caldwell Cleaves, pastor of the church in 1900 and 1901. In that sermon one Sunday he said, "When the horse paws in the valley, I'll be there."

"I never shall forget it," Alberta said.

The expectation that one day she would meet her Maker in no way altered Alberta's behavior at church. "Alberta was devilish like most smart children," said Katie Dublin-Currie, a neighbor and Sunday school pal of hers. Katie's mother played the piano at night at the same sporting house where Alberta's mother worked.

Katie was three years older than Alberta but smaller. The two of them worked together as child muggers. They beat up the smaller kids at church and stole the pennies they brought for the offering. "We didn't use knives like they do today," Mrs. Dublin-Currie said. "We just used little sticks to scare them." The little girls bought ice cream cones with the loot.

Both girls turned to more honest activities as they grew up. Katie married Patrick Henry Dublin, a graduate of Tuskegee Institute, whose print shop at 363 Beale Street was the first owned by a black in Memphis. She took it over on his death and was still running it out of her garage on her ninety-third birthday.

Because of the respectable kind of place Collins was, singing along with the choir and the harmonium was supposed to be refined. But that didn't suit Alberta. "I'd sit up front with my grandmother, and I'd get to singing those spirituals out loud. And ol' Sister Lyons be looking at me to tell me to shut up. I knew it made her mad, so I'd sing louder. I wasn't scared of Sister Lyons. Oh, my goodness. They thought that was awful."

Alberta admitted that she was "always too fresh," so much so

---

*David M. Black Tucker, *Pastors and Leaders: Memphis, 1819–1972* (Memphis: Memphis State University Press, 1975), p. 23.

that she never imagined that being a boy instead would be of any advantage. "I didn't think the boys had the guts I had. I always wanted to do things that other people were afraid to try, to undertake something difficult." That meant doing things during the summer with Katie like "sneaking" over to Loeb's Steam Laundry on Madison Avenue, where they earned a little money as "shake-out girls," shaking out sheets before feeding them into the mangle, the machine that ironed them.

Alberta's mother at the time had an extra job over at Fred Rozier's Memphis Steam Laundry. Seeing how this impressed everyone, Alberta wanted to do the same. "Those places were high-hat," she said. "You got a job there, and you were a big shot."

She never had as much luck getting into the Ringling Brothers Circus in the field on Jackson Avenue the few times it came to town. She'd flop down on the ground and wiggle under a flap of the canvas tent. But before she had a chance to dust herself off on the other side, there was always a guard towering over her. He'd grab her hand and escort her to the nearest exit before she had a chance to see what the tigers, lions, and elephants were up to. Out she'd go, time after time. She never did get to see the circus.

But she did get into Grant School over by the corner of Auction Avenue and North Seventh Street even before she was old enough to enroll. If La Tosca could go, so could she! She'd just plunk herself in the classroom of a sympathetic teacher, like Miss Minnie Lewis, and try not to attract any attention. "I'd never cause any trouble. She could see I was trying to learn."

Alberta spent a lot of time studying at home. She probably tackled numbers first so she'd be able to count money, her favorite hobby in life from the age of about four. Then she took on the alphabet and the meaning of every word she read, saw, or heard.

"If I didn't understand what something said, I would ask somebody, 'What does this mean?' I'd ask my sister what a word meant. And if I wasn't satisfied or if it didn't sound right, then I'd ask somebody else. I decided what I learned I would have to learn right. I wanted to learn the right way to speak. I wanted to learn the right things to say. I wanted my English to be good, understandable, not no baloney jive. I wanted to be absolutely perfect in all my under-takings."

Miss Laura made sure that Alberta spoke correctly. "I'd say, 'Those ladies is so funny.' And my mother would say, 'Not *is*. Ladies are more than one. So those ladies *are*.' And you know where my mother got it from? The sporting ladies would tell my mother right. And when she came home, if we said something wrong, she'd tell us right."

In 1903, when Alberta was eight, Miss Laura decided that she and her daughters were too much of a burden on her mother, and they made the first of many moves from one cheap room to another. Miss Laura rented a room at 170 Beale Street, across from the Beale Street Baptist Church. The E. S. Goens Tonsorial Parlor, a barber-shop, was at 175 Beale, and a hop, skip, and jump down the other way at 149 was Abraham Schwab's general store. You name it, Schwab sold it, and in any size.

Miss Laura's landlady was Josie McCoy, whose father, Levy McCoy, owned a funeral parlor nearby at 157 South Fourth Street as well as the Mount Zion Cemetery. Alberta thought he was something else because of an unusual asset at his funeral parlor.

"He had a dead man—deader than a doornail, honey—standing up there on the left with his back to the door," Alberta said. "He was like a statue, dressed up like a model with a suit on. He didn't look bad. He just looked like an old man standing there. He was a real man, baby. Levy McCoy had even taken his mustache and em-balmed it. He was a tall black man. If you called him black in those days, you'd have your head cut off. We used to resent that. We didn't want people to call us black."

Alberta wasn't telling a tall tale. A book entitled *The Bright Side of Memphis* by G. P. Hamilton (published in Memphis in 1908) carries a photograph of Levy, looking like a Harvard law professor in his three-piece suit and bow tie, and describes the undertaker as "one of the best embalmers of modern times" (p. 278). "Many undertakers are not very skillful, but Mr. McCoy is a happy exception to this rule. In his establishment may be seen the remains of a man in a state of perfect preservation, notwithstanding the fact that the man died several years ago. His methods of embalming seem to transform the remains into stone."

The old dead man was the only petrified thing on Beale Street in those days. Blacks by the thousands were abandoning the lower Mississippi Valley, selling whatever land or possessions they had acquired since the Civil War for absurdly low prices and hauling their dreams to the cities upriver. Many of the migrants settled in Memphis. Others used it as a stopping-off place on the way to St. Louis or Chicago. From 1890 to 1900 the population of Memphis grew from 64,495 to 102,647 as a result of this migration and the one moving easterners westward.

Memphis was a rough-and-ready port town. Beale Street started or ended, depending on which way you were going, at the Mississippi River, where burly roustabouts toted barrels and bales on and off the steamboats that plied the great waterway.

Up and down, Beale Street was one rambling, rousing, bargaining, hustling, pimping, gin-guzzling, crapshooting, preaching, banjo-strumming, dancing, laughing, flirting, killing, syncopating mass of humanity. Musicians and singers began to put all that commotion into notes and words that would profoundly color American music for decades with the "blues."

Author Albert Murray, born in Nokomis, Alabama, describes the blues as "a statement about perseverance and about resilience and thus also about the maintenance of equilibrium despite precarious circumstances and about achieving elegance in the very process of coping with the rudiments of subsistence."*

W. C. Handy, "Father of the Blues," born in Florence, Alabama, moved to Memphis in 1905, formed a band that became the city's liveliest and most famous, and established a publishing company the next year with a young singer and lyricist, Harry Pace. In 1909, while leaning against a cigar counter in Pee Wee's Saloon on Beale Street, Handy wrote the first blues composition as a campaign song for the successful mayoral candidate Edward H. Crump; he published it in 1912 as "Memphis Blues." In 1914 Handy published the "St. Louis

---

*Stomping the Blues. (New York: Random House, 1982), pp. 250–251.

Blues." Later he took it to Chicago and asked a young singer there to introduce it for him. Her name was Alberta Hunter.

Alberta showed no signs of being a musical prodigy in Memphis, although she did butter up a neighbor, Hattie Abrams, because she had a piano.

"I'd say, 'How are you, Miss Hattie?' And I'm jiving her, you know, to get on her piano. Isn't that funny? I don't know one note from another. I'm talking to her and jiving her at the same time. I've always been able to jive." (*Jiving* is musicians' slang meaning "to play jazz"; for Alberta it meant "to dupe, manipulate, or ingratiate herself with someone.")

"Miss Hattie was one of those swellheaded ones. We called people like her a dicty—someone who thought God made her and threw the pattern away."

Whether Miss Hattie disliked Alberta's dirty little fingers jabbing at her sparkling ivory keys or she just wasn't the jivable type, she always shooed right out her door the moppet who could be called a national treasure eight decades later.

So Alberta's musical education depended on her keeping her ears perked for the Handy band, flashing bright red uniforms and shiny brass instruments and jazzing down the streets of town. "We'd hear that ta-da, ta-da of the band, and Lord, we'd be out the door so fast," she said.

The most enjoyable place to catch the band was down at Dixie Park, built by the prominent black Robert Church. He was one of the South's first black millionaires, having bought up property at bargain-basement prices back in 1877 and 1878, when a yellow fever epidemic killed or frightened away thousands of people from the city.

The park had a flying jenny, a carousel, that was Alberta's favorite pastime. She'd have to run from her grandmother's macaroni and cheese on Sunday to get down to the park and be one of the first in line so that the minute the ride opened and the bell rang she'd be ready for the horses.

Memphis was a merry-go-round itself, with all that was happening there. It was also more than its reputation as home of the blues implied. As a plaque outside the Old Daisy Theater on Beale Street reads, quoting black entertainer A. J. Grant: Beale Street was the place to be.

"With the confines of segregation, it became the black capital of the Mid-South and a place where blacks and ethnic whites sought to fulfill their dream. As B. B. King remembered, 'When you walked down Beale Street, you felt you really had something, because you could get work on Beale Street, you could get justice on Beale, you could get whatever was available for people on Beale Street.' "

Blacks felt so good about themselves on Beale Street that they resented Booker T. Washington's coming to the auditorium there in the early 1900s to tell them that they ought to learn how to farm. "They thought he was tearing them down, trying to make them subservient to whites, instead of building them up," Alberta said.

"But they were wrong," she said decades later. "Washington could see that farmers were going to be able to make lots of money. Farming was not to be looked down on." His message, she said, was: "You might not be cut out to go to college. But you can learn something else that is just as valuable."

Even though blacks considered themselves "Negroes" on Beale Street, they were looked at and treated as "niggers" anywhere else in Memphis or the South. Children like Alberta said they were taught that they were different from white people "from the very beginning."

It didn't take many pushes and shoves off sidewalks before she learned either she would have to walk in the gutter when a white person was on the same sidewalk or have to cross the street. It didn't matter much which alternative you took. The humiliation of being displaced was just as bitter on either side.

Alberta wasn't one to let prejudice lower her self-esteem. "I was always equal," she said. "I always felt I was good enough to do anything else that anybody else could do, but I was not given a chance to do."

She boldly pushed segregationist barriers aside, as she would do throughout her life. When a Jim Crow law went into effect on July 5, 1905, in Memphis, it required blacks to sit behind a movable divider sign on the streetcar. She would simply take the sign down and sit where she pleased.

She found discrimination was just as prevalent within her own race, however. Blacks were trying so hard to look like or act like whites that they avoided association with anyone darker than themselves.

For example, Ann Deb—whom Alberta called Aunt Deb, although she was no relation—was lighter-skinned than most of her black neighbors. So she stayed pretty much to herself. Every afternoon Alberta would watch her bring home her pigs and cows, hoping to slip inside the yard and play with her granddaughter Daisey Topley. But Daisey looked like a white child. So Alberta and the other darker-skinned children had to talk across the fence to Daisey, if they were allowed even that close a contact.

Miss Laura must have thought that Beale Street offered too much rawness for the eyes and ears of her girls. In the next two or three years she moved her brood to a succession of other addresses: 33 Menager Street, 426 Manassas, and 362 North Dunlap. This last house, which they occupied in 1908, was on the property of Nellie Hunter, a white woman who lived in a big house in the front.

Since Alberta had started school precociously, she decided that by age thirteen it was time she started earning some money. So she talked Miss Nellie out of twenty-five cents a week in return for getting for her the newspaper or an occasional bag of rice or cornmeal down at the store. Even then Alberta gave part of any money she received to her mother when ragged ends wouldn't meet.

Another dividend of pleasing Miss Nellie was the horse and buggy she had. Alberta would climb up and sit back in that buggy all by herself. If she were lucky and happened to catch Miss Nellie in a cooperative mood when she was going out, she might get to ride along. On those occasions Alberta would sit up straight as a ramrod and wave to the other kids on the sidewalk as if she were the queen of Sheba going off to visit Solomon.

Unfortunately there was more than a horse and a buggy in Miss Nellie's stable. She had a boyfriend who owned racehorses.

"Know what he used to do?" Alberta asked. "He used to put me up on a horse and molest me. He'd be standing down beside the horse. He'd put his hands on me, not all over me, just on the one place. He was a child molester, the dirty dog."

Every time the man visited Nellie Hunter he went looking for Alberta and molested her again when he found her. "If Miss Nellie had known he was annoying me, she would have kicked him out of there. She was that type of lady," Alberta said.

He wasn't the only one. There was also the black principal of a school. "He was short and weighed two hundred or three hundred pounds." Whichever, he was big.

His wife, whom Alberta called Aunt Martha, though she, too, was no relation—*Aunt* was a term of affection and respect and a way blacks had of creating a protective and supportive network for everyone's kids—was the first person she remembers using a hot iron to straighten her hair.

"But now that I know life," said Alberta, "I know that he was a dirty, stinking puppy dog. 'Cause I used to spend weekends with his mother and father, and he'd go get me up in that stable and molest me.

"He molested many of the children. I think he'd try to have sex with them. He'd be dirty enough to have a horse. He molested me, but he didn't—" Alberta stopped, not wanting to get any more detailed.

All those scenes that she remembered vividly throughout her life made her fear or resent most men. "I got so down on some fellows that I hated to breathe the air that they breathed. 'Cause I thought they were taking advantage. I figured if I told somebody those old men were doing this to me, they wouldn't believe me.

"People think a child is a liar. Children can scream and cry and do everything to try to impress the person of the fact that they are being mistreated, that they're not lying, and still, they would not be believed. It's a crime. Oh, it's a crime."

It was bad enough having to keep the humiliation to herself. But it was downright painful walking around and having to look at the men who were constantly abusing her. "It just made me stay away from men."

Not all men were bad, she admitted. She liked L. H. Fields, principal of Grant School. "He was a little ol' short, fat man, fat as a pig. Had a daughter named Ruth. And I had every respect in the world for that man. He was a good man.

"And there was a Mr. Brown, a teacher. He had a glass eye. Kids would snicker at him.

"I didn't dislike all men, no. Because I was crazy about an old boy named John Young. He was ugly sure as you were born. But he was tall and could wear clothes. A girl named Everlina Anderson took him away from me. She married him. And there was another fellow named Thomas Kembrow. A girl named Calley Young took him away from me. She married Kembrow, too. Oh, I lost them all.

"Oh, Lord. God is so good. They got their marriage. And I got the fame."

She would never have wanted to trade places with them. "No, I'm glad I don't have to sit around and hold them babies," she said, imitating a bawling baby's cry. "No, Lord, look at me, stepping off one plane and getting on another, going up, up, up. But I love children. I like them, but I don't want them around me."

Alberta could usually avoid any entanglements with unwelcome suitors by saying her mother wanted her right back in the house, as was usually true, or that she was on an errand for Miss Nellie down to Jack Latura's grocery store at the corner of Lane Avenue and Dunlap Street.

The Laturas must have been rather ordinary white people because Alberta remembered nothing special about them other than that they sold the best hard wine ball candy in the neighborhood, three for a penny. And they had a bar in the back room, as most grocery stores did then.

Jack Latura's son, "Wild" Bill Latura, made news in December 1908, when he walked into a saloon at Fourth Street and Beale Avenue, shot three blacks to death, and fatally wounded a fourth. When apprehended later that night, he reportedly told the police, "I shot 'em, and that's all there is to it." Seven eyewitnesses testified at the ensuing trial that he had done just that, in cold blood. But all the witnesses were blacks. The jury, naturally, was white. The witnesses were held in jail during the trial.

Latura said his victims planned to kill him. His mother testified before a packed courtroom that she thought her son was insane, whereupon Wild Bill began sobbing like a child. The jury found him not guilty.

The unequal system of justice throughout the South stuck in the craws of generations of blacks. "White people were found guilty but always acquitted," said Alberta. "Things that happened years and years ago are still in Negroes. Some of the older parents still tell the children of the things that happened before they were born, and that keeps the black man bitter.

"I know we were mistreated," she said. "But I ask God to help me forgive."

Alberta had a harder time forgiving injustice in her own home. About 1906 or 1907 her mother remarried. The man was Theodore Beatty, whom everybody called Dode. He was fair-skinned and looked a bit like an Irishman. About all Alberta ever said of him, other than that she hated him, was that he played guitar, went to "chicken fights" on Saturday nights, and fought with her mother all the rest of the time.

"He was insanely jealous of my mother," she said. "He didn't want my mother to say good morning to anybody. He hated my intestines because I'd hit him when he'd hit my mother."

Alberta was also jealous of her half sister, Josephine Beatty, the daughter Dode had with Miss Laura. She resented the intrusion the two Beattys had in her relationship with her mother and consequently ignored Josephine's existence.

Not having a loving father fueled Alberta's ambition. "It made me more determined to come through with flying colors, to get to the point that I could say *I* did so-and-so," Alberta said.

She compensated for her frustration by attacking La Tosca. There was the day when she, La Tosca, and Josephine had to get all gussied up in their high-button shoes and frilly dresses to have their photo taken sitting on the back steps of their house on North Dunlap Street. It wasn't for anyone's birthday or anything like that. But, said Alberta, relishing the memory of the day, "it was an occasion for me 'cause I pushed her off the steps."

La Tosca hadn't done anything especially mean that day to Alberta, but all her wrongdoings of other days and years were tallied on the get-even chart in Alberta's mind.

"I waited for her," said Alberta. "I wanted to get her on the high steps, high as I could get her." The placid yet stoic expression on Alberta's face in the photo belies the anxiety she felt about possibly missing a golden opportunity to make the long-awaited hit.

"I jived her and got her over on this side," Alberta said, pointing to the right side of the steps, " 'cause I could push her farther. I waited till she was talking." Alberta stepped up to La Tosca, pushed with all her might, and, "Bang. She didn't know where she was going. I wasn't kind enough to push her sideways. I pushed her off backwards. God help me, it was a terrible thing," she said, laughing.

Alberta couldn't say if La Tosca was hurt. She didn't inquire at the time. "I know I intended to hurt her," she said.

La Tosca treated Alberta with due respect after that day.

In 1909, soon after that incident, the family moved to 465 North Manassas, where they shared a double-tenant house with Hattie Sykes, a dicty who didn't give Alberta the time of day, and vice versa.

About that time Alberta's grandmother went to Denver. Aunt Mary Fletcher was out there working for Judge Bissel, father of at least two of her children, and needed help taking care of some children she had with her there. La Tosca, Tom, Arthur, and Kenneth were sent out to join them soon after. Alberta lost her greatest ally and friend, her grandmother. She turned inward as she entered adolescence, with few interests to keep her company. She didn't care for pets. She didn't cut pictures out of magazines. She had no toys or dolls. She didn't paint or draw pictures. She didn't believe in haunted houses or fairytales. There were no movies, no radio, no television, no school sports, no Girl Scouts. And she couldn't manage to sneak into the circus. She didn't even dress up at Halloween the way other kids did.

Riding on the flying jenny or in Miss Nellie's buggy and stalking the Handy band were the only fun she ever admitted having, and these things she could do alone without other children.

Irma Watts was okay. "She was my pal," said Alberta. "But she always had a sweetheart." So much for her.

"I never was playful like a child," she said. "I was always like you'd expect a grown woman to be."

Miss Laura reinforced Alberta's introvertedness by concluding that her associating with any of the available playmates in the neighborhood could only be hazardous. She told Alberta to stay at home.

"My mother always had her nose in the air," said Alberta. In her mind there was never anything but trouble lurking right outside the door.

She wasn't far from wrong. Two houses down the street was the wildest child of them all, Dossie Mabin. "She calls herself Dorothy now," Alberta said in later years, lifting her eyes heavenward at the upgrading of the name.

Dossie as a little girl was innocent enough in organizing a circle of local kids and leading the singing of "A tisket, a tasket, a green and yellow basket. I wrote a letter to my ma . . ." And on the refrain—"I found it, I found it"—the person closest to a dropped handkerchief would pick it up if Dossie hadn't tripped him or her up so she could be in the desired position.

Or she'd command her legion to scavenge baking powder cans and fish bladder and cord to make play telephones so she could shout orders from her station on Manassas to a platoon of subordinates down on the corner of Lane Avenue, a few houses away.

A snoopy old lady who lived next door was always tattling on Dossie. One Valentine's Day Dossie decided it was time to take care of her. So she cut out of the newspaper a picture of an ugly old lady, tied it around a brick, and about nine that night, when nobody but her gang trembling in the bushes was watching, smashed her personalized valentine right through the glass pane of the tattletale's front door.

From among the "innocent" bystanders questioned in private came the unanimous verdict that Dossie was the culprit. She got switched up one side and down the other by her mama, but it didn't calm her down one bit.

About the only thing that set her back a notch was an incident at Grant School involving Alberta.

Recess was always the time for the rambunctious boys to hit the play yard and, on the basis of a slur against one anothers' mothers, beat the tar out of one another. For their part, the girls initiated their own aggression with a ritualistic testing of the pecking order among them.

One recess Alberta, looking like a smart aleck, walked outside carrying a little chip of wood on her shoulder. That was the dare. If someone was brave enough to knock that chip off her shoulder and strong enough to survive the aftermath, then she was better'n her.

Someone dared Dossie to go clean off Alberta's shoulder. The indomitable Dossie strutted right up to Alberta and knocked off the chip.

"I wasn't afraid of Pig," Dorothy Mabin Young remembered at age ninety in the living room of her Memphis home surrounded by a Raggedy Ann doll from childhood and red and yellow satin pillows. "But I was afraid afterwards. She beat the hell out of me!"

The two girls never became close. Dossie, like Irma, was crazy about boys. "If you got to talking with Dossie, before she was through she'd get to talking about some fellow," Alberta said. "And I didn't like that."

In late 1910 or early 1911 Alberta and her family moved to 884 Lane Avenue, the last little house in Memphis she lived in. She remembered nearby railroad tracks and trains hooting softly in the darkness like owls deep in piney woods.

No matter what time they passed they never seemed to interrupt dreams—good or bad. Alberta couldn't remember ever having dreams, not even daydreams.

"There weren't any options for us colored girls," she said. "I never knew what was going to happen to me, but I knew something was going to happen, and I knew one of those days would be my day.

"You see how I'm sitting here quietly," she said at age eighty-nine, on the edge of her bed in soft green hospital-issue pajamas she had brought home from a recent hospital stay. "I'd be sittin' there in the house [in Memphis] lookin' out the window, and I'd be thinking. Or I'd sit on the back steps, and I'd think maybe I'm being mistreated. But I'm gonna make it in life because I'm going to try hard. I figured as long as there was a God and there was a way to be made, I'd be part of that way.

"Inside of myself I'd say I don't have to worry because maybe tomorrow, no, maybe the next day, no, but maybe the next day, I'll make it."

She ran away from home once, she said. "I ran around the corner, then ran back home. I knew that I couldn't make it unless I went back home and had patience. I figured if I took my time, I would get there quicker. So that when I ease in there, I'd ease in the right way, and they can't push me out."

Alberta wasn't all that patient. Katie Dublin-Currie said Alberta "gave her mother trouble for two or three years" before she finally left home, quitting school and insisting that she was "going to go make me some money."

"Kids were talking that Alberta left home first to go sing on Beale Street," said Dorothy Young.

Mrs. Dublin-Currie couldn't confirm that. "I was too scared to go down there [to Beale Street]," she said.

Alberta flatly denied singing on Beale Street, ever. "I always wanted to stay away from anything that had a reputation of being bad," she said. And women who sang on Beale Street had that reputation. If that had been her only chance to start a singing career, she said, "I'd rather not have the chance."

Years later, however, when Alberta was in Memphis, the *Memphis World* (June 4, 1948) carried a front-page article that spoke of Alberta's "regret" that she wasn't able to see Anselmo Barrasso, owner of the famous Palace Theater, among others. (His brother F. A. Barrasso founded in 1909 the Theater Owners' Booking Association [TOBA] that hired many black singers to perform at its nationwide chain of theaters.)

"The veteran Beale Street Theatre executive was one of the first to note Miss Hunter's talent when she was a teen-aged girl and gave her an opportunity to appear on his stage," the newspaper reported.

Whatever singing she did in Memphis, Alberta said she "could go just so far" in her hometown. Furthermore, "If I had stayed in Memphis, my mother would never have let me out from under her wing."

Alberta kept hearing about Ellen Winston, the daughter of one of her mother's friends, from the letters Ellen sent home from Chicago, where she was working. She wrote her mother how young girls were being paid up to ten dollars a week singing in the Windy City.

"Imagine that," Ellen's mother told Miss Laura one day, reading the letter to her. Imagine that, thought Alberta, who was taking in every word of the conversation. Hadn't a teacher at school told Alberta she could sing very well?

"So I thought, Oh, yeah, I'm gonna get me some of that ten," Alberta said, savoring the idea of that much money then.

Her chance to escape came not long after that. She was picking up a loaf of bread for her mother at the store one hot July afternoon in 1911 when she met one of her teachers, Floyd Lillian Cummings. Because of her unusual name, the children all called her Miss Florida. Miss Florida told Alberta she was leaving for Chicago that evening. She was traveling with a man named Wyatt Edgerton, who no one at the time knew was really her husband.

"I sure wish I could go with you," Alberta said.

Miss Florida said she happened to have a child's pass to Chicago. An eight-year-old girl by the name of Charlotte who was to use the pass wasn't able to go. Alberta could use it, she said, if she got her mother's permission to go.

Alberta said she would go home and ask Miss Laura, knowing she wouldn't get back out of the house to go as far as the grocery store again if she did pose the question to her mother. "My mother always used to say, 'Chicago is so cold. Mother doesn't want you going to Chicago.' "

Alberta ran to find Dossie to tell her she was going to Chicago and needed some money quick. "I gave her the only dime she had when she left," said Dorothy Young, clarifying quickly that "a dime was a whole lot then."

At the previously agreed-upon time Alberta, clutching her dime, met her teacher and her husband at the Illinois Central Railroad station. Before long, the train started hissing steam, and the conductor chanted with a melancholy ring to his voice, "All out the northbound train. All out the northbound train."

"He said it three times," Alberta remembered. " 'All out the northbound train.' So I just stepped right on up. I got on that train, child, and sat in between Miss Florida and Mr. Wyatt. Then the conductor cried out, 'All aboard,' three times. I guess that was their trait.''

Soon after the train chugged off, the conductor started collecting tickets. Because Alberta, although sixteen years old at the time, was small and appeared much younger, the conductor didn't question her traveling on a child's pass. So began a lifetime of fibbing on the subject of her age.

The conductor took their tickets and went on about his business. As the train gathered speed, soot and cinders whirled in on the Jim Crow car, reserved for black passengers only, just behind the coal car. Alberta, dressed in a blue dress and red shoes, would be fitting her nickname, Pig, by the time they arrived in Chicago.

But she could not have cared less. All night long the sparks mingled with the bright summer stars flickering above Alberta's head like halos of lightning bugs bewitching the imagination of a young girl whose time had come to leave childhood and home behind, down the tracks.

CHAPTER TWO

Making It to the Dreamland

"It was just the hand of God that led me to the place where Ellen Winston was living," said Alberta.

As she liked to tell the story, she jumped on the streetcar in front of the Chicago railroad station after arriving from Memphis that summer morning of 1911 with Miss Florida and her husband, not having the slightest idea how she was going to find the daughter of her mother's friend.

"I didn't know where she lived," Alberta said. "But being young and not knowing, I thought I could go any place in Chicago, and people would know where she was."

Suddenly, according to her version, she bolted from the streetcar and found herself in front of the Burlington Building at 2918 South State Street. She must have overheard Ellen's mother say that was where Ellen lived. Alberta walked straight ahead to the front door, which was open, and entered a hall. One door off the hall led into a saloon.

"I could hear music from one of those old-fashioned pianos you pump with your feet, a player piano. And they were playing 'Where the River Shannon Flows.'"

She stood there for a while and listened to the song. Then she walked up the stairs to the second floor, where a woman, Sara Love, was doing some wash.

"Lady, do you know a girl around here by the name of Ellen Winston?" Alberta asked.

"No, I don't, child," the woman responded to the disappointed creature who looked like a chimney sweep after her train ride. "What you doing here? Where are you from?"

"Well, I'm looking for Ellen Winston," said Alberta.

"Well, I'm asking you where you're from."

"I'm from Memphis," Alberta, never one to be generous in giving out personal information, replied reluctantly.

"Memphis?" the lady asked.

"Yes, ma'am."

"Well, there's a girl that lives here by the name of Helen Winston. ["Helen's a big shot now living in Chicago, so she changed her name," Alberta said many years after the incident.] Helen lives here, but this is her day off," Mrs. Love added.

"Would you let me stay here until she gets back?" Alberta asked. The woman agreed.

When Helen returned, she was startled to see Miss Laura's daughter washed up and waiting for her. "Pig, what in the world are you doing here? What's Miss Laura going to think?"

Alberta told her about Miss Florida and the train pass.

"Well, you sit down there," Helen said. "Wait till I get my shoes off."

"I don't remember whether her feet were hurting, or whether it was snowing or what, but anyhow, I know she took her shoes off," Alberta said. A person going barefoot, even at home, impressed Alberta, whose mother never let her have that freedom. It wasn't a classy thing to do.

Helen was second cook in a boardinghouse in Hyde Park, a silk-stocking neighborhood in Chicago. The next day she brushed the pigtails out of her little friend's hair, put her in a longer, more grown-up-looking dress, and took her to the place she worked to ask the owner if she could possibly give her friend some little kind of job to do.

"A job? Doing what?" the woman thundered. "She's nothing but a child." On second thought, detecting persistence and a willingness to work in the little girl's serious face, she agreed to let her clean up tables and peel potatoes for six dollars a week plus room and board.

Actually "room" meant sleeping under "coats and things" in a little bed in the basement next to others occupied by Edna Love, Sara's mother-in-law, Helen on occasion, and several other hired helpers.

"I peeled potatoes till the cows came home," said Alberta, who then dropped them one by one into a tub.

Making money and making it honestly were more important at the time to Alberta than singing, she always said. "I just wanted to work, to think that I was earning an honest living. I've always been happy knowing that what I was doing was clean and honest. I think that's the reason my body is so strong," she said at age eighty-nine when getting up to walk was a struggle.

The first week she sent her mama two dollars from her pay with a note explaining where she was and telling her not to worry. Alberta said that from then on, throughout her life, she wrote her mother every week when they weren't together and sent her money. "I sent her so much money my mother wrote me once and said, 'For God's sake, stop sending me money. I'm tired of going to the bank.' "

Peeling potatoes was not what Alberta had in mind for the long run. And six dollars a week was a far cry from ten. If other girls were getting that much, she was going to get it, too. Before long she started slipping out of the boardinghouse late at night when her companions were sleeping. She'd head for South State Street with its flashing lights, swanky people, and hot entertainment. The fancy places had formidable-looking doormen and bouncers. So she set her sights on the unassuming dives where the guard was down.

"I tramped and tramped and tramped, trying to get that work," she said. She'd go into one place after another, repeatedly, and be tossed right out. Finally she spotted Dago Frank's at Archer and South State streets.

She cased the place and watched how women, often unaccompanied, went sashaying right in the front door with an air of knowing what they wanted and going after it. The heavily made-up ladies amply filled out their garish dresses while Alberta had to rely on safety pins to keep her borrowed dress pulled together over her skinny body. But the patrons, all of whom were white, looked as if they were out to have a good time. None of them looked particularly threatening.

So in she marched, to the amusement of the customers sitting in booths along a side wall, and bumped right into Roy, the manager. It was like trying to sneak into the circus in Memphis all over again. Before she had time to see the action, there she was back out on the street.

" 'Get her out of here,' he'd shout. 'She'll get my place closed.' The police were after him anyhow for other things," Alberta said. The "other things" were going on upstairs where women and their gents could get together more privately.

"But I kept going back every night," Alberta said. "You know, I'm determined." Each time she set foot in the door she politely greeted Bruce, the only black in the place. He was the piano player, a lousy one at that. But he was struck by the determination of the girl who paid him so much respect.

So one night, when she walked right up to his piano and started blurting out that first song she had learned from a player piano, "Where the River Shannon Flows," he tried to accompany her.

"He was worse than I was," Alberta said. To top it off, Bruce sagged to one side because one leg was shorter than the other, while Alberta looked and sounded as forlorn as an alley cat.

"Bruce, get her out of here," said Roy again. "She's terrible."

"They made fun of me, honey," Alberta remembered. "They laughed at me 'cause I was singing high soprano. What did I know about singing contralto?"

"Oh, come on, Roy, give her a chance," said Bruce. "You can see she's nothing but a kid."

Roy refused. Alberta kept on peeling potatoes, going into Dago Frank's, and being shown the door.

Although she was getting nowhere in that area, she advanced on another front. Always wanting privacy, she found herself a room for a dollar a week at 3210 Dearborn Street with a woman named Cora Durham and her husband, Louis Durham.

One night, weeks after her "audition" with Bruce, the telephone rang at the Durhams'. It was for Alberta. She was to start work immediately at Dago Frank's for ten dollars a week. Months and mounds of potatoes had passed since her arrival in Chicago. But her day had come.

Luckily she had heard and learned another song she liked called "All Night Long." That gave her a rather skimpy repertoire for her opening night. So each night she'd hang around a player piano somewhere and pick up one new song. Poor Bruce, whose specialty was Stephen Foster songs, had to scramble to keep up with his industrious partner, but the clients, with their minds on getting upstairs with their dates, were sympathetic. Sometimes they'd even leave a little tip for the pitiful duo that was making such an effort to entertain them.

Alberta started trying out her own words to songs she had learned. She thought nothing of substituting a word or phrase to someone else's song, especially if it added a little punch or color and made her audience pay more attention to her.

The first lyrics which she ever wrote down and which were probably her own are on the back of an envelope she saved. She sang them when the newsboys in Chicago first started hawking the headline TITANIC SINKS. The British steamer took 1,503 white people to the bottom of the North Atlantic early on the morning of April 15, 1912, and Alberta chirped for black mothers:

> . . . *shout for joy*
> *'Cause not a mother lost a girl or a boy*
> *So fare the* Titanic *farewell.*

Her next challenge was to outmaneuver the pimps who hung out at Dago Frank's. "They were ready for you," she said. "They had Chicago sewed up." But they were such gentlemen, she remembered, that no one would have guessed they were pimps.

Because everyone appeared so proper, Alberta thought it was respectable for her to perform at Dago Frank's, even though it was a bordello, in contrast with Memphis's notorious Beale Street, where sexual intentions and activity weren't at all discreet.

"You would think they were all ministers," Alberta said of the men who frequented Dago Frank's, "not that ministers are so grand and so good." She found they wouldn't bother someone like her who "had ambition, nerves, and a mind of her own," not to mention homely looks. "They protected me in a way because they taught me a lot that I know. They'd sit me down and talk to me. They would tell me how a man would take a girl downtown and dress her up and buy her gorgeous clothes and then make a hooker out of her, and how to watch for it."

The women at Dago Frank's also took Alberta under their wings. "They were very tenderhearted," she said. "They made their fellows give me money all the time. Then they would make me sing again, and they'd say, 'Now, don't sing it that way. Do it like this,' you know. And I would sing it that way, and finally I made good.

"And they'd go out and buy me little dresses. Paid a dollar and a half for a dress. Oh, my goodness, that was a lot of money.

"I want the world to know that a lot of those sportin' women do things because of circumstances," Alberta said. "Some of them have children, families to take care of. They're not all bad. They're trying to help their fellowman."

Little did Miss Laura learn from the letters Alberta regularly sent home of her daughter's new associates except that they all were well dressed, very nice, and taking good care of Alberta. Miss Laura might have described her own employers on Gayoso Street the same way, so she couldn't be sure what company her daughter was keeping. But she supported her daughter's ambitious start in life.

"She approved of anything that I did that was decent," said Alberta. "She was proud because she figured I was proud and that I was going to take care of myself. She knew that I knew right from wrong and that I'd strive for the best, whether I got it or not. She was right behind me in whatever I did, to let me know that I was not alone."

Alberta stayed at Dago Frank's for nearly two years, to the summer of 1913, "until they saw the cops were really coming this time."

She moved on to Hugh Hoskins, a very small club with an exclusively black clientele at Thirty-second and South State streets. Zella Hunter (no relation) played the upright piano just inside the door, with her back to the audience. It was important she have her eye on the door so she could signal when the cops came looking for one of the customers, like "Tack" Annie Williams, one of the city's cleverest pickpockets, who hung out at Hoskins.

"She was the ugliest woman that ever breathed a breath of life," Alberta said. "She looked like a horse with a hat on. It was a sin to put a woman on earth as ugly as Tack Annie.

"But she was as clever as she was unattractive. She could walk up to a man and tell him, 'Honey,' and come out with a suitcase if he had it in his pocket." Or if her prey were wearing a diamond stickpin, she would lean over him and, with a hook on the back of one of her front teeth, snatch it off him in a flash.

She and the other women pickpockets would go downtown where the traveling businessmen hung out. "They'd never harm them or anything but would just talk to them and get their money," Alberta said. "Every night the girls would come in and count their loot. Tack Annie always came in first with a handful of wallets and stickpins she had stolen all over town." After the money had been counted and the pimps paid off, they all would sit around and buy each other drinks and give Alberta good tips when she sang.

Harry Merrill also worked out of the place. He was called Big Harry, not to be confused with Little Harry, who was also a regular. They both were confidence men. Alberta found out years later that the two Harrys had "confidenced" her stepfather, Dode Beatty, out of a grocery store he owned in Chicago after separating from her mother and moving there. "They didn't know he was my stepfather," she said. "If they had known, they wouldn't have done it. You know those fellows had honor, as it went."

Alberta didn't know whether it was her mother or her stepfather who had walked out the door first in Memphis. As she said, "There was some leaving done." At any rate, while Alberta was still working at Hoskins, she brought her mother to live in Chicago.

One of the waiters there, Douglas McGee, called Shine, was madly in love with Alberta. Poor guy. He didn't get any attention from her. "I always ignored him just like he was a piece of tripe," she said.

Nevertheless, he did everything he could to help her. He even rented an apartment so Miss Laura would have a place to stay. Alberta stayed there, too, and neither of them gave him a penny toward the rent. He certainly didn't get paid otherwise. He stayed with them, but as Alberta insisted, "No funny business ever went on there."

Mother and daughter got along fine because neither intruded in the life of the other. Miss Laura never went to see Alberta sing. And it wasn't because she disapproved of her career. "She was proud of me, but she didn't know how to express it," Alberta said. "She was curious to see me perform; but she didn't know how to go about it, and I didn't know how to tell her to. It never crossed my mind that she should go."

The only thing Alberta ever knew about her mother's life in Memphis, and she found out about it only years later, was that Miss Laura had also worked for a hospital for a while. But her mother never talked about her work, much less her life. Alberta took after her, having to learn as a celebrity to reveal a certain minimum amount of detail about herself, which she did in a canned version that she repeated to journalists ad infinitum for decades.

"I never shared my private life with anybody in the world," Alberta said, "not even with my mother. I've always been a loner. The only thing that anyone knew about my private life was what they tried to guess. But nobody ever knew. I never sat around and told stories on myself to anybody. People used to say, 'Alberta is crazy about John Young.' That was in Memphis when I was a child. You know how a little boy and girl would stand by a gate looking at each other and grinning. That was the only way that anybody would find out about my life. They'd just sit looking." She'd let them form their own conclusions.

In spite of their not sharing experiences or feelings, Alberta became very close to her mother. The resentment she had toward her favored sister, La Tosca, did not extend to her mother once her sister was no longer present. Alberta appreciated the fact that her mother never judged her or made demands of her. And she certainly didn't want to know about Alberta's sex life.

"I was always an old-fashioned girl," Alberta said. "You see, sex was always vulgar where my mother was concerned. We never discussed her business with men or me going with a fellow."

Actually the two women shared the unspoken bond of having

been abused and humiliated by men. In providing well for her mother the rest of her life, Alberta was protecting her from ever needing to depend on a man and subjecting herself to such treatment again.

Alberta bade farewell to Hugh Hoskins late in 1914, fourteen months after she started there. "I had done all I could do. I had gone as high as I could go at Hoskins. So I looked for higher ground."

During her climb she stopped for a while at Elite Number One at Thirtieth and South State streets, owned by Teenan Jones, who was also in the pawnshop business. Tony Jackson did a great job accompanying her on the piano, and in return, she sang and helped make popular some of the songs he wrote, like "Some Sweet Day" and "Pretty Baby."

Some whites would come in there, but it was basically a cabaret for blacks. Teenan liked Alberta because he thought she was thrifty. "He knew I was trying to work and save what little I could," Alberta said.

"You're smart, kid, and I like you because you're clean," he told her. "Stay that way."

He wasn't so impressed with her smartness after he had let her wear a little forty-dollar diamond ring from his shop. She never returned or paid for it. Years after "he would look at me and laugh," she said. "I guess he thought, 'She's a deadbeat.'

"I conned him out of that ring." Alberta chuckled in old age, feeling comfortable with the respectable distinction in her mind between conning and outright stealing. Alberta wore that ring only once in public because she noticed all the other people who could afford such a ring were wearing theirs. And she wanted to be different.

Now that she had the ring as a fixed asset, Alberta decided that her life was valuable enough to insure. On November 2, 1914, she took out her first life insurance policy, with her mother as beneficiary. In exchange for a weekly premium of five cents, the Metropolitan Life Insurance Company promised to pay fifty-two dollars on her death—that is, if she died at least six months after taking the policy.

Little did she or they know how much more living she had to do. And climbing.

The next step in 1915 was to the Panama Café at Thirty-fifth and

South State streets, owned by Isadore ("Izzy") Levine and Izzy Shorr. The Panama was quite the place. It was packed every night with white people, mostly residents from Hyde Park and entertainers from the shows downtown. It had two long, very ordinary rooms, one upstairs, the other downstairs. But they represented two different styles. You chose the one that suited your mood.

Downstairs the nice, quiet girls sang sophisticated stuff, "opera jive," as Alberta called it. That was Cora Green, Mattie Hite, Nettie Compton, Florence Mills, and Ada Beatrice Queen Victoria Louise Virginia Smith (later du Conge was added; all the neighbors had wanted to name Ada, so her mother, not to offend them, threw all their suggestions together). In years to come she would be better known the world over as Bricktop. Nettie's husband, Glover Compton, sat kind of sideways on the piano bench, a cigar hanging out of his mouth, and accompanied that group without ever looking at the keys of his piano.

Mattie Hite was a tall, dark-brown-skinned young girl, with a heavy voice. She was full of life and very kind to Alberta, always telling her, "Girl, you ain't got no business here. You belong in New York."

Cora Green was "nice" and had an "in-between voice, between sweet and jazz. Everybody on that floor was a different type, had a different-type voice," said Alberta. "Brick couldn't sing. She talked most of her songs. But, boy, could she dance awhile. All five of them could dance."

Florence Mills was a smash hit whether she was singing sweet as a nightingale or impersonating men onstage.

Upstairs were the barrelhousers, which meant "you were kind of rough-and-ready," Alberta explained.

George Hall was the pianist for the rowdies. And he "could play a mess of piano," Alberta said. The bunch included Nellie Carr, Mamie Carter, Twinkle Davis, Goldie Crosby, and Alberta. They sang the blues, but actually Alberta did most of the singing. Goldie and Mamie could sing "a little," Alberta said. Nellie Carr could sing all right, but her strength was running across the floor and flopping into a split.

Many customers went upstairs to see Twinkle Davis, "whose legs made Marlene Dietrich look like a scarecrow. All she had to do was walk out on the floor," said Alberta. "But all she had were her legs. She tried to dance, but she was as bad a dancer as I was a storyteller."

Dressing up wasn't yet in vogue for cabaret performers in Chicago, so they all wore street clothes. "I featured smart blouses," said Alberta. "All my blouses had high collars." She had her blouses made with little tiny buttons, contrary to the style of the time, again to set herself apart. "I always wanted to be distinctive, to be my own self and not be like anybody else," she said, looking at a photo she saved of herself in her early twenties in a "mahogany brown" blouse.

She also made sure that her group upstairs set its own pace and that it was a winning one. "Get this straight," Alberta insisted. "The customers wouldn't stay downstairs. They'd go upstairs to hear us sing the blues. That's where I would stand there and make up verses and sing as I go along."

The successful competition made Bricktop and the rest of them downstairs mad. "Yeah, they got hot," Alberta said.

The Panama was a place to make good money. Whites were generally as good as blacks at tipping, Alberta said, "but you knew that Negroes would give you their last nickel even if they didn't have a dime left. And they'll still do it."

She and the other entertainers worked at the Panama from 8:00 P.M. to midnight, then headed for the after-hour clubs to perform.

Alberta also began to make money from the composers who came into the Panama and paid a singer like her, who was becoming one of the most popular in Chicago, to introduce one of their songs. "If I liked the songs, I would sing them," Alberta said. "I wouldn't do it just for the money."

She was one of the first to sing "Sweet Georgia Brown" for its composer, Maceo Pinkard. Porter Grainger asked her to sing his "Michigan Water Tastes Like Sherry Wine," and W. C. Handy asked her to sing his "St. Louis Blues."

"I became so popular that everybody was trying to get me then," Alberta said.

Not only songwriters were after her. One evening a finely dressed "yaller girl" caught Alberta's roving eyes at a table where a fun-loving theater crowd was seated. The young woman was Lottie Tyler, the oldest niece of the wife of Egbert Austin ("Bert") Williams, America's most beloved black comedian in those days. Lottie, who had far more glamour than money, was passing through Chicago, working as a maid for Fay Bainter, the last white actress to play Topsy in the play *Uncle Tom's Cabin* in a Players Club production in New York in 1933. "Lottie had the most beautiful legs that were ever on a person," Alberta said.

Lottie was obviously attracted to Alberta and told her, "If you ever want to come to New York, you come to this address." Alberta guarded that address with the same reverence with which she stowed away her first diamond.

With her career she never knew where she'd be next. As it happened, she was out of the Panama before she knew it. A man named Curley killed someone there in 1917, and the police closed the place overnight. Florence Mills, Bricktop, and Cora Green, who had already formed a group called the Panama Trio, traveled west on the Pantages theater circuit. Bricktop and Cora Green soon accepted other offers, leaving Florence to finish the group's contracted tour by herself. Florence was such a success by herself that no one mourned the passing of the trio.

Alberta went next door to the De Luxe Café, owned by Frank Preer, husband of the stage and screen actress Evelyn Preer. Jimmie Noone's band played in the cabaret upstairs, over a billiards parlor. Freddie Keppard, one of the all-time great trumpet players, was there, covering his fingerwork with a handkerchief so no one could steal his style. He was a very nice fellow, Alberta said, "but he seemed to stay to himself more or less. I don't remember having very much to do with him."

Actually Alberta never hung around or socialized with any of the musicians or performers. For one thing, she never drank, smoked, or took dope. It was just as well from the musicians' point of view because she made them feel that they had to say, "Excuse me, Alberta," when they used their colorful language in front of her.

"They used to say I was swellheaded, that I thought I was better than the rest of them because I didn't sit around in bars. I was reared by an old, old, old lady, what rearing I had, when I was at home."

About the only major excitement she remembered in those days was a visit her half sister, Josephine, made to her mother, who was then living in a fifth-floor walk-up apartment on Thirty-first Street.

"I remember Josephine came to stay one day. She was about fourteen or fifteen years old. With a fellow. Josephine was big enough to try to go with a fellow. They had just come in town. They came into the apartment, and as they started talking, bang. He shot at Josephine. He missed her, but still, they went out of the house together. My mother made them go. And I never did see Josephine again."

Josephine died a couple of years later, Alberta said, but she didn't know the circumstances.

Alberta stayed at the De Luxe for only a week because Bill Bottoms, the dapper owner of the Dreamland Ballroom and later Joe Louis's dietitian, invited her to cross the street and sing at his cabaret. "That's where the Lord put His arms around me," Alberta said. "Honey, I went from there to everything. I just sang and sang and sang."

Everybody knew Alberta was there from the day she started because of Jones, the barker, who stood out front and hollered, "Ladies and gentlemen, come in and . . ."

"He'd holler like we were a circus inside," Alberta said. "He was a mess, Jones was. Yeah, but he finally got married." That took care of him.

Even without him Chicagoans went inside to hear the glory of Joseph ("King") Oliver's band. Oliver, a big, tall man with one eye, was on trumpet, and he could play it as soft and sweet as the voice of Florence Mills. Accompanying Oliver at various times were Wellman Braud on bass; George ("Pops") Foster on bass; Sidney Bechet on clarinet; Warren ("Baby") Dodds on drums; and Lillian ("Lil") Hardin, also born in Memphis (three years later than Alberta), on piano.

"And she was a pianist, too, baby," said Alberta. "You know one thing? All you had to do—we knew nothing about arrangements, keys, nothing—all you had to do was sing something like 'Make Me Love You,' and she would have that one gone. She could play anything in this world and could play awhile. She was marvelous."

King Oliver was playing at Lincoln Gardens in 1922 when he

asked Louis Armstrong to come to Chicago from New Orleans to play second trumpet in his Creole Jazz Band.

They formed an incomparable team. The two of them would play a duet of "Holy City" that "would make the hair on your head rise," Alberta said. "Louis was like a great big, overgrown kid. He was just as sweet, nice, and kind as he could be. And he loved his music. Louis used to play with all the heart he had. You could see he enjoyed what he was doing. Everybody loved him."

Including Lil, who left her husband and started going out with Louis, to the chagrin of her mother, who financed Lil's passion for clothes and who insisted that her daughter was too good for Louis.

Lil and Louis Armstrong did get married finally in 1924. Louis left Lil in 1932 for a woman named Lucille, whom he later married. "Lil never got over it," Alberta said sadly, remembering that Lil died onstage shortly after Louis's death in July 1971, playing a tribute to him.

Songs like "After All Those Years" and "Don't Say You Don't Want Me" were written for Lil and all the other women having domestic troubles who came to the Dreamland to hear Ollie Powers sing.

"He was a great big, fat guy who looked like an ofay [a white man in the black slang of the era], the most wonderful disposition you ever saw in your life and just as sweet as he could be," Alberta said. "And what a voice!"

Ollie, who was a tenor, and Alberta were lucky to have such strong voices since there was no such thing as a microphone in those days, and the Dreamland was almost a block long. Alberta would go up to the platform and hum a tune to Lil. Alberta didn't know, and never did learn, how to read or write music, much less indicate the key in which she wanted something played. But, as she said, "Let somebody strike a wrong note, and I'll tell 'em right away. I know exactly what I want."

Lil would start playing the song, and the band would pick it up. When Alberta finished, she raised her arm to signal for them to stop. Alberta had both the band and the audience at her command. She became known as the "South Side's Sweetheart."

P. L. Prattis, a renowned black journalist writing for the *Pittsburgh Courier* (September 2, 1961, section 2, p. 9), recalled:

> Chicagoans of that day never said: "I'm going to the Dreamland."
> They said: "I'm going to hear Alberta."
> Just a slim, brown figure, a velvet voice, somewhat throaty, sparkling eyes which gave meaning to what she sang, and above all, friendliness.
> She was friendly with everyone but indiscreet with no one.
> Just a night club singer, you might say. But you'd be wrong. Every song she sang carried a message, and those to whom she sang took home the message and never forgot it. She paid for life's journey by comforting people and making them feel good all over.

Having a message and telling it well were Alberta's demands on a song and on herself in delivering it. She could croon a ballad as well as she could pour out the blues. Throughout her life she didn't want to be categorized as a blues singer or anything else. "Just call me a singer of songs," she always said.

From her earliest days as an entertainer she wanted to be able to size up an audience and its moods and give it what it wanted at any particular moment. Her tips and popularity suggested that her timing and choices were finely tuned.

Of course, there were those who wouldn't set foot in a place like the Dreamland to listen to her or anyone else sing the blues. That music, they were sure, was a one-way ticket to hell.

"Blues aren't sinful," Alberta said. "You're telling a story. Blues are a song from your soul. When you're singing the blues, you're singing."

The blues did break social conventions when singers, especially women, referred freely to sex, infidelity, loneliness, and frustration—"letting it all hang out" long before another generation coined that expression and thought it was doing something new.

Alberta found out how strongly some people disapproved of the blues when she tried once to visit her aunt Babe after she had moved to St. Louis. "She ignored me," Alberta said. "I guess 'cause she was supposed to be a Christian lady, and I'm singing jazz. And you know, you sing blues and jazz, and you're on your way to the devil with a hat on."

That's not what a lot of the elite, black and white, of Chicago who came in to pay her tribute thought. Nor did her pimp friends from Dago Frank's who came to see how their "little girl" was doing. Even the pickpockets came in after cleaning up downtown. They didn't bother anyone at the Dreamland, Alberta insisted.

"They came to enjoy themselves, and they did," she said. No booze was served at the Dreamland at the time because the city told club owners they had to choose between serving liquor or providing entertainment. Customers could bring their own bottles. But there were almost never any fights. People went there to have fun. Admittedly the fun got out of hand now and then when a person of one race passed to someone of the other, via one of the waiters or singers, a flirtatious note suggesting a rendezvous. The notes were called grenades for good reason. "If you got caught with one, things could get a little hot," Alberta said.

Alberta turned her nose up at anyone unrefined or too close to her own humble origins with whom others might associate her. She preferred to be seen greeting a young, handsome hulk from Rutgers University, an all-American football player who exuded charm and gentility. This was Paul Robeson, the man who would become the nation's greatest and most mistreated black actor.

"Paul used to come in and sit there by himself and have a beer," Alberta said. She would politely say hello to him, never guessing that one of her greatest moments onstage would occur with him in London many years later.

White entertainers came to the Dreamland after performing in the Loop because they wanted to imitate the style of the blacks, so popular at the time. "People from downtown would say we had something they just didn't have," Alberta said. One thing the black performers had was an incredible facility for improvisation, something basic to jazz, a special talent Alberta shared. "Some of the time I'd just sit there and make up something and start humming it, and the orchestra would pick it up. Now, how would they know what I had on my mind? How would they know to go from one note to the other? It's just that kindred feeling."

Musicians like Bix Beiderbecke and Frankie Trumbauer were entranced with what they heard from their counterparts who had come to Chicago from New Orleans, people like Lawrence Duhe, Sugar Johnny, Roy Palmer, Tubby Garland, Wellman Braud, Minor Hall, Tubby Hall, and Herbert Lindsay.

Al Jolson was there asking Alberta to sing his favorite song, "Mammy's Little Coal Black Rose."

Sophie Tucker, called a coon shouter because she tried to sing like a black, wanted to learn whatever it was that was making Alberta such a star. Before long she sent her maid, Belle, to ask Alberta to come back with her to the Tucker's dressing room at the Palace Theater, where she was appearing. She wanted Alberta to teach her how to sing "A Good Man Is Hard to Find," a song written by Eddie Green that Alberta introduced for him in 1918 and sang often for years.

"I never did go," said Alberta. "Something wouldn't let me. I think she would have liked to learn some of my tricks and to take advantage of me by getting popular on my style. But nobody can learn my style because I don't know it myself. It's always changing."

Finally Sophie sent her pianist, Ed Shapiro, over to take down notes as he listened to Alberta sing.

Whatever Alberta did, she did it right and made a killing from it. She started singing at the Dreamland in 1917 for $17.50 a week. Over the next five years there she worked up to $35, big money for a guaranteed salary in those days. Bottoms paid in cash—no checks—and always on payday. "No withholding tax," Alberta clarified. "Lord have mercy, nothing. But I'm afraid of the law," she said. "I was always taught to do right. So when I found that it was time for me to go in to pay income tax, I went on down there and paid it. Because I don't want no police coming near me. I'm afraid of them." Her fear lessened as she grew older and richer.

"But why is it every time I pay my income tax, I pay what the man tells me I owe, and then he always comes and says, 'You owe ten dollars more.' It's not my fault if he doesn't get it right, is it?"

What the tax man never heard about were the tips Alberta pulled in from big-time gamblers like Dan Gaines. "I used to go home with four hundred and five hundred dollars some nights in twenty and fifty-dollar bills," she said of her Dreamland days.

"Alberta wore heavily beaded dresses that glittered and sparkled as she shimmied around the room and sang," Lil Armstrong said (in an interview with jazz critic Chris Albertson). "Every now and then she'd make her breasts jump, and then the cats really loosened up on their bankrolls."

As much as Alberta made at the Dreamland, she still wanted to earn more. So she worked on days off or after hours as a drop-in girl, a singer who circulated from one club to another, at places like the Pekin, Packy McFarland's, Lorraine Garden #2 (formerly known as the Paradise Gardens), Elite Number Two and the Entertainer Café in Chicago.

Lillian Curry saw Alberta at most of those places in 1917. "Alberta wasn't a beauty," she said. "But she had a certain flair. When she sang, people listened, and I thought that was a big compliment."

"I was glad I went along," said Mrs. Curry, "because some of those girls, like Alberta, went on to great heights."

Some of the after-hour places would stay open as long as customers wanted to be there, sometimes until nine or ten the next morning. And no one would bother anyone else. "If you'd lose a hundred dollars, someone would see you drop it and say, 'Hey, fellow, you dropped this money,' " Alberta said.

She would even catch a train late at night to go about half an hour out to the Burnham Inn on the outskirts of Chicago. The trip was worth it because she could clean up in tips there.

That was the first time she knew she was working with gangsters. Many of them ran the clubs where she had been singing, but she said she was not aware of their other activities. As long as she got her money, she didn't care who was up to what. Besides, they were good to artists, protecting them, helping them out as they had the money and influence to do, and really enjoying them.

In Burnham she saw how nonchalantly gangsters killed each other off. "In those days you could kill a horse in Chicago, and they didn't care," she said. "Fighting was an amusement in Chicago." One night the lights went out at the inn while she was singing. Bang. When the lights came back on, a guy was lying dead by the piano at Alberta's feet.

Alberta always refused to name any gangsters involved in this or any other incident. "I'm not calling a living gangster's name," she said. "No, baby. Because they would snap me off in a minute."

That was probably the first time, too, that the gangsters knew they were associating with an entertainer who was a thief. There may have been a dead man at Alberta's feet when the lights came on, but her hand was alive and well in the cigar box on top of the piano, snatching a fistful of the dollar tips that musicians and singers were supposed to divide equally at the end of the night.

"I was paralyzed. I couldn't move," said Alberta, cackling as she remembered getting caught. "I just kept my hand in the box. Course, the musicians said we had been doing it all along, which we had been doing."

Normally she was a bit more subtle in making off with the loot. Alberta was known for always having a long scarf dangling from a ring on her finger. "I like to be different," she said. "I'd always pay a lot of money for them. If I had on a black dress, I'd get a gorgeous red or yellow one, something that would be a contrast. I'd just handle it unconsciously but with flair. Jiving."

Those scarves may have made her look distinctive. But they also camouflaged the bills in her hand that she was supposed to share with the musicians. If the wad in her hand got too big, she would just "scratch a little itch" over the bottom of her V-shaped neckline and let a little something fall in there.

Another trick was to drop some of the money on the floor just as a certain waiter was coming along. By previous agreement, he would manage to scoop up the loot that the two of them would split later. "It was a shame, but I did it just the same. I guess everything was dirty."

And to milk more tips out of her customers, Alberta would move from one table to another and sing so low that only the people at one table would be able to hear her. If people at another table wanted to hear the same song or any other, they'd have to tip her for a similarly intimate appearance.

One white woman, Bea Palmer, used to tear a fifty-dollar bill in two and give Alberta half to start singing a song. The other half was paid at the end of that song. So Alberta would bait her with the beginning of the first song, get half a bill working in her hands, then start into another number she knew the woman liked to get part of another bill. "I knew her weakness," said Alberta. "Yeah. So I'd get both of them bills."

To "break the monotony of singing at the Dreamland" Alberta often accepted out-of-town engagements. In January 1919 she sang for a couple of weeks at Michaelson's in Cincinnati. One of the waiters there, a good-looking guy a year older than she, by the name of Willard Saxby Townsend, was just back from the war. He was still wearing his soldier's overcoat and cap. "He had the prettiest eyes you ever saw in your life," she said. "Oh, he was handsome!"

Some eyeing got done both ways because the two of them crossed the river to Covington, Kentucky, on January 27, 1919, and got married. Amanda Randolph, who was playing the piano at Michaelson's at the time, stood up for Alberta at the ceremony. (Years later she played Sapphire's hussy of a mother on the *Amos 'n' Andy* television show.)

"Lord, it's a shame the way I treated him," Alberta said of Willard. "It's not that he wasn't a decent character." Willard presented a good image of a protector, something most black female entertainers at that time found both necessary and convenient. Some of them wanted a man to put order into their lives, if not to dominate them, to tell them what to do.

Alberta, proud of being able to take care of herself from an early age, thought a handsome husband would be useful as a status symbol. He might also undermine the conclusion she knew many people drew that she was a "bulldiker," a lesbian. All the better if Willard's presence would stop their wagging tongues.

But Alberta was a lesbian. As a child she refused to play with boys to avoid their sexual advances. Her inability at a young age to protect herself from being molested by men reinforced her proclivity to limit her sexual relationships to women.

She grew up in a household and an era that did not permit discussion of sexuality, much less acceptance of homosexuality. The subject remained one she refused to discuss. But she went further.

Alberta did everything to conceal this preference all her life. In her mind lesbianisn tarnished the image of propriety and respectability she struggled so hard to achieve.

Alberta said that she really loved Willard. "Yes, I did. I only knew him a couple of days. But I loved him. I could see he was a fine young man and a perfect gentleman. I've always been crazy about class." (She laughed off their later separation by saying she "wasn't the type to stay at home and see that the man's underwear is clean or get him a good meal and all. I wasn't cut out to be a good wife.")

They went back to Chicago together and stayed with her mother, who charged Willard nine-dollars-a-week rent, according to the divorce suit he filed in 1923. Alberta didn't give their relationship a chance to develop. She didn't even sleep with Willard. She said she was embarrassed to sleep with her husband in her mother's house, so she slept with her mother. (He didn't mention that to the court.)

Alberta went back to work at the Dreamland, but Willard didn't get a job right away. "The fellows around Chicago, you know, the ones that were in the sporting life, they wanted him to just hang around and see me work," Alberta said. "I told him to get a job."

She worked late at the Dreamland and then normally went to an after-hours place to earn another buck or two or twenty. He usually went with her but then didn't want to get up in the morning and look for a job. "So I told him to just try to find another place to go," she said, laughing. "If you step back and don't step up for yourself," she rationalized, "somebody else is going to step ahead of you. So I pushed him. I helped myself by helping him."

Willard Townsend told the judge he tried to keep Alberta at home. "She insisted on going on entertaining at cabarets," he said. "She told me that she could make more money than I could give her and that she did not like domestic life. I kept after her and told her I would rather she would stay at home and not do that kind of work. After I told her the last time, she left." That was on March 18, 1919, two months after their marriage.

Willard never criticized Alberta. Years later he and Ed Welch, brother of singer Elizabeth Welch, visited the home in Annandale, Virginia, of a man named Kenneth L. Kramer.

"Bill asked if I had records by Alberta Hunter," Kramer said in a letter dated November 28, 1977, to *New Yorker* magazine writer Whitney Balliett. "I played several of them. He listened with pleasure, and I asked the source of his interest. He said he had been married to her a long time before, when he was a young man and when she was already a star. I asked what had happened, being far brasher then, and he replied, somewhat sadly, 'I was just too damn young.' "

Willard went back to Cincinnati to live with his mother, said Alberta, who didn't answer a court summons four years later. The divorce was decreed on March 23, 1923.

Alberta went to New York to visit soon after separating from Willard in 1919. Singer Revella Hughes remembers meeting her and singer Maude Russell, known as the Slim Princess, briefly early that year in front of the Alhambra Theater in Harlem. Revella immediately liked Alberta.

"She was nice to everyone," Revella said. "And her bearing! They should have called her Lady Hunter."

Alberta had read in the March 1, 1919, edition of the *Chicago Defender* the society column review of the party Mrs. Bert Williams gave in her palatial home at 2309 Seventh Avenue in Harlem. Among the "gowned and bejeweled" present was Miss Lottie Tyler. Alberta was impressed. It encouraged her to look up the winsome young woman who had been so friendly when they met at the Panama Café in Chicago.

Alberta found Lottie at her aunt's house. She went up to the door and knocked. "I didn't know you had to meet people formally," Alberta said. "I didn't know you had to at least walk in and say, 'Good morning,' graciously. You don't go knocking on the door and say [as she did to Lottie's uncle] 'Lottie here?' "

"That's how I met Bert Williams, out of the clear blue sky, for no rhyme or reason," Alberta said. "He didn't pay any attention to me. I wasn't even alive. He was a West Indian. They're full of baloney, a lot of them. Thought they were better than God made little apples. Forgive me for saying it, because so many of my friends are West Indians and I love 'em so. But they've always been big shots."

The snub she received from Williams made Alberta more careful in the future about her manners. She didn't hold the incident against him because she respected him. "I admired him and was proud of him. Because at the time colored people weren't getting the breaks that I thought they deserved. I was happy to see somebody get them, especially those who were ladies and gentlemen."

Williams, a light-skinned black from Antigua, had trained to be a Shakespearean actor. Not finding work, he joined George Walker to form the comedy team of Williams and Walker. They were allowed to perform only if Williams used black face, a humiliation that he accepted but that tormented him.

While in New York Alberta also dropped in to say hello to her old friend W. C. Handy who with Harry Pace had opened the Pace and Handy Music Company on Broadway and published that spring, among other titles, a new song called "Uncle Sam Ain't No Woman, But He Sure Can Take Your Man."

There is no record of Alberta's having performed in New York that year, so she probably stayed only a short time. She was back in Chicago by late July 1919, for she remembered being at the Dreamland the day the race riot, one of the worst in U.S. history, broke out.

Blacks faced increased discrimination in urban areas in the North, where they were migrating in large numbers and challenging poor whites for housing and menial jobs. Black newspapers were filled with stories of victims of lynchings, brutality, church bombings, and injustice in the courtroom. The Ku Klux Klan was again on a rampage throughout the country. Black veterans were embittered because they had fought overseas for democracy and their country only to return and be treated as inferior civilians, a complaint still voiced fifty years later by black veterans of the Vietnam War. *The Birth of a Nation*, a film banned in a number of northern cities for fear it would spark riots, ridiculed the black race. It didn't take much to light a fuse.

On July 27, 1919, a group of whites hurled rocks at black teenager Eugene Williams while he was swimming near a "whites only" beach on Lake Michigan near Twenty-ninth Street in Chicago. Williams was struck on the head and drowned. In the four days of rioting that ensued thirty-eight people were killed and hundreds were injured, the majority in both categories being blacks.

Alberta weathered that storm as she did all others, minding her own business. She remained in Chicago until the end of the year, when she went to New York to celebrate New Year's Eve with Lottie. The two of them enjoyed being together so much they even thought of traveling together to Europe. On January 1, 1920, Alberta wrote the U.S. Department of Commerce asking for a copy of her birth certificate so that she could apply for a passport. She gave her address as 109 West 139th Street, c/o Miss Lottie Tyler. Lottie was renting an apartment there at the time from a woman by the name of Mrs. Pauline Reid.

One or both of them changed their mind about the trip. Alberta returned to Chicago shortly after the new year. She and Lottie were to be friends and lovers for many years, but their relationship did not require their living together or even being in the same city or country at the same time. Alberta was strong-willed and independent and wanted to travel and pursue her career when and where it suited her.

She very much wanted to appear onstage. While she was singing at the Dreamland, she met Eloise Scott, a performer with J. Rosamond Johnson's vaudeville act, and said to her, "Gee, I wish I could get on the stage. How do you go about it?" (Eloise wrote Alberta on June 20, 1944, reminding her of this conversation and that Alberta was the only person she ever let use a song of hers called "Wild Oats." "We are old cronies who had much in common in days gone by," she wrote.) She told Alberta, "It only takes guts and nerve" to get into the theater.

Alberta put herself to it and appeared for the first time in her life in a musical comedy revue called *Canary Cottage*, which opened on August 23, 1920, for a two-week engagement at the Avenue Theater at Thirty-first Street and Indiana Avenue in Chicago. Songwriter and comedian Shelton Brooks produced and starred in this the first show for his recently created theatrical group, which included Ollie Powers, Evelyn Preer, Marguerite Lee, and Alberta.

The only press comments Alberta received for her performance were brief notes in the *Chicago Defender* (August 28, 1920, p. 4) saying she wore a gown that brought "gasps" from the audience and made four encores with the chorus of a song she sang called "Wake Me Up with the Blues."

The group's next show, *Miss Nobody from Starland*, opened on September 6, also at the Avenue. Alberta played Nina, an Egyptian princess who was a stowaway on board the *Aquitania*. The son of a "hair restorer maker" convinces the captain not to deliver the princess, with whom he has fallen in love, over to the authorities. A *Chicago Defender* review merely said, "Alberta does fairly well in her lines, but her real forte is her singing" (Sept. 11, 1920, p. 4).

September Morn was the last of Brooks's series. It ran from September 19 to October 2. Alberta played the role of Argentina, a Persian dancer about to make her New York debut. Her enterprising agent tells the press that Argentina was the model for a famous painting by the same name. He steals the painting and has his client's face painted over the original but then makes the mistake of having it delivered to the home of the artist rather than of the owner. The *Chicago Defender* called it a "classy musical comedy," not to be missed.

The company played *Canary Cottage* at the Dunbar Theater in Philadelphia for the next two weeks and opened with it on October 18 at the Lafayette Theater in Harlem. Alberta left the company the next week and returned to Chicago.

Shelton Brooks picked Maude Russell, whom Alberta had met the year before in New York, to replace her in the play. He asked her to go by the Dreamland to pick up the script that Alberta still had with her.

"Alberta got bitchy," said Maude.

"What you hanging around here for? Trying to take my job away?" Alberta said to her. When Maude explained her mission, Alberta treated her more politely.

Alberta was in no danger of losing her job. She was again the queen of the Dreamland, the new Dreamland. Bill Bottoms had just finished structural changes and renamed his place the Dreamland Café. He had added a balcony where the musicians would perform. Below it, there were tables set with crisp white linens, giving space for a new dance floor made of glass with colored lights underneath it. The Chinese chef was serving the best chop suey in Chicago.

The Dreamland was also perfecting the art practiced by many clubs in Chicago of staying open past the official closing hour. "They were supposed to close at midnight," said Alberta. "But the minute they turned the key that way, the door was locked. Then they turned it back this way, and the club would be open for breakfast dance."

With its new sophisticated look, the Dreamland Café was the most spectacular night spot in black America. And its image made Chicago the place to be for a black entertainer. Said Alberta: "If you had worked in Chicago and had been recognized there, you were somebody, baby. New York didn't count then."

Songwriters like W. C. Handy recognized that, too. Alberta had introduced and made famous his "Beale Street Blues" and Eddie Green's "A Good Man Is Hard to Find." As the *Chicago Defender* said, "Miss Alberta Hunter . . . contributed as much to putting over these two song numbers as any headlined artist on Broadway, for it was her continued use of them that brought these songs to the attention of the best vaudeville singers" (October 23, 1920, p.4).

So it was natural that when Handy had another new song to introduce, he took it to Alberta. That was early in November 1920. Handy had been in Brownlee's Barber Shop in Chicago, where he wrote the lyrics and orchestration for "Loveless Love." The song begins, "Love is like a gold brick in a bunco game."* Once it and his haircut were through, he took it next door to the Vendome Theater where he had Professor Erskine Tate, the orchestra director, play it for him. Handy liked it, so even before he had it printed, he took it to Alberta and taught it to her.

"Brought it in on a piece of brown paper like you wrap groceries in," Alberta said. She introduced his song and helped make it one of his most popular. "It made a bull's-eye," Handy recalled in his autobiography, *Father of the Blues.* "Before Alberta reached my table on the night she introduced the song, her tips amounted to sixty-seven dollars. A moment later I saw another lady give her twelve dollars for 'just one more chorus.' I knew then and there that we had something on our hands, and the later history of the song bore this out."

The Dreamland became the place not only to hear new music but

---

*Copyright MCMXXI by Pace & Handy Music Co., Inc. Revised edition copyrighted MCML by W. C. Handy. Permission granted by Handy Brothers Music Co., Inc., New York, N.Y.

also to see the latest fashions. Alberta was determined to be the best-dressed woman there. "I don't like to sound like I'm boasting," she said, "but they used to say I wore such smart clothes. I paid a lot of money for my clothes." She had a tailor make a coat that was mole on top and seal on the bottom. "I paid eighteen hundred dollars for it then, so you know it must have been all right." (Years later she gave it away.) "That's where I started putting on clothes."

Alberta fell in love with a woman by the name of Carrie Mae Ward who owned a house at 3641 Prairie Avenue where her mother was then renting a room. She and Carrie Mae took an apartment at 4428 Prairie Avenue across the street from Jack Johnson, who in 1908 became the first black to win the heavyweight championship of the world, a title he held until 1915. (Joe Gans had already captured the lightweight trophy from a white man in 1902, so the two were folk heroes in being among the first blacks permitted to make it in the white sports world. Johnson, elected to the Boxing Hall of Fame in the year of its founding—1954—gained further notoriety by his two marriages to white women.)

Dr. Daniel Hale Williams lived on the second floor beneath Carrie and Alberta. Doc Williams, born near Pittsburgh in 1858 and a graduate of Northwestern Medical School, founded Chicago's Provident Hospital, the first open to all patients and doctors, regardless of race or creed, where in 1893 he performed the nation's first successful heart surgery.

"Carrie was a beautiful woman, and now that I know life, Carrie was a pretty smart woman," said Alberta, trying to put a smoke screen over their relationship. "There was a man . . . at the railroad company, who was keeping her. Not only he, but others, too.

"I remember Carrie saying, 'I'm going to make you the best dresser in Chicago.' " She started by putting Alberta in big bloomers, "like the Turks wore," Alberta said, making her the first entertainer in Chicago to dress exotically. "Boy, I wore some clothes. Chicks today think they're dressing up, but I was dressing up when they were in the cornfields."

She started dressing all right. But one dress in particular people seemed to remember, to Alberta's chagrin. It was a bright red dress, much too flashy for Alberta's taste. As rumor had it, every time the two women had a lovers' quarrel, Carrie locked up all of Alberta's clothes except the red dress, leaving her nothing else to wear. Considering Alberta's feisty nature, that red dress must have been worn out soon.

Lovie Austin, who later became accompanist for the great blues singers Ma Rainey and Ida Cox, was another fancy dresser in those days. At the time she was the music director of a little vaudeville house called the Monogram Theater at Thirty-fifth and South State streets associated with the Theater Owners' Booking Association.

Lovie had a Stutz Bearcat upholstered in leopardskin to match the outfit she liked to wear while tearing around in the car. Alberta took a drive with her once. Never again. "She drove it like someone who had just bought an oil field," Alberta said. "She'd go so fast."

Alberta never had a car. She always preferred to take a bus or streetcar and save her money. A friend tried to teach her how to drive, but every time she drove at night and saw lights, she wanted to jump out. "So I knew I would either injure or kill somebody," she said.

Alberta worked at the Dreamland through 1921, a good year for black singers in general. The year before, Mamie Smith's recording of "Crazy Blues" for Okeh, the first vocal blues record, had sold more than a hundred thousand copies the month it was released, convincing recording executives there was a market for black singers. Mamie, wearing flashy gowns and diamonds, was a big hit at a concert in March 1921 at the Avenue Theater in Chicago.

That same year Harry Pace launched the Pace Phonograph Company of New York with the first black-owned label, Black Swan. Its slogan was "The Only Genuine Colored Record—Others Are Only Passing for Colored."

Black Swan's first recording was of Revella Hughes, a refined singer, singing "Thank God for a Garden." The seventh record was a bit more adventurous, with Ethel Waters singing "I'm Wild About Moonshine" and "It's Getting So You Can't Trust Nobody." Alberta made a brief trip to New York to cut Black Swan's next record—her first—in May 1921 with "How Long, Sweet Daddy, How Long" and "Bring Back the Joys," accompanied by Fletcher Henderson on the piano. At the same time she did a second Black Swan recording of two more songs, "He's a Darned Good Man (to Have Hanging Round)" and "Some Day Sweetheart."

Alberta described Pace's "little bitty studio" in New York. She stood in one room singing through a horn placed in a small, square window. In the adjoining room a needle cut into a thick brown wax on the revolving matrix, spinning off a curlicue shaving that a technician brushed off onto the floor. "And this fellow took so much pains to try to see that the recording would be good," she said.

Alberta's self-taught, classy diction and her smooth voice got her on records, but these qualities weren't enough to get her in the cast of *Shuffle Along*, a major musical event of 1921 and the first all-black show on Broadway since the famous Williams and Walker shows more than ten years earlier. The book was written by Flournoy Miller and Aubrey Lyles; the musical score by Eubie Blake; the lyrics by Noble Sissle. As J. A. Jackson, a black columnist for *Billboard*, wrote (June 11, 1921, p. 45), "This show is a rainbow of hope and encouragement to every artist of the race." It opened the doors for the appearance of many other black shows for the next decade.

Blake and Sissle hit the jackpot with songs of theirs like "Love Will Find a Way" and "I'm Just Wild About Harry." The show opened on May 21, 1921, at the Sixty-third Street Theater with a cast that in New York and on the road included Florence Mills, Adelaide Hall, Josephine Baker, and Paul Robeson. It grossed eight million dollars.

Alberta called Sissle a dicty because he had an air of superiority coupled with a "color complex." He considered her too dark to be in his show, she said. (Sissle also overlooked Alberta in 1924 when casting for his musical comedy *The Chocolate Dandies*.) "I lived to tell him what I thought about him," said Alberta. Better yet, she outlived him, although even that satisfaction didn't totally assuage her bitterness toward him.

In spite of that rejection, Alberta's reputation continued to grow. In November 1921, when Bill Bottoms took on two new partners at the Dreamland, Clarence McFarland and James H. Williams, and expanded the orchestra to twelve pieces, fifteen hundred people turned out for the reopening to hear the "ragtime song bird deluxe" as the *Chicago Defender* called Alberta. Her fans kept the place jammed every night and on Sunday afternoons, when the show was accompanied by the one-dollar dinner of either creamed chicken and rice or stewed chicken and spaghetti followed by peach cobbler.

By year's end Alberta was even featuring some of the songs from *Shuffle Along* like "If You Haven't Been Vamped by a Brownskin, You Haven't Been Vamped at All."

In January 1922 Alberta gave what was one of the few dinner parties in her life. Black Swan Records must have put her up to it, if not paid for the groceries as well, to help promote the company and its singer Ethel Waters, known as "Sweet Mama Stringbean," who was in Chicago on tour with the Black Swan Troubadours. Four of her northern musicians quit there rather than go south with her, but she was determined to go ahead. (It was on that trip that the body of a young black boy, lynched because he supposedly talked back to a white man, was thrown into the lobby of a theater where she was to appear. Ethel fled Atlanta one night because of threats on her life as well.)

Ethel, like Alberta, was a reject for the famed musical *Shuffle Along*. The casting director turned her down because he considered her "just a cheap honky-tonk singer."* By the next year, however, she was fast becoming one of the most popular black recording stars of the era.

The dinner guests included Miss Waters, Ethel Williams (a lover of Ethel Waters for several years), Martha Briscoe, Marguerite Ricks, and Alvin Malone.

"All voted Miss Hunter a charming hostess," said the *Chicago Defender*, probably copying a press release since the typically foulmouthed Ethel Waters never found anyone else "charming," certainly no one like Alberta, whose good manners and talent would take any attention away from her.

No mention was made of the presence of Carrie Mae, Alberta's lover. But since they still lived together and Alberta didn't know how to cook, Carrie Mae must have been the one who prepared the meal.

Alberta was disenchanted with Black Swan for doing so little promotion of her records in contrast with the big buildup it was

---

*Jervis Anderson, *This Was Harlem* (New York: Farrar Straus Giroux, 1981), p. 133.

giving Ethel Waters. So when Paramount asked her to come to New York and make the first record on its new "race" series in July 1922, she readily accepted. She signed an exclusive contract on August 19 following her first two recording sessions earlier that summer. The agreement made a regular commuter out of her on the train between Chicago and New York.

That first release, recorded in July, was of "Daddy Blues" and "Don't Pan Me." At the same time she recorded "Why Did You Pick Me Up When I Was Down, Why Didn't You Let Me Lay" and "After All These Years" for one release. For another she sang "Gonna Have You, Ain't Gonna Leave You Alone" and, for the first time, one of her own songs. It was called "Down Hearted Blues."

She hummed her song one day when she was with Lovie Austin back in Chicago, then sang one of the verses:

> *Gee! but it's hard to love someone*
> *When that someone don't love you,*
> *I'm so disgusted, heart broken too*
> *I've got the down hearted blues . . .*

"Ooh, that's wonderful, honey," Lovie told her. As Alberta sang, she improvised with some new words. "Different little things would come to me that rhymed," she said.

> *Got the world in a jug, got the stopper in my hand*
> *Got the world in a jug got the stopper in my hand*
> *And if you want me, you must come under my*
> *command.*

Lovie, who already had some recording experience, told Alberta this was a song that ought to be recorded. ("Lovie was a wonderful woman," Alberta said. "She was kindhearted. She tried to help anybody and everybody that she could.")

"Well, okay," Alberta told her, needing her help to write down the music. "If you think it could be a good song, you can have the tune that I'm humming, and I'll take the words."

Lovie sent the manuscript of the music and lyrics to Washington,

D.C., where they were copyrighted on April 25, 1922. The fact that she put the lyrics in Alberta's name forever impressed Alberta with Lovie's honesty when everyone else was taking advantage of other composers. "She could have stolen the whole thing from me, and I would never have known the difference," Alberta said.

"Down Hearted Blues" became a big hit. It was recorded by every other label at the time, according to Alberta, becoming the first song to achieve that popularity. And it was distributed widely throughout the country by Pete Wendling and Max Kortlander on their piano rolls.

Alberta recorded another two sides with Paramount in New York in July 1922, with Eubie Blake on the piano. They were "I'm Going Away Just to Wear You Off My Mind" and "Jazzin' Baby Blues."

Then she appeared along with the great comedy team of Moss and Frye in a variety show that opened on August 14 at the Lafayette Theater in Harlem. She recorded at Paramount again in early September, this time "You Can't Have It All" and "Lonesome Monday Morning Blues."

On September 11 she appeared in a new show called *Dumb Luck* with music and lyrics by Donald Haywood and Porter Grainger. It opened at the Lyceum Theater in Stamford, Connecticut, and ran for two days. "The show was lousy, so they closed it," said Alberta.

Black music critic J. A. Jackson criticized the promoter for taking ninety-three black performers out on the road and hoping through good press to raise the money to bring the show into New York and pay the cast. "Another colored show numbering many artists of unusual merit has come upon evil days because of the callous-heartedness of a mountebank promoter," Jackson wrote in the *Afro-American* (October 6, 1922, p. 13). "These fellows with a lot of nerve, very little cash, less knowledge of the show business and a total lack of any sense of moral responsibility have preyed upon the confidence of the colored performer. The handicap of so often being denied their fair chance has made the Negro actor anxious to the point of gullibility."

Ethel Waters, who was in the cast, took the costumes and either sold or pawned them to raise enough money to get the performers back to New York. Those who were stranded included a who's who of black entertainers: Moss and Frye, Boots Marshall, Cleo Desmond, Dick Wells, Ruby Mason, the Will Elkins Glee Club, Revella Hughes, Lena Horne's mother, Edna, and Lottie Tyler, who was in the chorus line.

But Waters, infuriated by having a strong competitor in Alberta for the affection of both the audience and the cast, bought rail tickets only for herself and her girlfriend, Ethel Williams. Not to be outdone, ever, Alberta pulled a wad of bills from her bosom, to the wonderment and cheers of the cast, and got the rest of them safely back home.

Alberta decided Chicago was safer territory for the time being and headed back just in time to be at the Dreamland on the afternoon of September 22 to perform for singer Cora Green, the leading lady, and the rest of the cast of *Strut Miss Lizzie*, a musical on tour from New York that had opened at the Auditorium Theater. Dreamland owner Bill Bottoms had the habit of inviting the entire casts of visiting shows to his café.

"We had never seen anything like it," said Harry Watkins, a tall, lanky dancer in the chorus line of that particular production. First on the program at the Dreamland was Mae Alix, singing and doing splits. Then the master of ceremonies announced, "And now, ladies and gentlemen, the pièce de résistance."

"And out came Alberta with an act bigger than Pavarotti's," said Harry. She sang "Chicago, Chicago, that toddling town . . ." then did a risqué number, for which she was becoming famous, called "If You Want to Keep Your Daddy at Home."

After hearty rounds of applause Alberta went over to the table where Harry was sitting with Al Moiret, another good-looking chorus boy. Harry, although from a poor family in North Carolina, talked and carried himself gallantly. Yet he could tell dirty jokes and carry on like a "yard dog," as he says. He was one of the few people Alberta ever met who truly amused her.

It was friendship at first sight for both of them, a devoted one that was to last for sixty years. Alberta loved Harry's authenticity and flair, his willingness to let her boss him around, and, above all, his discretion in not talking with others about her private life, an attitude he continued even after her death. To him she gave her highest accolade: "I can trust Harry."

Alberta was at the height of her success in Chicago and as a recording star. Paramount bought half pages in newspapers to advertise the "prima donna of blues singers." In an ad for "Down Hearted Blues" it even offered to its sales representatives a large, autographed "original photo of beautiful Alberta Hunter in a striking pose," which was nothing more than her sitting with her legs crossed, on a piano bench, a hat on her head and bundled in a mink coat.

Early in 1923 she became the first black singer to be accompanied by an all-white band, the Original Memphis Five, on her Paramount recording of " 'Tain't Nobody's Biz-ness If I Do," a song she introduced for its composer, Porter Grainger, and "If You Want to Keep Your Daddy Home."

Her achievements attracted attention from Paramount's competitors. On January 19, 1923, Frank Walker of the Columbia Graphophone Company in New York tried to lure Alberta into his fold. ("I loved Mr. Walker," Alberta said. "He was a prince. He was fine.")

"No doubt you know that the Paramount Company is very small indeed, and the prestige that you gain from singing for them is very limited," the sly prince wrote to Alberta. He asked her to advise him when her exclusive contract expired.

He must have inquired earlier about both her and King Oliver's availability. She obviously recommended he recruit Oliver in spite of her not being free herself because in the same letter he said, "Regarding Joe Oliver's band, my only idea in this respect was to use them as an accompaniment for you in case you did work for us. It will therefore be necessary for us to forget them until such a time as you will be ready to do a test record for us." Columbia wasn't after Oliver. It wanted Alberta.

Alberta, realizing how desirable she was as a singer, decided to cash in on that popularity by offering her talents to other, less scrupulous recording companies by using a pseudonym. Mae Alix—a woman she helped escape a dismal job in the Chicago stockyards (one of the few major employers of blacks) for a singing slot at the

Dreamland—owed her a favor. So several of the songs Alberta recorded for Paramount in New York in February 1923—among them "You Shall Reap Just What You Sow," Lovie Austin's "Bleeding Hearted Blues," W. C. Handy's Loveless Love," and her own "Chirpin' the Blues"—were also issued by the Harmograph, Famous, and Puritan labels under the name of Mae Alix.

She sang other songs recorded for Paramount that year on the Silvertone label as Helen Roberts and on the Harmograph label under the name of Monette Moore, a singer who was just starting to record and whom Alberta was helping promote by using her name. (Monette later used her own pseudonym, Susie Smith.)

Alberta thought she was putting one over on Paramount—"slickology," as she called it. "I used those other names to stay out of trouble," she said. "I didn't realize they could trace me down just the same. At that time I wasn't as slick as I am now," she said just before she died.

Paramount stepped up its promotional effort with a full-page ad for "Bleeding Hearted Blues" in the *Chicago Defender*. Darkened drops of blood dripped off the word *bleeding* on the page. The text was equally ardent. It read: "She craved love. Wild, passionate kisses—long, dizzy embraces. And so she sings 'Bleeding Hearted Blues'—a song of recklessness—of burning desire—of desperate longing. Don't miss this daring new Blues hit, sung by dashing Alberta Hunter—the Race Songstress who has startled the world with her sensational Blues songs."

About the only person Alberta really startled was Mae Alix's boyfriend, who thought her association with Alberta was too close for his comfort. Paramount must have put blood on Alberta's mind because she smelled serious trouble one night at a small club on Wabash where she often sang after her stint at the Dreamland. Just as she was about to enter a swinging door at the club, the boyfriend, having spotted her approach, slammed the door into her when he left.

"I went right on, did my work that night," Alberta said. "But afterwards I went straight home, packed my trunk, and left the next morning for New York because he looked like he had fire in his eyes. He was going to try to hurt me one way or the other."

Before leaving, however, Alberta asked Bill Bottoms to let Mae take her place heading the show at the Dreamland, a request he granted. Again she helped someone else by helping herself.

Alberta rationalized her hasty departure by saying it was again time for her to climb another step toward success. And that, in her mind, could only mean a move to Broadway.

"I conquered Chicago. What did I want to stay there for?" she said. "I wanted to go to New York, where there was publicity, celebrity. 'Cause if you make it on Broadway, you have nothing to worry about. You've gone as far as you can go, except to heaven."

CHAPTER THREE

Climbing to Higher Ground

So again, on Saturday evening, April 14, 1923, Alberta caught a train, "moving up," but this time heading east, following the stars that would light up the Great White Way for her. On the following Wednesday she opened on Broadway and became a star.

Comedian Eddie Hunter's new show *How Come?*, for which he wrote the book and Ben Harris wrote the music and lyrics, opened at the Apollo Theater on Forty-second Street at Broadway on Monday, April 16. Sam H. Grisman, the producer, had great expectations for the show that he advertised as "a girlie musical darkomedy." With reason. More money, eighty thousand dollars, had been invested in it than in any other black show to date, including *Shuffle Along* in 1921.

Eddie Hunter was nervous about the opening because they still hadn't found the right "specialty singer" (as opposed to a singer cast in a role) to introduce the finale with a song. Ethel Waters, Trixie Smith, and Bessie Smith all had been tried out, but none of them fitted the bill. When Hunter learned that Alberta had just arrived in New York, he asked her to come see him right away. She went to the theater for an audition late Monday morning, the day the show was to open.

Alberta went to the front door of the Apollo even though she knew that show people were supposed to use the backstage door. But they let her in anyway. Bill ("Bojangles") Robinson, the great tap dancer, was there and showed her down the aisle. Ethel Cavalier, who knew of Alberta from their mutual friend, Geraldyn Dismond, a member of Harlem society and a noted journalist, greeted her and introduced her to Will Vodery, the show's bandleader. Vodery, an arranger and bandleader, was Florenz Ziegfeld's orchestrator for many years.

"Ethel introduced me to this old dog," Alberta said. Vodery, who considered himself a lady-killer, insisted that Alberta accompany him alone to his office over the lunch hour to discuss her audition. He made a pass at her, and she bashed her knee in his groin, according to Chris Albertson, to whom she told the story years later. So, of course, when they got back to the theater, she suspected he would try to sabotage her audition. "I told him not to play me any vamps [repeated opening bars of music], just an introduction," she said. "Instead, he started vamping it." The result was disastrous. Grisman turned her down.

Billboard reported that Alberta; Lottie Tyler, with whom Alberta was staying again at 233 West 135th Street; and Lottie's aunt, Mrs. Bert Williams, were in the audience at the Apollo that evening for the opening. They and other blacks were allowed to sit on the main floor of the theater—a rare occurrence even for black musicals in the 1920s—although only to the far right or left of the center section, which was reserved for whites.*

J. A. Jackson, the black columnist for *Billboard*, called *How Come?* "the most stupendous colored production ever offered for Broadway's consideration" (April 28, 1928, p. 50).

None of the white newspapers praised the plot, comedy, acting, or singing. " 'How Come's?' chief defect is an unsuccessful attempt to imitate Broadway musical comedy," said the *New York Sun* (April 17, 1923, p. 14).

But a few of the papers were taken by the forty exotic dancers in the cast. "The ensembles are cyclonic, rhythmic gyrations, synco-

---

*Allen Woll, *Dictionary of the Black Theatre: Broadway, Off-Broadway—Selected Harlem Theatre* (Westport, Conn.: Greenwood Press, 1983), p. 82.

pated contortions, a maze of movement which are the essence of Afro-American jazz," said the *New York Evening Journal* (April 17, 1923, p. 20). "Those girls and boys strut their stuff—yes suh!"

The *New York Times*, a killjoy even in 1923, said, "The business of Negro musical comedies on Broadway was last night reduced to an absurdity with the production of 'How Come?' at the Apollo." It called the cast "mightily undistinguished and incapable" (April 17, 1923, p. 26). It didn't even note the appearance of by-then world-famous musician Sidney Bechet in the role of a clarinet-playing Chinaman or Andrew Tribble impersonating a female, Orphelia Snow, who is in love with Rastus, the leading male, a much rarer act onstage at that time than a woman impersonating a man.

Nor, obviously, did it find any humor in Eddie Hunter's performance as Rastus Skunktom Lime, convicted embezzler of the Mobile Chicken Trust Corporation in the little town of How Come?, who escapes from jail and, with his partner, Rufus "Buddy" Wise, played by George W. Cooper, sets up a bootblack parlor in Chicago as a front for a bootlegging operation. If you wanted gin, you asked to have your white shoes polished. If you wanted whiskey, you high-stepped in with your tan shoes.

Threatened with imminent failure after the dismal reviews, Grisman approved drastic changes in the show, including a trial run with Alberta beginning on Wednesday, April 18. She was sensational, said Harry Watkins, a chorus boy in the production. People weren't used to seeing a singer dress up the way Alberta did. That night she had on a white dress with pink rosebuds. She was introduced as "the songbird of the West."

Harry peeked out from behind the curtain and saw Sophie Tucker, Belle Baker, and Al Jolson in the front row going wild, just like the rest of the audience, hooting and hollering. He and several other members of the cast pushed Alberta back onstage after her first number, saying, "You're stopping the show, girl. Get back on out there."

"I didn't realize what that meant," Alberta said. "I thought I had taken a brody [flopped]."

She sang two songs, "You Shall Reap Just What You Sow," a song she said Alexander Robinson had written for her when she was still at the Dreamland, and "If You Want to Keep Your Daddy Home."

The white critics didn't go back a second time to review the revised show. But the black press was right there and took it all in. The *Baltimore Afro-American* (May 11, 1923) printed a big photo of Alberta on its front page with the caption "New Broadway star." *Billboard*'s J. A. Jackson, writing an updated review, called her an "instantaneous hit." He referred to her "stopping the show" as "the highest tribute that can be accorded any artist." He praised her "clarity of voice, mellowness of tone, a clear pronunciation, all blended and sent over the footlights with a savoir faire that has to place her in a class by herself."

Alberta's celebrity status in New York brought many invitations for her to perform at benefits. As tightfisted as she was with her money, she was always ready to give her time and talent to any benefit for members of her race. On May 20, 1923, soon after arriving in New York, she performed along with Paul Robeson, Revella Hughes, Georgette Harvey, and Will Marion Cook's Orchestra at the Shubert-Century Theater to raise money for a black women's charity.

Unfortunately Alberta's stardom didn't shine brightly enough to keep *How Come?* on Broadway. It closed after five weeks, unable to bring in enough revenue to pay the theater the guaranteed minimum of $4,000 a week. So the troupe hit the road. Alberta was to receive $140 a week but never did as ticket sales continued weak. But more important to her than the money at the time was her own success onstage.

After a two-week engagement at Philadelphia's Dunbar Theater the show opened on June 11 at the Lafayette Theater in Harlem. The *Amsterdam News* (June 13, 1923, p. 5) raved about "Alberta Hunter, the sensation, who stopped the show every night while it was at the Apollo Theatre . . . and, judging from the enthusiastic manner in which she was received, it is not farfetched to say that she is one of the best in her line today, barring none."

Four weeks later the group moved on to a succession of one-week stands at Newark's Shubert, Washington's Howard and Baltimore's Gayety theaters, then to Ithaca, New York, Harrisburg, Pennsylvania, and Binghamton and Buffalo, New York.

John Scott, a ballet student at the time who was visiting a friend in Buffalo on Labor Day 1923, remembers seeing Alberta there onstage. "She stood alone," he said. "If you saw her one time, you saw her all your life. Her presence and style marked you forever. She was motivated from within and had that inner something that projects."

The next stops were Toronto, Chicago, and the Michigan Theater in Detroit. By mid-October management problems had developed. The cast had agreed to accept lower than its contractual salaries until such time as the show produced more revenue. Now that it was doing so, the performers wanted their original salaries restored. When producer Grisman, who had been arraigned on July 2 on charges of forgery, refused the increase, the cast resigned and the show closed.

Before returning to New York, Alberta visited her mother and recorded four songs at the studios Paramount then was operating in Chicago: "Experience Blues" and "Sad 'n' Lonely Blues," with Tommy Ladnier on cornet, Jimmy O'Bryant on clarinet, and Lovie Austin at the piano; and "Miss Anna Brown" and "Maybe Someday" also with Lovie Austin and Jimmy O'Bryant.

Advertisements soon appeared in the major black newspapers for these records as well as for the songs Alberta had recorded in New York for Paramount in May—"Mistreated Blues," "Down South Blues," and "Michigan Water Blues," the first two with her own music and lyrics, and all accompanied by Fletcher Henderson at the piano—and in July—"Stingeree Blues" and "You Can't Do What My Last Man Did," with Fats Waller on piano.

In these early recordings Alberta's voice sounds screechy. Jazz critic Chris Albertson explains this: "She recorded in the beginning, unfortunately, for recording companies like Paramount that had inadequate equipment. When other companies were recording electrically, Paramount had a light bulb in the studio and that was the extent of their electricity and electrical process."

The strength of Alberta's voice, even in later years, could never be compared to that of a Bessie Smith or an Ethel Waters, Albertson has said, but as a live entertainer who could measure the mood of an audience and sing a song in a style and language it would appreciate, she was one of the best.

Bessie and Alberta had been recording many of the same songs, such as "T'Aint Nobody's Business If I Do," "Aggravatin' Papa," and "Bleeding Hearted Blues." Alberta liked Bessie's singing. "Her voice was so outstanding," she said. "You couldn't help but admire her."

The two women never met—not, however, because of any antipathy between them. "I don't think she disliked me," Alberta said. "She didn't have a chance to like or dislike me. She was a woman that just didn't bother."

Alberta certainly didn't go out of her way to meet Bessie either because she thought her a "little rough." Alberta disliked women who cursed, shouted, and fought, especially in public, and who were gaudy, as she found Bessie. "She wore feathers all over her head," Alberta said.

"Bessie had trouble with her men," she added. "Not me. 'Cause I was evil. If I thought someone was going to try to put something over on me, I'd laugh them off and go on about my business. Bessie would suffer."

Alberta never bought Bessie's records or those of any other blues singers. She didn't buy a gramophone until 1928, when she was in London, and then someone stole it from her. "It wasn't that I felt that I was better than anybody else or didn't have to listen, because you can always learn something from other people. It was just that I was so wrapped up in my work that I didn't listen to anybody's records."

Alberta did occasionally go to hear other singers but would never try to sing like them. "I always had my own style," she said emphatically.

In 1923 Bessie recorded a song Alberta wrote, "Down Hearted Blues," for Columbia. In six months it sold 780,000 copies, according to Albertson, becoming Columbia's first pop hit and the beginning of its "race" record series.

That success didn't do Alberta much good. For years she got no royalty payments for most of the songs she recorded, much less for the songs she wrote that other people recorded. In the early days Alberta would receive a contract and seventy-five dollars per side of each record she cut. The royalty was to be a fourth of a penny per record sold.

Alberta said her mother, thinking all those record contracts weren't important, threw them out. That is hard to believe. Miss Laura was a fastidious woman, compared to her daughter, who misplaced important documents throughout her life. It's more probable that Alberta herself lost the contracts and blamed her mother rather than accept the responsibility for having been taken advantage of all those years. Or it may be that Lottie or some other disgruntled lover threw them out to get even with Alberta after a quarrel.

Aiberta remembered getting $368 once for "Down Hearted Blues" from M. A. Super, a white man who was head of Paramount Records. "He was an honest man," she said. But that was the sum total of her royalties for many years for her most famous song.

She said J. Mayo ("Ink") Williams, the black manager of Paramount's "race" record series, kept most of the money due her. Without her knowledge or assent, he negotiated with other recording companies rights she thought she had sold only to Paramount, and he collected money in her name. "He was swiping my money," she said. He would also register other people as having written a particular song in addition to her and simply not distribute their cut of the royalties. The addition of famous names was a common practice with most of the recording companies in those days as a way of adding prestige to a record. "They wouldn't ask if it was all right to put Fletcher Henderson and Ethel Waters and eight or ten other people on your song as authors, too. That's the way they'd cheat you," Alberta noted.

Years later, when Alberta wised up to what had happened, she asked for, and received, a letter from Lovie Austin saying she had "had absolutely nothing to do with" the song "Chirpin' the Blues" that Alberta had written by herself.

"Ethel Waters was, I must say, nice," Alberta said begrudgingly, since Ethel had written another letter, as did Fletcher Henderson, saying they had not participated in writing the lyrics or music of Alberta's "Down South Blues." Both were listed on a royalty contract dated August 23, 1923, that Alberta later acquired and hung on to as proof of the hanky-panky.

Mayo Williams and Lester Melrose, a recording scout for OKeh, Victor, and Bluebird, eventually set up their own publishing companies and for a pittance acquired full rights to the music and lyrics of a number of people. Having no intention to publish anything, they held on to their properties, hoping to sell them one day to other publishers.

In 1984 Alberta heard that Williams was very ill. "I'm sorry he's sick," Alberta said. "He's lying there now in Chicago. He's a vegetable." She had no malicious satisfaction from seeing someone sick. Yet she believed strongly that people paid for their sins and that Williams was undoubtedly being punished for his.

Alberta returned to New York on October 25, 1923, days after *How Come?* had closed in Detroit. Eddie Hunter, not one to give up easily on his show, invited Alberta and some of the other members of the cast, including Amon Davis, George Cooper, and Andrew Tribble, to form a small traveling company called *Stars of How Come?* to perform some of its hit numbers. They opened at Harlem's Lincoln Theater in November, then moved on to the Douglass Theater in Baltimore.

William E. Ready, a journalist for the *Afro-American*, was intrigued with Alberta's presence onstage after so short a time performing in theaters. "During the past three years, the writer in his capacity as theatrical reviewer of this paper, has heard many 'blues' singers, ranging all the way from that brilliant galaxy in which scintillate such lights as Ethel Waters, Mamie Smith, Lucille Hegeman, Sarah Martin, etc. down to the frowsy little soubrette in the tab shows," he wrote (November 30, 1923, p. 4). "But we say without equivocation and in all honesty, Alberta Hunter . . . in our judgment stands at the forefront of them all."

Ready was also impressed by Alberta's lack of formal education and of her saying she had "picked up" what she learned as she "came up." He continued: "In 'picking up' she has done well, for her conversation and bearing have all the earmarks of one who has the advantage of fairly good schooling as well as cultural surroundings."

But what really surprised him was the fact she didn't want to use the income from her "instant success" to buy a car. "No, I haven't got one," she said. "And I don't intend to buy one. They are only excess baggage. I am saving my money to buy a home."

Surprisingly, Alberta let some money slip through her hands to buy a large ad in the *Chicago Defender* at the end of 1923 to promote herself while greeting her friends. It read: "Merry Xmas—Happy New Year, Alberta Hunter, Internationally known blues singer, affectionately called 'Brown Sugar' by New York's Theater Going Public."

The *Stars of How Come?* didn't last long. In December 1923 Alberta was back in New York, singing at the Hollywood Inn at Broadway and Forty-ninth Street. In early February 1924, she recorded again for Paramount with the Elkins-Payne Jubilee Quartette accompanying her singing of "Old-Fashioned Love" and "If the Rest of the World Don't Want You (Go Back to Your Mother and Dad)."

Alberta sang for the first time on radio on a WJZ broadcast on March 8, 1924, with Porter Grainger and Ethel Finnie. She also started rehearsals for another Eddie Hunter show.

Struttin' Time opened on May 18 at the Howard Theater in Washington. Eddie Hunter played Sherman Douglass Howard Washington Moppton, who flees his southern birthplace under the mistaken impression that he has accidentally shot the constable's wife. He goes to New York and works at the Hotel Strutt, where he falls in love with Dusty Snow, the head housemaid, none other than Andrew Tribble again in drag. Alberta had a minor role as Grenadine Green but did her usual showstopping by singing "Laugh Your Blues Away" and "Sweet Poppover." Catherine Yarborough, a chorus girl in *Shuffle Along* in 1921, who made her operatic debut in the United States in 1933 in the title role of *Aida* with the Chicago Opera Company, played the switchboard operator.

Paul Bass and Harry Watkins, whom Alberta often referred to as her "brother," were bellhops in the play. Among the total cast of seventy were Ada Brown, Dink Stewart, Nina Hunter, and Lena Roberts.

Although the *Washington Daily News* complained of the show's four-hour length, it applauded the performance: "When the soulgate becomes dry and creaks on its hinges; when a weary spirit fails to respond to such normal restoratives as spirit of ammonia, shellac and peptona—try a colored musical show. As the boys say—it will do you a world of good. . . . It's dance, dance, dance and sing, sing—with low comedy a-plenty."

Something was missing. Six weeks later, on June 30, when it closed at the Dunbar Theater in Philadelphia, only thirty-seven members of the cast were still hanging on. The performers, who had been receiving only twenty-five to fifty percent of their contracted salaries, received a final twelve dollars each to pay board bills and get home.

By that time Alberta had been in enough theaters and met enough performers, agents, and owners to know how she could make it on her own. She formed her own vaudeville act, Alberta Hunter and Company, later adding "Syncopation De Luxe" to the title, and opened at the Keith Theater in Jersey City on August 21, 1924. Keeping an act together was harder than it looked, because members of the group were constantly drifting off. But she typically kept two other people with her, doing a combination of singing, dancing, and comedy routines.

More troublesome for Alberta were the humiliating conditions imposed on black entertainers. About the only way then to survive was to work for the black vaudeville circuit, TOBA, with many of its theaters in the South. Pay was low, dressing rooms and rest rooms were decrepit or nonexistent, and the hours were dismal. One of its theaters, the Monogram in Chicago, required performers to put on ten shows a day.

"You had to have true grit to go on it because the conditions were so deplorable," said "Doll" Thomas, electrician for the Apollo in New York. And you had to take being treated like a dog outside the theaters in the South. He remembered a trip he took in the 1920s to Atlanta to resolve an electrical problem in the TOBA theater there. On finishing his work, he went to the train station to buy his ticket back to New York. The redneck clerk turned his head, spit on the floor, and said contemptuously, "Ain't no more niggers leaving here."

Alberta refused to work the TOBA circuit. But even at white theaters in the North where she did work, black women had to perform wearing bandannas, Aunt Jemima dresses, and gingham aprons; the men wore overalls.

"They wouldn't accept us Negro girls in smart clothes," said Alberta, who had been known onstage for her gorgeous gowns. "That's why Ethel Waters made up like a washerwoman for so many years."

And blacks were never given top billing. They were placed early in a show to warm it up. But if they were too good at doing that, white acts refused to follow them for fear of appearing bland by comparison. "We made it too hot for them," Alberta said.

She constantly had to swallow her pride to get work. "We resented it, but we wanted to get on the big time," Alberta said. "When you want to do something, you accept what you can get until you're in a position to speak out."

Alberta put up with the treatment because she was able to book her act on the East Coast at some of the Keith theaters, the most prestigious white vaudeville circuit in the country, which to her represented another important step up in her career.

The *Chicago Defender* (October 11, 1924, p. 8) reported her success on her own: "She is tying the bill into knots at every performance. Alberta Hunter has made a great name for herself in the East."

Alberta also gave two acclaimed performances at benefits in New York, one for the nearly blind prizefighter Sam Langford on August 15 at the Lafayette Theater, the other for the NAACP (National Association for the Advancement of Colored People) on November 17 at Happy Rhone's Club. The *Pittsburgh Courier* (November 22, 1924, p. 10) said the latter was the great social event of Harlem that year and described the entertainment provided by Amanda Kemps Dancing Dolls, Sissle and Blake, Fletcher Henderson's Band, and Alberta. She "was a scream" and "captivated the audience," it reported.

Traveling the vaudeville circuit had its limitations, Alberta found. She received little press coverage. The newspapers that year of 1924 were filled with rave reviews of Josephine Baker, Elizabeth Welch, and Amanda Randolph attaining stardom in the new Sissle and Blake musical comedy on Broadway called *The Chocolate Dandies* and of the fabulous Florence Mills in Will Vodery's *From Dixie to Broadway* at the Plantation restaurant on Broadway.

Record companies had big, splashy ads for Bessie Smith, Trixie Smith, Mamie Smith, Ida Cox, and Ma Rainey, whom Alberta called the "ugliest woman in the business."

And one could miss golden opportunities by not being in New York. That was the case with an offer to go to Paris. It happened while Alberta was out of town. Gene Bullard, manager of a little bistro in Paris called Le Grand Duc, at 52 Rue Pigalle, tried to get a singer from New York to replace Florence Embry, the temperamental star who had left him to open her own place called Chez Florence. Bricktop, in her autobiography by the same name, says Bullard sent for her.

Alberta had her own version of the event, which she learned of several years later. She personally wouldn't tell on Bricktop but expected Harry Watkins to do so. He would talk about it only after Alberta's death. Even then he looked heavenward and said, "Now, don't you all hit me." According to him, Kid Coles (a black American Harry believes was Florence's husband) sent the telegram for Bullard to Alberta c/o Eva Blanche, a former chorus girl who served meals around the clock to black entertainers in the large dining room of her Harlem apartment and held messages and mail for them when they were on the road. Bricktop picked up the telegram for Alberta, saying she was going to deliver it, read it instead, then took off immediately for Paris. As Harry said, "In those days you had to survive. You got a job wherever you could, however you could."

Joe Attles, a singer and dancer who took care of Bricktop in New York before she died, said, "If anybody stole a message for a job, it was Alberta Hunter, not Bricktop."

Harry said Bricktop did the same thing in 1935, swiping a message from a woman who had seen Alberta perform at Fred Payne's Bar in Paris and invited her to an engagement in Budapest. As he tells the story, Bricktop got off the train in Budapest. Once the woman who was there to meet Alberta understood what had happened, she took one fierce look at the light-skinned, freckle-faced Bricktop and shouted, "You get on the next train and go back because you're not the nigger I sent for."

So, while Bricktop was getting set up at the end of 1924 as a grand hostess in Paris, Alberta resumed her recording career in New York. Her last record had been with Paramount in February of that year. A month later Paramount absorbed Black Swan and reissued all of that company's records, including those Alberta had made.

She was upset that Paramount did so little promotion of her records and wasn't enthusiastic to have her do new ones. So she violated her exclusive contract by recording on the sly with Gennett in New York, using her dead half sister's name, Josephine Beatty.

On November 6 she recorded "Everybody Loves My Baby" with the Red Onion Jazz Babies. Louis Armstrong was on cornet; Aaron Thompson, trombone; Buster Bailey, clarinet; Lil Armstrong, piano; and Buddy Christian, banjo. Two days later she recorded "Texas Moaner Blues" with the same accompaniment, and on December 22, "Nobody Knows the Way I Feel Dis Mornin'," "Early Every Morn," and "Cake Walking Babies." That last session was with the Red Onion Jazz Babies, including the two Armstrongs, Christian on banjo, Sidney Bechet on clarinet and soprano saxophone, Charlie Irvis on trombone, and vocalist Clarence Todd.

Paramount discovered Alberta's subterfuge with Gennett. It "dropped" her before the end of the year, according to Robert M. W. Dixon and John Godrich.* Years later Alberta told a reporter for the *Amsterdam News* (November 5, 1938, p. 21) that her contract at Paramount was not renewed "because they said I sang too softly."

There was no quibbling about her voice when she went looking for a job at the Hot Feet Club, a small, intimate place on Houston Street in New York. She heard about the opening from Mae Barnes, a tap dancer and singer in *Runnin' Wild* whom she met at a party just before Christmas 1924. Robert H. ("Feet") Edson had contracted Mae and singer/dancer Mercy Marquez to join a show at his club. Mae told Alberta he wanted another singer. Alberta always expressed her gratitude to the few people like Mae who helped her find work.

Feet Edson was a gangster, said Mae. "He could blow you away or anybody else. He had his mob. But that's where the money was going to be made. You could make two hundred and fifty dollars a night there."

That is, if you cheated the musicians out of their full share. While Alberta was building up her bosom with tips, Mae was doing splits the better to stash bills in her bloomers. Their pianist, Garland Wilson, must have gone home broke most nights working with those two highway robbers. He held no grudges, though, and the three

Recording the Blues (New York: Stein & Day, 1970), p. 27.

of them became inseparable whether they were going to parties or to silent films. Garland always had to pay his way because according to Mae, "Alberta hung on to a dollar until the eagle cried. She even had Confederate dollars. That's how much she saved money! If she had a dollar, she put ninety-nine cents away."

Alberta was "a very plain person," Mae said. "She couldn't stand people who put on airs." And among intimate friends, she would tell as good a dirty joke as anyone. "She could get lonely, but you'd hardly know it because she wouldn't give vent to her feelings." One thing she let you know about her was that she was bossy. "She could be very domineering outside of work," Mae said. "She liked to have her own way. If she didn't get it, she'd sulk and wouldn't talk to nobody."

Although Mae lived a few blocks from Alberta, she said she never met Lottie, with whom Alberta was living, so well did Alberta protect that relationship from public view.

"When Alberta went out somewhere with Lottie, they were always correct, never mushy," said Harry Watkins, who was the only person who regularly frequented Alberta's apartment. "They were like two friends ordinarily would be in public. Lottie was very sedate," he said. "She was brought up that way. She was raised to be a dicty nigger. She liked me, and she didn't," Harry added. He loved to act silly, tell funny dirty jokes, and humor Alberta. "I would just be myself. Alberta and I could stay in the house and have a ball all by ourselves, laughing at everybody but ourselves." Lottie would say in a "very fancy and formal way, 'Oh, Alberta, you just laugh at everything.' "

Even after Alberta's death Harry refused to comment on Alberta's long affair with Lottie. "I knew they were very close," he said with dramatic flair. He rolled his eyes mischievously as if back on a vaudeville stage and sang a few lines of "Tain't Nobody's Business If I Do."

Alberta recoiled every time a lesbian performer like Ethel Waters fought with one of her girlfriends in public. "What will people say?" Alberta asked.

Harry tried unsuccessfully to explain to her, "People think and talk even more if you try to hide something."

If Alberta went around with anyone else, it was most likely to be with boys who were in show business, said Mae. "They made her feel gay, and they kept her young. I never saw her pal out with no woman."

One of those boys was singer Jimmy Daniels, whom Alberta met at Henry Brannon's (a mutual friend) house on 135th Street. Lottie used to take her there every Sunday to eat one of the delicious meals Henry liked to cook for his good-looking and sociable friends.

Alberta remembered meeting Jimmy soon after he arrived in New York from Texas, where he had been brought up. "This one was just a little one," she said. "They'd just brought him in. Handsome? Oh, was he handsome! He had hair as red as fire, and his folks had money."

At age eighty-nine, holding her head high like a dowager, Alberta said: "People thought we were the swank group, the Sugar Hill group."

Alberta didn't stay long in New York. Forever anxious to be on the move, she teamed up with comedian Sam Bailey early in 1925 and struck out again on the vaudeville trail through various states in the East. The *Shamokin* (Pennsylvania) *Dispatch* (undated article) said that Alberta and Sam in their act called "Let 'Em Roll" were equally at home singing and dancing. Alberta, though never proud of her dancing skills, apparently knew how to cut a rug when she wanted to.

In March Alberta was back in New York celebrating Lottie's birthday. *Billboard* (March 14, 1925, p. 52) reported that Alberta, "a frugal young lady," invited six other women to a Harlem night spot. (The women were not identified.) Alberta gasped when she got the bill for two rounds of ginger ale and six little sandwiches. It came to $23.70. "Her economical soul was stunned when she saw the total," *Billboard* reported. "She said that she was through with night clubs as sources of pleasure."

She was also through with New York for a while. "Alberta Hunter and Her Boys" (Herman Taylor and Bobbie Shields), as her new act was called, headed for the hills of West Virginia, where they were one of the few black acts headed by and featuring a woman to play the Keith theaters, according to *Billboard* (May 30, 1925, p. 49). She even sent the first recommendations to the black newspapers on where black entertainers could find room and board in these little towns, where no white establishments would take them in. For example, *Billboard* printed her tip to go directly to Mrs. Matthew Obie's home in Fairmont, West Virginia, because she served such good meals.

Alberta's "Boys" were pacesetters in their own right, introducing to a number of hillbilly towns on the circuit the new dance of the era, the Charleston, first performed on Broadway in 1923 by Maude Russel in Maceo Pinkard's show *Liza*.

Alberta herself is attributed with popularizing the next fashionable dance, the Black Bottom, if not actually originating it.* Dancing star Ann Pennington, known for her 1½-C-size feet, rouged knees, and nicknames Pipsy, Bananas, and the Countess, made the dance known in New York in 1926 at the Apollo Theater in the production *George White's Scandals*. On Ann Pennington's death in 1971 the *New York Times* (November 5, 1971, p. 46) suggested that Alberta might have been the first to perform the dance in 1925, on the vaudeville circuit for white audiences.

Abel Green and Joe Laurie, Jr., in their book *Show Biz—From Vaude to Video*† said Alberta was the first to present the dance and even had it copyrighted. They said the name of the dance "was derived from the muddy black bottom of the Suwannee River, and the movements suggested the dragging of feet through the mud." The dance became very popular in London, they said, but people there "balked at the name, which had a different significance in England. They presented it as the Black Base, or Black Bed. Actually, no one in America either believed that the 'Bottom' of the name referred to anything but the spot slapped by its dancer."

Alberta was embarrassed by the suggestion that she had much to do with a dance that was heavy bump and grind. When asked to describe it, she said, "Oh, it was just a certain, tricky kind of step."

However, her childhood friend Dorothy ("Dossie") Mabin Young,

---

*David Ewen, *New Complete Book of the American Musical Theater* (New York: Holt, Rinehart & Winston, 1970), p. 175.

†(New York: Garland Publishers, 1985), p. 220.

at age ninety, enjoyed showing just how to do it. "You clap your hands on your rear end," she said. "Then you bend your legs and go down, down to the floor, twisting and turning, close to your partner. Then you come back up and move away from your partner and give him the come-on with your fingers down here," she said, beckoning with her hands high between her legs. "Yeah, I done that. And I'm still doing it."

Suffice it to say that the dance caused police raids on the Sunset Café and the Plantation Café in Chicago over the Christmas holidays in 1926. It was soon replaced by the less provocative Sugar Foot Strut.

Traveling the vaudeville circuit could be hectic and lonely. But camaraderie paved the long road through the American countryside. Alberta crossed paths with the elite of the black entertainers, people like Miller and Lyle, Butterbeans and Susie, and Sippie Wallace. She enjoyed even more the less known, simple groups she found along the way. Because blacks were loners among all the white acts in each theater, they stuck together and helped each other out as much as they could. They kept each other's addresses so they could send word about job openings. And they signed each other's autograph books with folk wisdom and messages of praise, hope, encouragement, and affection.

Some of the notations in Alberta's book, which she kept as a fond memory of those days, suggest she was more respected and admired by these companions than she was by her sophisticated counterparts in the city. She adored simplicity, always, and felt more at home with these humble folk who weren't so quick to criticize their peers.

"How could one wish anything but the finest and best in life to a modestly charming and wonderfully clever girl who never allows her own success to keep her from saying the nicest things about her fellow artists." That was the message Louise Elliott of Faye, Elliott, and King wrote into Alberta's book.

"True wisdom begins when a man starts thinking for himself. When you allow others to do your thinking you become but an imitation of those you follow. It's a pleasure to meet with one who has realized this. Your name is significant, for if we hunt for a thing with unfailing perseverance, we must find the prize. That Miss Hunter will find it, I am sure. 'Bo Pink Toes,' Sincerely, Leo Hyland."

She continued in 1925, persevering through places like Niagara Falls and Utica in June; Albany in July. On July 7, 1925, she and her new partners, Herman Taylor and C. Beasley, along with Florence Mills, Sissle and Blake, Miller and Lyles, and Moss and Frye, performed at a benefit that Bojangles Robinson organized at the Lafayette Theater in New York for actress May Kemp, who was dying.

The *Chicago Defender* (July 11, 1925, p. 6) blessed Alberta's new act: "So many race acts have been using piano players in their acts, and, to tell the truth, they are looked upon as merely crutches for weak acts. Alberta has proved she needs no crutches for she was the hit of the May Kemp benefit. . . ."

In August Alberta performed in New York, Newport, and Boston; in September, in Salem, Massachusetts, Binghamton, New York, and Akron and Wheeling, Ohio; in October, in Sharon, Pennsylvania.

Alberta reportedly canceled a "western tour" in November so that her mother could visit her for the first time in New York. Miss Laura didn't like the sight of Harlem, and she didn't approve of her daughter's relationship, as concealed as Alberta tried to make it, with Lottie Tyler. She left for Chicago the day she arrived in New York. "I spent my hard-earned change to bring my mother to New York," Alberta complained. "And she didn't stay long enough to take her hat off. I had to send her back the same day. She didn't like New York."

Thinking her mother might one day live with her, Alberta had purchased an apartment the year before at 133 West 138th Street, across from the Abyssinian Baptist Church, made famous years later by its flamboyant preacher-politician Adam Clayton Powell, Jr. The apartment was in one of the first co-op buildings for blacks and was sold by John E. ("Jack") Nail of Nail and Parker, Inc. Real Estate who worked with John D. Rockefeller, Jr., on some of his many Harlem properties. The building was less than a block away from the row of Georgian town houses built in the 1890s for wealthy whites that became a historic district. By 1920 the area had been taken over by black doctors, lawyers, dentists striving to get ahead. Thus it and the block immediately to the north of 139th Street, also between Seventh and Eighth avenues, took on the name of Strivers' Row.

Rather than have Lottie live rent-free in this, her own large apartment, Alberta preferred to collect a good rent on it from someone else and split the cost of a smaller, cheaper rental apartment with Lottie, stashing the difference in one of her bank accounts.

Alberta insisted that she paid her share of the food that Lottie cooked for them on occasion. "I never was a leech," she explained. It was Lottie who sometimes had difficulty paying her share. Although Lottie was from a socially prominent family, she didn't have much money. She worked as everything from a chorus girl to a stacker of balls in a billiards hall, Alberta said, and saved none of what she earned.

"I think she was a little promiscuous with men," Alberta once said, to explain how Lottie lived better than her earnings permitted. Alberta was known for being generous in giving gifts to women she favored, but she certainly would not put them on her dole.

Alberta enjoyed being back in New York. Her relationship with Lottie had turned into an enduring friendship. It was always good to see Lottie again. And Alberta loved being spoiled and entertained by her faithful and spirited escorts, Harry Watkins and Jimmy Daniels. She sang at Kenney's in Brooklyn in November and at the Lafayette Theater in Harlem in December 1925.

And she began working for OKeh in New York. In three sessions she recorded "Your Jelly Roll Is Good," "Take That Thing Away," accompanied by Perry ("Mule") Bradford's Mean Four; "Everybody Does It Now," "A Master Man with a Master Mind," and "Don't Want It All"; and "Empty Cellar Blues," "Double Crossin' Papa," and "I'm Hard to Satisfy," a song she wrote.

Harlem was astir that winter with the recent court decision favoring Alice Beatrice Jones, an ex-laundress whose husband, white New York millionaire Leonard Kip Rhinelander, tried to annul their recent marriage after reading in the newspapers that his bride was not as white as he thought she was. The court said she had only twelve percent "Negro blood" and, therefore, was "legally colored, not Negro," leaving him without recourse under New York State laws. Harlem was stunned by the liberality of the initial judgment. Rhinelander was later granted a divorce.

Harlem was an exciting place to be in the late twenties. As Louis Armstrong said in his autobiography,* Harlem was the "biggest Negro city in the world." From the first white suburb of New York City at the turn of the century, Harlem in the next three decades became home for some two hundred thousand blacks. They moved up from their enclave centered on West Fifty-sixth Street, and they came in droves from the South.

Harlem became big and brassy. It became the home of the city's poorest residents and the playground of the richest. Poor blacks got off the subway at night and went home to cots in hallways or parts of subdivided rooms in railroad flats in Harlem. Rich whites, in diamonds, furs, and black ties, were driven in their Rolls-Royces or Duesenbergs to 142d Street and Lenox Avenue to the Cotton Club, the "aristocrat of Harlem" nightclubs, or to the lesser but nonetheless fun and glamorous Connie's Inn, Barron Wilkins' Exclusive Club, or Small's Paradise.

"White people went to Harlem and couldn't believe their eyes," said Harry Watkins. "It was like when we went to Paris. It was all so wonderful and new."

Blacks were normally allowed in those places only to entertain or wait on tables. Whites were there to watch blacks at their exotic best, not to socialize with them. Even people like W. C. Handy were barred from entering the Cotton Club.

But almost everyone, black and white, managed to have a good time in Harlem in the 1920s. "High Harlem" blacks went to fashionable clubs that made them feel at home, places like Happy Rhone's, the Lenox Club, and the Bamboo Inn.

Anyone with a dime to a quarter could get into a rent party, a tradition brought up from the South to raise money to keep a landlord off one's back at the end of the month. You paid the entrance fee at the door. If you still had a quarter left, you could buy a plate of pig's feet or tails, chitlins, black-eyed peas, or ham hocks and cabbage, all

---

Swing That Music (New York: Longmans, Green & Co., 1936), p. 81.

accompanied with a piece or two of fresh corn bread. There was plenty of beer and bathtub gin to wash it all down, again for a reasonable price.

Once you got feeling good, you could always find a partner to take into a dimly lit separate room to dance the Charleston, Black Bottom, Monkey Hunch, or Mess Around. A piano player like Fats Waller or Jelly Roll Smith and perhaps one or two other musicians were always on hand to keep the place bouncing.

Rent parties were often the cause of marital problems. A judge in a Washington Heights court ruled that these affairs were indeed a "menace to the community" and upheld a husband's complaint that his wife should either end her "craving" for going to them or move out (*Amsterdam News*, October 28, 1925, p. 1).

Even more notorious were "buffet flats," usually in a private railroad flat, where you could select just what you wanted, and were ready to pay for, from a good meal or drink to a smorgasbord of gambling, dope, erotic fantasy, or sex. Women typically owned and ran these establishments and made good reputations among their clients by knowing exactly what their fancies were and providing them. They often supplied safekeeping for money or other valuables because many of their clients either didn't trust banks or didn't want others' knowing about their sometimes sizable assets, frequently of suspicious origin. Eva Blanche's apartment, where Bricktop allegedly made off with Alberta's Paris job offer, was such a place.

"I found it [Harlem] had all kinds, like any big city," wrote Louis Armstrong.* "It had no-good floaters from all over the country, and it had thousands and thousands of good, hard-working colored people, and on top of that the most brilliant and talented musicians and actors and poets and artists of our race, mixing there together—they had come from everywhere to Harlem, which is the capital city and the city where most of our colored genius today is to be found, more than in all other places in the world, as I know."

While white people were riding back downtown after the Cotton Club show saying they had been to Harlem, most of them completely missed what was really happening in Harlem. All that black creative

*Ibid.

genius that didn't fit into a tap dancer's show was turning inward. The result was an extraordinary period of cultural expression that came to be known as the Harlem Renaissance.

Some of the names associated with that rich movement, most of which are foreign to white people even today (their loss!), are painter Aaron Douglas; diplomat and intellectual James Weldon Johnson; writers Claude McKay, Zora Neale Hurston, and Arna Bontemps; poet Countee Cullen; bibliophile Arthur Schomburg; and scholar W. E. B. Du Bois. It was a time when A. Philip Randolph was actively promoting trade unionism for blacks and Marcus Garvey was busy riding down Seventh Avenue in a crimson cape trying to get everyone to go back to Africa. Few people wanted to leave.

Langston Hughes, a poet, lyricist, short-story writer, playwright, world traveler, and a friend of Alberta's, was one of its brightest proponents of the Harlem Renaissance. Hughes had rebellion in his blood. He was the grandson of Lewis Sheridan Leary, the first man killed in John Brown's raid on Harpers Ferry in 1859. Another relative, Charles Langston, operated the underground railroad in Cleveland that spirited slaves to freedom. Hughes, who died in 1967, lived for a while in a little house at 20 West 127th Street just up from a storefront church named God's Bathtub.

One of Hughes's poems that Alberta liked best was "I, Too":

> I, too, sing America.
> I am the darker brother.
> They send me to eat in the kitchen
> When company comes;
> But I laugh,
> And eat well,
> And grow strong.
> Tomorrow
> I'll sit at the table
> When company comes.
> Nobody'll dare
> Say to me,
> "Eat in the kitchen"
> Then.
> Besides, they'll see how beautiful I am

And be ashamed—
*I, too, am America.**

Many of his race criticized Hughes for writing about the rough edges of black life, reinforcing, they charged, stereotypes of the black as good-for-nothing. He contended that he was writing about life as he saw it. He daringly criticized the black nouveaux riches for their "slavish devotion to Nordic standards, their snobbishness, their detachment from the Negro masses and their vast sense of importance to themselves" and the black media for perpetuating the idea that whites were better than blacks and were, therefore, to be imitated (*Pittsburgh Courier*, April 9, 1927, section 2, p. 1).

Alberta greatly admired Hughes for his talent and his biting tongue, and when she was in New York, she often attended his poetry readings. He frequently asked her to read his poetry before such a gathering. "I was never any good at that," she said. She did sing some of the songs he wrote from time to time. Alberta was also a friend of Langston's aunt Toy Brown, who for years did the alterations on all the fancy dresses Alberta bought for her performances.

One of Hughes's benefactors was A'Lelia Walker, the only child of cosmetics millionairess Madame C. J. Walker, who died in 1919. A'Lelia's prestige as America's wealthiest woman didn't buy her social acceptance from upper-class Harlem. They looked down on her because she was dark-skinned, wasn't a college graduate, and was the daughter of a woman who had started out as a washerwoman. Also, she was just too chummy with Carl Van Vechten, the *New York Times* writer who offended many of them with the realistic description of Harlem and its people in his book *Nigger Heaven*, named after the balcony of Harlem's Apollo Theater.

A'Lelia outclassed them all, buying the most exquisite European furnishings money could obtain for her two Harlem apartments and Hudson River estate. And she opened her salons to black artists, intellectuals, and entertainers, most of whom jumped at any chance

*Reprinted from *Selected Poems of Langston Hughes*, by Langston Hughes, by permission of Alfred A. Knopf, Inc. Copyright 1926 by Alfred A. Knopf, Inc., and renewed 1954 by Langston Hughes.

to satirize the snobbish dicties. The ground floor of her town house at West 136th Street became known as the Dark Tower Tea Club, named after the "Dark Tower" column Countee Cullen wrote for *Opportunity* magazine.

She threw parties that attracted some of the most fashionable and prominent whites from both sides of the Atlantic and, for the sheer fun of it, threw them all together with racketeers and numbers bankers. The entertainers she befriended—Adelaide Hall, Paul Bass, Maude Russell, Freddie Washington, Al Moiret, Jimmy Daniels, and Alberta Hunter, among others—were more than happy to perform at her parties. Alberta approved of A'Lelia's snubbing of Harlem society and felt very much at home with her and her guests.

Occasionally Alberta took some of A'Lelia's more adventurous wealthy white friends to speakeasies for blacks where they needed a personal introduction to get in the door. Black writer Dorothy West once went to Harlem with two carloads of "Park Avenue people" and a few English friends of theirs. When Alberta hopped out of the other car to talk the club's doorman into letting her mixed group go in, the elegant white gentleman in the car next to Dorothy West said of Alberta, "She is the most sophisticated woman in New York."

West preferred to describe Alberta as "giving the appearance of being a very simple woman" and not being much fun, at least not with a crowd like that. "How much fun can you be if you don't smoke or drink?" she said.

A'Lelia Walker's death on August 17, 1931, is often associated with the end of the Harlem Renaissance. The attention, respect, and support it focused on black culture and heritage waned for more than thirty years. The work produced during the Renaissance gave generations of blacks something to be proud of. Unfortunately its inability to bring about more dignified, if not equal, treatment of blacks by whites produced bitterness and frustration for two more generations of blacks.

Black entertainers who entered the white world daily, who depended on it for their survival were among the most eloquent of their race in this struggle. Bert Williams expressed the pain of discrimination in 1915. A black newspaper repeated his words to a black audience:

> Singing a half dozen coon songs and telling a few Negro dialect stories does not satisfy my ambition.
>
> I want to be the interpreter of the Negro on the stage, not the Negro you see me as now—that is the burlesque Negro, just as the stage Jew's a Jew drawn with red paint and not with faithful black ink. The Negro has a place and a big one in the history of this country, and he has to be shown in the drama just as he exists in real life.
>
> For hasn't he heart throbs? Doesn't he lie awake nights smarting under the customs that make him a pariah in the life of the community? Isn't the flow of his life being checked as it gets underway? In fact are there comparable dramatic situations possible in the life of the average white man today?
>
> I want to be the expositor of all this sort of thing [*Chicago Defender*, March 27, 1915, pp. 1 and 7].

Bert Williams did move hundreds of audiences with his heartthrobs until he died in 1922.

Blake and Sissle were the first black vaudeville team (the Dixie Duo) to refuse to blacken their faces for the stage. They created another first with their 1921 production of *Shuffle Along*. Among the great songs they wrote for that show were, as noted, "I'm Just Wild About Harry" and the romantic "Love Will Find a Way." Including the latter number in the show was an audacious move, opposed by several of its backers. After all, blacks weren't supposed to have the same emotions as white people, much less express them onstage to a mixed audience. But Sissle and Blake would not be intimidated.

Paul Robeson was the next courageous—read "scandalous"— black of the 1920s. He played the role of Jim Harris in Eugene O'Neill's play *All God's Chillun Got Wings*, which opened in New York at the Provincetown Playhouse on May 20, 1924, after a delay caused by the controversy it generated. The play offended many because of a scene in which Jim's white wife (played by Lillian Greene) kisses his hand. (He was even more bitterly attacked, mostly by white

Americans, when as Othello he kissed a white Desdemona, played by the great English actress Peggy Ashcroft.) A *New York World* editorial (March 4, 1924, p. 10) referred to *All God's Chillun*, then in rehearsal, as "needlessly offensive, perhaps dangerous. It can serve no artistic or moral purpose."

The *Chicago Defender* (April 5, 1924, part 2, p. 1) quoted O'Neill's response to public charges that he was trying to stir up racial unrest. "Nothing could be farther from my wish than to stir up racial feeling," he said. "I hate it. It is because I am certain 'God's Chillun' does not do this, but on the contrary, will help toward a more sympathetic understanding between races, through the sense of mutual tragedy involved, that I will stand by it to the end. I know that I am right."

The black press disliked the play for other reasons. The *Afro-American* (May 23, 1924, p. 5) called it "a hard play to sit thru. To see a big, respectable and cultured character as the slave of a slim, depraved and silly white woman isn't the kind of enjoyment calculated to make up a good evening's entertainment."

The play opened in New York without eight children who had rehearsed their parts. It was considered improper for them to perform in the midst of such debauchery.

Alberta continued working on the Keith circuit, having signed a one-year contract in June 1926. Almost every week of that year she and Sam Bailey were in a different town. The *Afro-American*, having a hard time keeping up with her, ran a photo of her in July 1926 and said she had disappeared. She was pictured in what she called her "King Tut" pose—one hand on hip, the other against her forehead, her long, angular nose in profile, her curvy hips hugged by a sleek long dress.

Because a number of the Keith theaters were in the New York area, Alberta could live at home with Lottie, who had moved to an apartment on Edgecombe Avenue in Sugar Hill, the district that was a big step up on the social ladder from Strivers' Row, where they had been living.

Alberta was there on August 3, 1926, the day she made a rare entry in a diary. It read: "Thompson called about 2 o'clock-afternoon—on house phone. Asked for Miss Tyler. About 8:40 evening came to door."

"Oh, this is the guy who tried to rape me," she remembered when asked about the entry. "I didn't know him. This man said he knew Buffalo, a fellow from Chicago who used to come into the Dreamland. So this man came and rang the doorbell and said Buffalo had told him to come to see me. That he had some stockings or something to sell. When he came to the door later, he asked for Lottie and tried to push the door open.

"I screamed," Alberta said. "The man ran down the steps. Fortunately Mrs. Bert Williams and a man named Justin Gatineau, a Frenchman who was living with us, happened to be there. He chased after the man but didn't catch him."

A few days later, Alberta said, a friend of Lottie's sister by the name of Lillie Mae, who had been raped by this same man, saw him on a bus and had a policeman arrest him. The man was tried for several offenses, convicted, and sentenced to eighty-one years in prison, according to Alberta. "I've always been too slick to open my door for anybody," she bragged.

Getting back to New York also helped Alberta keep up her recording schedule. In August and September she recorded for OKeh "If You Can't Hold the Man You Love (Don't Cry When He's Gone)" and "You for Me, Me for You" with Clarence Williams on piano; "I'm Tired Blues," "Wasn't It Nice?" "I Didn't Come to Steal Nobody's Man," and "Everybody Mess Around"; and "Don't Forget to Mess Around" and "Heebie Jeebies." She recorded three other sides toward the end of 1926 in Chicago for Vocalion, but they were never issued.

Alberta always had running battles with her recording companies because they did not adequately promote her records, especially in the cities where she performed. An official at OKeh sent her a letter dated January 20, 1927, addressed to the Boston theater where she was singing. He advised her that to promote her properly, he needed to know with sufficient advance notice where she would be working, and when. That took some doing because she was zigzagging back and forth, often on last-minute notice of engagements, as she was doing that very winter, to places like Allentown, Pennsylvania; Ithaca, New York; Wheeling, West Virginia; and Waterbury, Connecticut. In other words, the promotion was never done satisfactorily.

Discouraged with OKeh, Alberta went to work for Victor, although it didn't do much better on the promotional side. In February she recorded "My Old Daddy's Got a Brand-New Way to Love," "I'm Gonna Lose Myself 'Way Down in Louisville," and two songs she wrote, "I'll Forgive You 'Cause I Love You" and "I'm Down Right Now but I Won't Be Down Always." In May she recorded again for Victor: "Beale Street Blues," "Sugar," and "I'm Going to See My Ma," accompanied by Fats Waller on the pipe organ. Alberta was one of the first singers to use both Fats and the pipe organ for accompaniment.

In between recordings she and Sam Bailey continued to work the Keith circuit, where they were well received. The *Springfield* (Massachusetts) *Union* (February 4, 1927) said of their appearance at the Palace Theater: "It appears that this reviewer is continually praising colored entertainers and no wonder. When they succeed in entertaining at all, they are lavish. Hunter and Bailey are lavish. They talk the extravagant quarreling talk that is supposed to be typical and then they dance."

Hunter and Bailey carried their song-and-dance routine successfully into New York again in April 1927, when they appeared at the 81st Street Theater.

With all their bookings and good reviews, Alberta still felt like a black bird caged by a white world. She, like so many others of the best black entertainers, turned her mind toward Europe.

CHAPTER FOUR

Getting Her Name Up in Lights

Charles A. Lindbergh shortened the distance across the Atlantic Ocean by landing in Paris on May 21, 1927, after his thirty-three-hour flight in *The Spirit of St. Louis*. The French were delighted with his pioneering feat. But they were more enamored of the spirit of black America that had landed on their shores years before. Josephine Baker had been there for two years and had made black the beautiful color of Paris. And a string of hot black musicians, starting with James Reese Europe more than a decade earlier, made jazz its heartbeat.

Bricktop opened her own club on the Rue Pigalle in February 1927 and regally entertained people like Cole Porter, Scott and Zelda Fitzgerald, Elsa Maxwell, and the prince of Wales. Heads of state called her "Madame" Bricktop, a term her mother, who lived with her in later years, said she should have them stop using. "It isn't nice," she said.

"Wah Wah dolls" were selling like hotcakes on the Champs-Élysées, in the image of pantomimist Johnny Hudgins and named after one of his songs. Hudgins managed a small club, the Jardin des Cacias, that featured afternoon tea dances and champagne at midnight. Later that year he headlined a revue called *Paris aux Étoiles* at the Moulin Rouge.

Tenor Roland Hayes was living in Paris and giving concerts in most of the European capitals. Florence Mills was an enormous success in *Blackbirds of 1927*, a musical production, in London. The Four Harmony Kings were singing in London and Paris. And Mutt and Jeff were cavorting across the stages of Berlin with their vaudeville act.

"The Negro artists went to Europe because we were recognized and given a chance," Alberta said. "In Europe they had your name up in lights. People in the United States would not give us that chance."

Alberta wanted her chance. She told people she was going to Europe on vacation "to tour the principal cities of the old world" and to make a few records. Actually she went job hunting but didn't want that known so that if she failed to find work she wouldn't have to return home empty-handed and embarrassed. She convinced Lottie to accompany her and paid her way. Alberta talked Lottie's aunt, Lottie Williams, into signing a statement to accompany her passport application of July 22, which Lottie also signed as a witness, saying that Mrs. Williams had known Alberta since she was born.

Mrs. Williams saw the two women off on August 5, 1927, and waved as the French liner *De Grasse* steamed off toward France. She did so with some trepidation, for the front page of the morning newspapers that day announced that Governor Alvan T. Fuller of Massachusetts had refused to postpone the execution on August 22 of Nicola Sacco and Bartolomeo Vanzetti, two Italian radicals convicted for the killing of a shoe company guard in that state. U.S. embassies in Europe were on alert for violent demonstrations to protest the sentence. The only turbulence Alberta found, however, was on their rough crossing. "I got so sick," she said, "I thought I was dying."

Nettie and Glover Compton met Alberta and Lottie in Paris at the Gare St.-Lazare railroad station and took them to stay at their apartment at 35 Rue Victor-Massé.

In a few days the visitors moved to the Hôtel de Paris at 55 Rue

Pigalle, where Catherine Yarborough (now an opera singer and calling herself Caterina Jarboro) also lived. Caterina showed them the way to the Flea Pit on the Rue Pigalle and the Rue Bergère in Montmartre, a combination poolroom, public bar, cigar stand, and place to drop in and hear news of home or friends. It also sold small Sterno stoves. Many people on a budget put the stoves on the square of floor tiles normally found underneath the sinks in hotel rooms.

"We used to cook on those stoves," Alberta revealed. "Now [Caterina] she's jiving. She doesn't want me to tell it, but I'm going to 'cause I'm talking about myself too. We used to buy a can of Sterno and light it and cook cans of Franco-American spaghetti. That's the way we ate.

"I love Franco-American spaghetti," she said. "This is an ad. No, it's not, 'cause I'm not getting paid for it."

On October 1 the *Chicago Defender* (p. 9) reported that Alberta and Lottie had recently been the guests of Johnny Hudgins and his wife, Mildred, to see Josephine Baker at the Folies Bergère. Alberta had known "La Baker" in New York when Josephine was put on the tail end of a chorus line because she was too dark. She went to Paris in 1925 with a show called *Revue Nègre*, starring Maude de Forrest.

"When they got to Paris, Maude, as some people do, lost her head," said Alberta. "She thought they couldn't do without her. So they gave Maude her walking papers and put the bananas on Josephine."

Now here was Josephine with her voluptuous brown body, gold fingernail polish, a tutu with bananas hanging on it, spit curl, and pet cheetah. She was as talked about as some of the other glitterati of Paris, people like Coco Chanel, Sergei Prokofiev, Igor Stravinsky, Gertrude Stein, Sylvia Beach, Ezra Pound, Ernest Hemingway, Sergei Diaghilev, Pablo Picasso, James Joyce, and Man Ray.

Travel for Alberta was a substitute for the formal education she never had. She was genuinely curious about the history of the places she visited and took notes on what she learned. Telling about what she saw was also a means of gaining the social respectability she craved.

The few other black entertainers, like Johnny Hudgins, who wrote letters about their experiences abroad, to be published in black American newspapers, spoke mostly about themselves and who was performing where. (Since most black newspapers couldn't afford staff reporters in Europe, they depended on black performers abroad to tell them what they and their colleagues were doing there. Failures were rarely mentioned, but then most blacks were big hits on the stages and in the clubs of Europe.)

In contrast with Johnny's self-promotion, Alberta's first letter, dated October 23, 1927, published by the *Amsterdam News* (November 16, 1927, p. 9), was a travelogue. She wrote about visiting Versailles, Fontainebleau (with descriptions room by room), the Cathedral of Notre-Dame, the Louvre Museum, and the "beauty and elegance" of Napoleon's tomb.

Alberta was most taken by the Paris that was architecturally and artistically monumental. It was a picture-postcard paradise. But Paris was also flamboyant, self-indulgent, narcissistic, sexual. There was Natalie Barney, a wealthy American lesbian who had lived in Paris from 1900. Nicknamed the Amazon, she dressed in a bowler hat and black bow tie and galloped her horse daily through the Bois de Boulogne.

Bricktop dyed her hair orange.

Black men and white women were on the stage together. Roi Ottley wrote of the phenomenon in his book *No Green Pastures*:* "Back in the days when America was outraged by Paul Robeson's kissing the hand of a white actress in a Eugene O'Neill play, 'All God's Chillun Got Wings,' Habib Benglia, a magnificent-looking Senegalese, was, to the delight of French audiences, dancing at the Folies Bergère in a g-string with white girls surrounding him."

Jean Cocteau orchestrated nights away for the connoisseurs of the predawn hours, a wild, wacky, and wonderful mélange of followers at his club, Le Boeuf sur le Toit (The Ox on the Roof), named appropriately after a circus-ballet-comic opera he helped create after World War I. It was the place to order a gin fizz from Moysès, the barman with devotees from the theatrical crowd, hear Jean Wiener at the jazz piano, sway on the sensuously crowded dance floor, or

---

*(New York: Charles Scribner's Sons, 1951), p. 73.

ogle at some of the more extravagant clients and try to figure out if someone named Barbette was a he or a she. Barbette was a transvestite from Round Rock, Texas, who, dressed as an ostrich-plumed nymph, glided nightly across a tightrope for the Médrano Circus. His real name was Vander Clyde, and he/she was a regular at the Boeuf.

Alberta didn't want to be associated with all that hedonism. She was there to work and to be appreciated for it, not to play. She openly criticized the Paris night life. "The shows here are most spectacular but lack the real punch and talent we have in America," she wrote the *Amsterdam News* that October 23. "They depend solely upon nudity, which has a tendency to get on one's nerves." Worse, she said, they didn't even know how to do the Charleston onstage.

She was more enthusiastic about the boxing match she saw on October 19 between Al Brown and Albert Ryall. "It was the quickest knock-out I ever saw. Mr. Brown knocked Ryall out in the second round, and he stayed out twenty minutes." The French "idolize" Brown, she said. "He is one of the most refined little gentlemen I have ever met."

She gave her first indication that her vacation was not to be a short one. "I do not know when I will be home," she wrote. "I am mad about the freedom of Paris. Color means nothing over here. If anything they treat the colored people better."

She wrote about an American Legion parade she saw with Nettie Compton, Florence Mills, and her husband, U. S. ("Kid") Thompson, from a "dandy spot" in front of the grandstand.

The most thrilling thing in the whole parade was a little brown-skinned fellow carrying the flag that led Kansas. He had the most beautiful smile, and when the people saw him, they cheered and threw up their hats. Officers saluted and we filled up our hearts with pride and our eyes with tears.

The white Americans positively look silly over here. They do their utmost to start trouble—to start the color question—but to no avail. To begin with, the French people do not like them. I am only praying no colored person will ever cause the French people to dislike us; as Paris, in fact, all of France, is a heaven on earth for the Negro man or woman.

As Alberta suggested, white Americans weren't entirely welcomed in Paris. The French were angry enough in 1927 about the execution of Sacco and Vanzetti. Then the U.S. government demanded that France, just when it was suffering hard times economically, repay its war debts. It didn't help that the estimated forty thousand Americans who were living at that time in Paris and the hordes of U.S. tourists were spending wildly and ostentatiously in France.

In contrast, Parisians were crazy about black people in general. That's why Nancy Cunard, heiress to the British shipping fortune, found it far more comfortable to live with her black lover in Paris than in London.

Shops were filled with African artifacts—bracelets made of carved wood and ivory, fetishes, and tribal masks of the type that inspired so many of Picasso's cubist paintings and sculptures. On the streets or in sidewalk cafés Parisians found blacks such an attractive novelty that they walked up, touched their dark skins with their inimitable expression of "Oo-la-la," and offered to buy them drinks.

"Black people couldn't do wrong in Paris," said singer Adelaide Hall. That is, if they didn't act like Sidney Bechet and Mike McKendrick, who got in a fight at Chez Florence in 1928. Out on the street Bechet, who shot at McKendrick, hit and wounded a passing Frenchman instead. He was sentenced to eleven months in prison but was expelled from the country after serving two months.

Blacks were in all the clubs and most of the hotels and restaurants. White Americans were apoplectic about this mixing and often refused to patronize an establishment that permitted it. Their dollars made many owners respect their wishes, but not without a great deal of resentment.

The French truly loved the pure rhythm and musicality of the black jazz musicians. In fact, it was after playing with his band in France during World War I that James Reese Europe returned to the United States and argued with many of his critics, including those among his race, who insisted that serious black musicians should imitate white music. They dismissed jazz as dishonest, a waste of time or downright sinful. "We have our own racial feeling and if we try to copy whites we will make bad copies," Europe wrote.* ". . . We won France by playing music which was ours and not a pale imitation of others, and if we are to develop in America we must develop along our own lines. . . . The music of our race springs from the soil, and this is true today with no other race, except possibly the Russian."

The French were bored with the white Americans' inability to appreciate their own black people and more so by their rabid insistence on rudely discriminating against them, especially in France. Not only did the French people accept the American blacks, but many blacks made an effort to learn the French language and often spoke it very well. The white American not only wouldn't bother to learn a few words of French but proclaimed noisily that the French damn well ought to learn English.

Alberta and Lottie received invitations to elegant parties and were introduced to European monarchs, socialites, diplomats, writers, artists, curators, couturiers, photographers, and an assortment of American tycoons and movie stars. One of the people Alberta met and liked immediately was Elsie de Wolfe, a Broadway stage star and often called America's first decorator, who lived for years in New York with her lover, Elizabeth ("Bessie") Marbury, before marrying Sir Charles Mendl, the press attaché at the British Embassy in Paris. Lady Mendl was one of the most fashionably dressed women on either side of the Atlantic, yet she thought nothing of standing on her head during parties at her Villa Trianon, just outside Paris at Versailles, and liked to meet and help talented young people with their careers. (She was one of the backers of Cole Porter's first musical, *See America First*.) Alberta especially liked two of Lady Mendl's mottoes: "Never complain" and "Never explain anything."

"I thought she was one of the most honest, wonderful, kind-hearted, unselfish, brilliant—everything that the word *good* stands for," Alberta said.

Lottie wasn't nearly so impressed as Alberta by Paris, Parisians,

---

*"A Negro Explains Jazz," *Literary Digest* (April 26, 1919), pp. 28–29.

or anyone else there. Alberta noted in a little book called "My Trip Abroad," inscribed in the front simply "From Amanda [Randolph]," that Lottie left Paris by boat train on October 29 at 10:46 to sail home on the *Mauretania*. "Mrs. Nellie Compton, Henry George Walton [a trumpet player at Chez Florence], Catherine Yarborough, Al Brown and I went to the station with her."

The large party might have been more to console Alberta than to see Lottie off. Lottie had fallen in love with the wife of her attorney and wanted to be with her back in America. Alberta resented being rejected by Lottie and carried a chip on her shoulder toward women for the rest of her life. Still, as hurt as she was, she and Lottie remained close friends until Lottie died.

If Alberta was grieving that day, she wasn't showing it. She made another entry in the book for the same date: "At 8:15 a beautiful Minerva automobile was waiting in front of my door for me. I got in and proceeded to 'Salle Gaveau' to hear Paul Robeson and Lawrence Brown. The concert was a triumphant success. In the party were Joslin "Frisco" Bingham, Mr. & Mrs. San Lazaro (banker), Mrs. Chrysler of Chrysler Automobiles, the nephew of the King of Egypt and I."

Unfortunately Alberta almost never wrote in the diaries or notebooks she kept, probably so that no one would ever be able to trace too many of her steps. However, on the following day, Sunday, October 30, 1927, she wrote: "I was the guest of honor at tea at the Embassy Balzac and Champs-Élysées. In the party were Mr. and Mrs. Henri de Poutand (Mr. Poutand is director general of Cie. Francaises des Disques et Phonographes 'Brunswich.') Mrs. Havermeyer, wife of the sugar king. An Indian princess, I can't spell her name, Mr. and Mrs. Davis, English notables, and the nephew of the King of Egypt and I."

Alberta also met at about this time and saw on occasion Serge Voronoff, a noted scientist, and Somerset Maugham. Maugham wrote a long article, inspired by Alberta, she said, but she didn't know its name. She remembered his scolding her for appearing to be so low-key about herself and her talent. "He said he didn't want me to be so modest. He wanted me to speak up. He said people weren't just being kind. It was my ability that attracted people. They had to be kind. 'What else could they be?' he asked."

On November 1, 1927, Alberta received a telegram from singer Edith Wilson, a close friend in New York, telling her that Florence Mills had died that morning, a week after having had an appendectomy. Harlem stopped to mourn the passing of its most beloved songbird. Montmartre was hushed. Blacks remembered where they were when they heard the news of her death, the way they recalled vividly decades later the moment they heard of the assassination of Martin Luther King, Jr., or of John F. Kennedy. In all cases an inner light was snuffed out. Streets and schools and housing projects and nurseries and libraries were named after King and Kennedy. Little Flo got a ten-thousand-dollar bronze coffin, a replica of the one that took Rudolph Valentino to heaven, and eternal glory.

On November 4 Florence Embry Jones and her husband sailed for New York and left Alberta in charge of the entertainment at Chez Florence, the small, very smart club owned by Louis Hamilton on the Rue Blanche.

"Well, I became very popular," Alberta said. She packed people into that place, singing a really risqué song called "Organ Grinders." Typically Alberta couldn't remember the words. But she did remember Elsa Maxwell's coming in to see her and bringing the prince of Wales on her arm. The prince might have enjoyed "Organ Grinders" as well, but he asked Alberta to sing "I Can't Give You Anything but Love."

As much as Alberta liked to sing Cole Porter's songs, she learned right away not to sing them when she saw him coming into the club, as he often did. "He didn't like you to do that," she said. "But he was a fine ol' boy. Little, tiny guy."

Alberta dressed elegantly for such courtly attention, outdoing even Florence Embry Jones, who was known for her stylish clothes. Mildred Hudgins, no slouch herself, took Alberta to some of the most fashionable couturiers for private showings. One afternoon the two of them dressed up and headed for the Grand Prix race at Longchamps, where they were hounded by photographers thinking they were models. Alberta kept a photograph one of them took of the two women. In all the papers only Mildred's photo appeared, however. Alberta was dressed in raven black. Mildred, a more attractive woman to start with, had on a lighter, more chic blue-gray outfit.

Florence Jones told Alberta about Bricktop's coming to Paris in 1924 and of her acceptance of the invitation meant for Alberta. So the two women, "Bert" and "Brick," picked up on their petty quarreling from the days of the Panama Café in Chicago. "They were always fussin'," said Bessy De Saussure, who was playing the piano at Fred Payne's Bar nearby and knew both women. "But it didn't mean a thing."

Alberta didn't have time to fret over bygones because, a few weeks after starting at Chez Florence, she was already receiving offers to entertain on the Riviera. She opened at the Princess Palace in Nice on December 10 with the Toumanoff Sisters, the Nevelskaya ballet, the Seven Stars Band, and the L'Ortega Orchestra. She sent a letter to the *Amsterdam News* (published on January 11, 1928, p. 11), saying she was a "decided hit." She wrote:

> The people applauded, stamped, yelled bravos, and I did encore after encore. I did the "Black Bottom" in my humble way, but to them it was great. I came here for one week, have been asked to stay three months, but cannot accept as I have signed contracts for one month in Monte Carlo at the Knickerbocker.
>
> This is a very beautiful city and it is quite like Paris. I am in headline position and have top billing. You would be very proud if you could see my billing and how I am received. I also feel my friends at home will be proud to hear of my success.

Alberta opened the new year working for a Mr. Frederick at the Knickerbocker Nightclub along with Princesse Helal doing her Persian dances and the Tix Sisters (also known as the Parisian Dancing Dolls), assisted by the Michigan Orchestra. She and Fredi Washington, a friend from Harlem, stayed together there for a few days. Fredi was touring Cannes, Monte Carlo, and Nice with Al Moiret as Moiret and Fredi, a sophisticated ballroom dance team. One night the two women sat on the hotel's terrace, looked up at the stars over the

Mediterranean Sea, and talked about the good turns their lives were taking.

Alberta loved the classiness of the Riviera, but her sights were set toward the north. She was determined to get to England but had no luck in acquiring one of the necessary work permits sparingly given foreign entertainers by British authorities. Then out of the blue came a telegram from London. Noble Sissle was helping organize "the greatest all-star coloured show ever staged" in England to raise money for victims of flooding caused by the swollen Thames River. Having heard that Alberta was on the Riviera and needing all the talented performers he could find quickly, he wired her that this was her chance to come to London. She would have to pay her own expenses and mention the lord mayor's name at the passport checkpoint on arrival in England. Alberta never moved so fast. She reached London on January 27, 1928. The show was scheduled for Sunday, January 29, at 3:00 P.M. at the London Pavilion at Piccadilly Circus.

Other performers on the bill were Layton and Johnstone, Williams and Taylor, Russel and Vivian, the Four Harmony Kings, Jackson and Blake, Leslie Hutchinson, James B. Lowe (the Uncle Tom of the film *Uncle Tom's Cabin*) and the "South Before the War Company," both acts "by kind permission of the European Motion Picture Co." At the last minute, when the program was already printed, Sissle convinced Josephine Baker to join the show. After working at her nightclub all night, she boarded a plane in Paris in the morning and arrived just in time to perform.

Alberta "tore the place up," as she said. "I put my foot down and went to town." Accompanied by Leslie Hutchinson at the piano, she sang "Just Another Day Wasted Away." Despite the song's title, it certainly wasn't lost time for her because Oscar Hammerstein II and Jerome Kern were in the audience, taking notes for future casting of the London version of their musical *Show Boat*.

Also, she had both feet down and in England. Her temporary work permit was valid for five weeks. She went to work right away at the Florida Club on Bond Street in London, then moved on to the Argyle Theater in Birkenhead, one of England's great vaudeville theaters.

Press critics liked her. "After building up a meritorious reputation for herself in the States as a 'Blues' singer, Miss Hunter soon had London at her feet on her arrival there a few weeks ago," one unidentified news clipping said. "Her appearance at the Argyle this week is her first in the provinces, and judged by her loudly acclaimed performance on Monday evening her success should be as devastating in the North as it has elsewhere. Her voice is a triumph of the Blues type of vocalism, with everything in it of that inexplicable 'catchy' quality peculiar to this class of American artiste."

Alberta moved on to the Empress Room at the Royal Palace Hotel in Kensington, London, for the month of March. With that engagement she was able to obtain an extension of her work permit. She was home safe.

Ivan H. Browning, star of *Shuffle Along* and *The Chocolate Dandies*, one of the Four Harmony Kings, and a correspondent for black American newspapers, echoed that reaction in his column for the *Amsterdam News* (March 14, 1928, p. 9): "Coming to London a total stranger, it is indeed remarkable the success she has had. She is billed as 'America's Foremost Brown Blues Singer.' It is a good title, and she lives up to her billing in every way."

Upon arrival in London, Alberta went directly to a simple but sturdy house at 17 Regents Park Road and rented a room from John Payne, an American baritone and choirmaster who had moved to London in 1919. Among American blacks in Europe he had the reputation of being their ambassador to the Court of St. James's. The back of the house was opposite the zoo in the beautifully manicured Regents Park, bordered on the near side by a row of some of London's most aristocratic homes.

Few American blacks knew anyone in London when they first arrived. So they all went directly to Payne, if not for a place to stay, at least for introductions to new friends in the academic, professional, entertainment, and social circles of England.

"See Johnny, and you'll be all right," said Leslie Thompson, a Jamaican musician and orchestra leader who visited the house in the 1930s. "His home was a mecca for colored artists." Paul Robeson and other entertainers gathered around the handsome grand piano in the drawing room for the open-house parties Payne gave on Sundays.

There were always extra lamb chops on the table, prepared by his housekeeper, Miss Kitchenside. That was okay if you didn't eat all your meals there as a boarder, said Alberta. "They were the worst lamb chops I ever tasted since I was born. She'd cook them, and you could see through the fat, it was so clear. It was nothing but mutton. You know how that old mutton is. It even smells mutton. Oh, Lord. Lamb chops for breakfast! Every day!"

Payne's hospitality was subsidized by Lady Mary Cook, wife of Sir Herbert Cook, a wealthy businessman and art critic and collector. Lady Cook had a special attraction to blacks—who she insisted should call her Mother—and to Payne in particular. Gene Brame, John Payne's nephew, who lived at his uncle's house in 1924, said Lady Cook believed in reincarnation. She believed that in her last life she and Payne had been married, with the twist that she had been the husband and he the wife.

There was no romantic involvement between the two of them—in this, the life they were living in the 1920s, that is. Payne cared very much for Lady Cook but also enjoyed the life-style she afforded him. Several times a week she bought theater, concert, or opera tickets for him and his guests. She paid for Brame's passage to England and for a private tutor for him, as she did for other worthy and talented young people who came to her attention.

She even acted as a press agent for her "children." For example, in 1923 she sponsored a concert for Payne in London, one that was unusual for the time in that there were only spirituals on the program. She encouraged him to be proud of his heritage and to help others come to know it and appreciate it. Then she sent letters to American newspapers about the concert.

"I wish to tell you of a concert given by Mr. John Payne at Wigmore Hall on October 13th," she wrote in a letter published by the *New York Age* (November 10, 1923, p. 6). "He was assisted by Mr. Lawrence Brown [who later played for Paul Robeson] who accompanied him on the piano and also occasionally vocally. It was a great success in every way. The audience was a large one and very enthusiastic and included many distinguished people." She sent reviews of the recital from the *London Morning Post* and *Daily Telegraph* to support her opinion.

Lady Cook not only provided Payne with a house but gave elegant parties for him to host which were among the liveliest in London. And on many a weekend she piled anyone who wished into one of her chauffeur-driven cars for a drive out to her country home, Doughty House, in Richmond, Surrey. The house, built in 1751 and often called Byways, was perched prominently on a hill overlooking the Thames River. In the entrance hall was a marble plaque showing the lineage of Lady Cook, the daughter of Viscount Bridgeport, the half brother of Viscount Nelson, England's greatest naval hero.

Sir Herbert Cook, a trustee of the National Gallery, had one of the largest private art collections in England. Among the six hundred paintings at this house were Rembrandt's *Portrait of a Boy* and *Tobit and His Wife*, Fra Filippo Lippi's *Adoration of the Maji*, Hubert van Eyck's *The Three Marys at the Sepulchre*, as well as works by Raphael, Titian, and Rubens.

Sir Herbert enjoyed telling his guests of the visit to his gallery of a brash American millionaire by the name of J. P. Morgan. Morgan saw one of the paintings in the collection and said he just had to have it. Sir Herbert thanked him for his admiration of the work but informed him that it was not for sale. Several weeks later a check arrived in the mail with Morgan's instructions for Sir Herbert to fill in whatever price was necessary to complete the sale. Sir Herbert crisply returned the check to Mr. Morgan.

Lady Cook wasn't one for formality. She dressed very simply. Payne kept after her to buy more feminine clothes, but she preferred basic, rather severely tailored suits. And she had no fondness for life at court. She was far happier sitting in Payne's parlor, knitting a sweater for him, chatting with visitors, and making them feel comfortable in her home away from home.

Life with patrons like the Cooks made living in London very glamorous for Alberta. She enjoyed being invited to teas and the theater with people who acted like lords, whether they were or not, and who treated her like a lady. But she most wanted to be accepted and applauded by them when she was where she felt most at home, onstage.

She got that chance on April 19, when Sir Alfred Butt, managing director of the Drury Lane Theater, asked her to accept the part of Queenie in the forthcoming production of *Show Boat*.

Show Boat was first staged in New York, opening on December 27, 1927, at the Ziegfeld Theater. The play, adapted from Edna Ferber's novel of the same name, depicts the life of Magnolia Hawkes, daughter of Parthy Ann and Cap'n Andy, owners of the *Cotton Blossom*, a Mississippi River showboat. While in Natchez, the nearly white Julie La Verne, who sings on the boat, rejects the sexual advances of the boat's engineer. He gets even with her by telling the local redneck sheriff that she is married to Steve, a white man in the cast. The sheriff goes to arrest the couple for breaking the state's law prohibiting miscegenation. Steve cuts Julie's finger, drinks some of her blood, and proclaims himself thereby part black, too. All the sheriff can do then is ban the racially mixed cast from performing.

Then a fancy-talking gambler named Gaylord Ravenal woos Magnolia, marries her, and takes her to Chicago only to abandon her and their daughter, Kim, who in time becomes a famous singer. In the end Gaylord and Magnolia have a happy reunion on the *Cotton Blossom*.

Paul Robeson was asked to join the New York cast as Joe, a hand on the boat, but because of major delays in the show's opening, he left the cast to fulfill previous commitments. A white vaudeville star by the name of Aunt Jemima played Queenie, the boat's cook and Joe's wife.

Robeson did take the role in the English version after convincing Hammerstein to substitute the word *darkies* for *niggers* in the lyrics of "Ol' Man River." Alberta won the part of Queenie over a "big, fat, white English woman." Hammerstein "wanted the real thing," said Alberta. "I don't think they would have let her play the part anyhow because she was typically English. *Show Boat* didn't want that English jive. *Show Boat* wanted America. If you're singing 'Ol' Man River,' don't come putting all that mess in there about I *can't* [she pronounced that word as the English do] do this, I *can't* do that. Don't put that jive in there, not in 'Ol' Man River.' "

So Alberta was the real thing as the curtain rose at the Drury Lane on May 3, 1928, "at 8 o'clock precisely," as advertised. American singer Edith Day starred as Magnolia, Sir Cedric Hardwicke as Cap'n Andy, and Marie Burke as Julie. Mabel Mercer was a chorus girl. It was the most spectacular show Alberta had ever been in, with sixteen settings that ranged from the riverboat to the Chicago exposition of 1893 and the Trocadero Music Hall in 1904. The *Daily Herald* of London described the play the next morning on its front page as "the most expensive and spectacular of all Drury Lane's big productions."

Alberta basked in the spotlights of that grand theater: "To think that I—me—poor, little, humble me was walking out onto the stage at the Drury Lane Theater in London, the theater of the world . . . where 'most everybody would give their lives to walk out on. . . ." She saw the audience looking at her, "smiling as if to say, 'Look at her. Look at her.' That was the thrill of my life, one of them anyhow."

Another thrill was performing with Robeson. At one point in the show he tenderly embraced her shoulder with his massive black hand and said he couldn't help lovin' his gal. "I'd look up at old Paul and sing, oh, Lord, 'Can't Help Lovin' Dat Man.' Oh, that was a knockout," she said.

"He tied that show up in a knot," she said. "There was something about his voice that was most alarming. Sometimes when he'd hum to himself, he'd sound like a moan, like the resonance of a bell in the distance. Oh, what a voice!"

Only once did that magnificent voice fail, of all nights on June 15, 1928, when King George V and Queen Mary came to see the play. "Paul started singing off-key and stayed off-key the whole night," said Alberta. "Later he cried like a baby."

Robeson received so much attention from the press and the audience that the stars of the show became jealous of him, Alberta said.

Alberta had her own problems of that sort. Originally she was to sing a number called "C'mon Folks" with the twelve black chorus girls imported from America for the show. But because it was such a big success early in the show, Edith Day created a fuss and had it removed.

Not to worry, as the English say. What was left in the show was enough to make Alberta a star of the London stage. The prestigious publication *Theatre World* carried a half page photograph of her and Paul Robeson with Edith Day and Marie Burke. Such equal attention with white stars would never have occurred in the United States, Alberta said.

An unidentified, yellowed press clipping in one of her scrapbooks read: "Miss Alberta Hunter, another coloured artist, was responsible for the continuity of the show—that is to say, it was her inexhaustible energy, drollery and indigenous sense of rhythm which set the pace. The numerous coloured artists and dancers who helped to form the musical and artistic background for the big scenes gave her a most loyal support and displayed an individual originality in their coordinated effort which would have shamed many an English chorus." Whatever newspaper that was, it was not the *Times* of London; it complained that the story of the play was not well told by the songs and dancing (May 4, 1928, p. 14). It made no mention of Alberta. It did give Robeson credit for singing one of the show's two hits, "Ol' Man River."

Alberta became very attached to Robeson, whom she called a "big hunk of humanity." She saw him often; he would come to John Payne's open-house gatherings on Sundays and often sang there. She felt very sorry about the persecution he suffered later in the United States. "They said he was a Communist," she said. "Paul was not a Communist. Paul was a man that wanted everybody to get a chance in life. And he used to speak his thoughts, and wishes and desires where people were concerned, and he'd try to help them. He was a fine young man."

Robeson refused to answer the question put to so many entertainers in the early 1950s by the U.S. House of Representatives Committee on Un-American Activities: "Are you a Communist?" The State Department refused to issue him a passport for nine years. His name was stricken from the record book of 1917–1918 as having been a member of the All-American football team. For years after his appearance before the committee Robeson found it hard to book concerts in the United States.

Alberta remembered meeting Paul on Seventh Avenue in Harlem about that time. He ran across the street, grabbed her, threw her up in his arms, and called her Queenie. "He didn't look so well, and he says, 'It's tough out here, Alberta.' "

That was the last time she saw Paul Robeson. His income decreased, and he became ill in the late 1960s. She said she tried several times to see him before his death in 1976 in Philadelphia but was turned away by his family. "He died with a broken heart because he was misunderstood," Alberta said.

London introduced Alberta to someone else whom she admired for the rest of her life: Marian Anderson, who was living at John Payne's house following her arrival in England in November 1927. Marian had a room with a piano, on the third floor, next to Alberta's room. "Marian was in London getting her register straightened out with Miss Amanda Aldridge, Ira Aldridge's daughter," Alberta said.

"She was cold as ice," Alberta said of Marian Anderson. "She had no soul. She had soul but not for her songs. We used to do things to hurt her feelings to help her. She didn't know we were trying to help her, but that's what we were doing."

In cahoots on that project were two other black Americans who also lived at the house: F. H. Robb, who was studying law in London, and Errington Kerr, a violinist who was studying medicine.

"She [Marian] was in love with somebody who wasn't quite as nice as he should have been," Alberta said. "That hurt her, too."

Offsetting the conniving of this little group, Lady Cook did everything she could to help Marian, Alberta said. Without Marian's knowing, she would buy up many of the tickets to her concerts and distribute them to her friends to make sure the halls would be full and heartily supportive of Marian's performances.

Alberta said she and Marian would ride for hours on top of the double-decker buses of London, taking in the beautiful sights of the city. Alberta really liked Marian. "She was never spoiled. She was sweet and quiet. I loved her so."

Alberta always considered Marian a friend. She was one of the few people from her past whom Alberta even liked to talk to in later years. When Alberta died, the only photographs of other people that she displayed in her apartment were of Marian Anderson and Paul Robeson. The former was autographed: "To dear Alberta, Show Boat's most marvelous Queenie. Sincerely, Marian Anderson, London, England."

Alberta also saved several telegrams from Marian. One was sent on February 13, 1928, to Alberta at the Florida Club in London, saying, "Heaps of love and best wishes for your success tonight." It was signed by Marian and John Payne. The next was sent on February 20, 1928, to Alberta at the Argyle Theater in Birkenhead, wishing "Success to you with all our love" and signed by both again. Finally, she saved a telegram Marian sent her in London from America on December 23, 1928, reading, "May the new year bring you health, happiness and prosperity."

In 1984, when asked any questions about Alberta, Marian Anderson refused to comment other than finally to say, "You know, I really didn't care for Alberta." Some black entertainers who knew both women are sure Marian's disdain toward Alberta in later years was due to her having discovered that Alberta was a lesbian, a fact, they said, that was repugnant to her.

Alberta sang at the going-away party Lady Cook and John Payne threw for Marian when she returned to America in September 1928. Beatrice Lillie (Lady Peel in private life) did a comical reading. Anton Dolin, the dashing English ballet dancer, was there, as were Mabel Mercer, the Duncan sisters, and Zaidee Jackson.

Alberta almost had to leave England before Marian. Late in June 1928 Sir Alfred Butt wrote her that she was going to be cut from *Show Boat*. "I want to say to you I have no criticism whatever to make in regard to your performance in our show," he wrote (letter reprinted by *Amsterdam News*, July 4, 1928, p. 10). "I think it is an admirable one in every way, and the only reason that we are, with reluctance, dispensing with your services is that our expenses are so extremely heavy that we are obliged to keep them as low as possible, and I came to the conclusion that I ought to fill the part of 'Queenie' at a lesser salary than you are now receiving. Yours faithfully, Alfred Butt, Drury Lane."

Alberta, dejected, booked passage on the *Île de France* departing for New York on July 11. Days before she was to leave, Sir Alfred had a change of heart. Alberta was to stay in the show. Lady Cook probably had something to do with that reversal, by lobbying either Sir Alfred or his superiors, if not personally agreeing to finance part or all of the differential in salary for Alberta to remain in the show.

The close call that almost sent Alberta home unwillingly made her think about her future in Europe. She knew it was far easier to stay in France than in England because of the former's more lenient work restrictions. So she started studying French in London. She wanted to impress audiences by being able to sing in French. But she also wanted to know the meaning of the words she sang and of many others so she could converse well wherever she went. "I didn't want to talk like a parrot," she said.

Alberta said she also took a few music lessons from Louis Drysdale whom she met through John Payne. "I never wanted to become an opera star," she said, explaining why she went to Drysdale, a noted tutor of opera singers. "I knew I didn't have the voice for that. But I wanted to be able to discuss my work intelligently."

Alberta had plenty of familiar faces to keep her company in London that fall. As Ivan Browning noted in his column for the *Chicago Defender* (October 13, 1928, p. 6), "London is full of Race artists at the moment, and to see them strolling around Leicester Square, Piccadilly and other streets reminds one of Seventh Avenue in New York."

There were also dangerous elements—white ones—on the streets, according to a letter Alberta penned on October 10, published in the *Amsterdam News* (October 24, 1928, p. 7): "Mrs. Aimee McPherson, the California evangelist, arrived in London a few days ago, after spending some time trying to drive the devil out of Paris. Instead of preaching the gospel, she was spreading prejudice. In one of her articles she spoke of the wickedness of Paris, etc., and she concluded by saying that Negroes were allowed to speak to white girls as freely as they cared to.

"She has been a complete failure here," Alberta happily reported. In the same letter she asked the paper to transmit a message to friends. "Please tell Mildred and Johnny Hudgins to write. I'm beginning to think they've forgotten me."

The black newspapers in America were printing so much about Alberta's success in Europe that all sorts of people were hearing about her. A man on Chicago's South Side who read about her decided to write her in London on November 27, 1928. His grammar and post-Victorian language indicated he was well educated. His address was the Omega Psi Phi Fraternity House, 5720 South Parkway, Chicago. The letter started: While perusing over the various papers this week,

I happily read the glowing news of your triumphant invasion of the British Isles. Congratulations.

"Prompted by the spirit of elation and thoroughly happy to read of your successes, hence this letter."

Lest she misinterpret his praise and think he had ulterior motives, he said, "It is not my intention to come out of the past and intrude into the serene tranquility of your well deserved happiness.

"Simply a salutation conveying that secret pride all men entertain concerning the woman who has won. With every good wish for your continued success permit me to remain, Sincerely, Willard."

Alberta saved that letter for the rest of her life, but she didn't answer her ex-husband. Let him praise her conquests, but let him, and everyone else, keep their distance.

London's social season, as reported by America's black newspapers, ended that year with the party Paul Robeson threw for the *New York Times* writer Carl Van Vechten and his wife, Fania Marinoff. The guests included Lord Beaverbrook, Fred and Adele Astaire, author Hugh Walpole, Lady Cook, publisher Alfred Knopf, Edith Day, and black entertainers Ivan H. Browning, Leslie Hutchinson, Tandy Johnstone, Turner Layton, and Alberta Hunter.

As a footnote to that year, Lady Cook gave a Christmas party for poor black children in London at the Friends' House on Euston Road. Alberta sang along with Paul Robeson, the Four Harmony Kings, and John Payne, among others.

Three months later *Show Boat* closed, after 350 performances. John Payne gave another of his celebrated parties, this one a farewell to Alberta. The usual types of guest—theater people, movie stars, journalists, and a peppering of nobility—showed up to pay their respects and have a jolly good time.

Several clubs in London invited Alberta to stay on, but she had a longing to get home to America and to her mother. It was only because of a financially irresistible offer that she committed herself for a month to open the Cotton Club, under the management of Jack Landorff, in Paris. Days after her departure on March 5, 1929, singer Nell Hunter (no relation) wrote a letter about Alberta to the *Pittsburgh Courier* (published March 30, 1929, second section, p. 8): "Socially she is quite the vogue here and has been highly entertained by Hon.

Lady Cook and others of her standing. Not since Florence Mills has anyone been so well loved in London. She has made and saved lots of money too."

Alberta had the fashionable Parisian designer Patou make a gown for her opening at the Cotton Club, located at 6 Rue Fontaine in Montmartre. Ivan Browning reviewed her performance for the *Chicago Defender* (April 6, 1929, p. 6). "She is billed like a circus," he said. "Her opening was a tremendous success, and whether it be variety, musical comedy or cabaret, Miss Hunter can always hold her own." Two of her numbers that went over biggest were "Why Do I Love You?" from *Show Boat* and a song called "Chiquita," which she sang in French.

Alberta was dressed to kill again for the opening of *Mississippi*, the French version of *Show Boat*, which she attended with her good friends Edith Wilson and Mae Alix. Alberta had been invited to join the cast of that show but for the price the producers were willing to pay she didn't want to commit herself to another long engagement before returning to the United States.

It was just as well that the Cotton Club flopped and closed several days after opening. Alberta sang for a few weeks at the Le Florence, owned by Peppy de Albrew. On her last night, May 21, while she was at the club, someone broke into her room at the Victor-Massé Hôtel and stole some of her clothes. By coincidence, Alberta the previous night had dreamed of being robbed. So the next evening she left her room wearing a diamond ring she had with her. Otherwise, it, too, would have been stolen. She immediately advised the American Consulate of her loss only to become infuriated because it did nothing to assist her.

She sailed for New York on May 22, 1929, aboard the *Île de France* with Mae Alix and Edith Wilson.

It was good that she was among friends on the crossing, for she was to find her destination, New York, even more inhospitable to her than it had ever been before.

Granny Nancy Peterson, who made macaroni, cheese, and tomatoes on Sundays.

(From left to right) La Tosca, Josephine, and Alberta minutes before Alberta knocked La Tosca off the steps.

Alberta as the "Sweet-
heart" of the Dream-
land Café.

Lottie Tyler, Bert Williams's
niece and Alberta's closest
friend for many years.
(*Peter P. Jones—Chicago*)

Florence Mills sang at Chicago's Panama Café the same time Alberta did. (*Joe Davis —London*)

Ethel Waters, Alberta's "Buddy Girl" and rival.

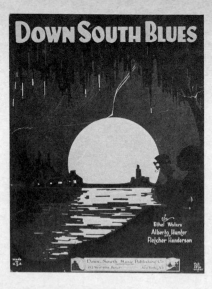

In 1923 the first of Alberta's blues songs were published.

Paramount Records began its "Race" record series with Alberta.

⫻

"If you're gonna sing the blues, make it classy," she said.

⫻

With unidentified members of
one of her vaudeville teams in
the mid-1920s.

Amanda Randolph, who stood
up at Alberta's wedding. She
became famous as Sapphire's
mother in *Amos 'n' Andy*.

Paris photographers thought Alberta and Mildred Hudgins were models.

Johnny Hudgins welcomed her to Paris in 1927. (*Waléry—Paris*)

Alberta had this portrait taken in Paris to distribute to agents and club owners on the continent. (*G. Ubidjian—Paris*)

They wanted the "real thing," a black, to play Queenie in the London version of *Showboat*. Alberta is center stage.

Alberta (left) in another *Showboat* scene.

Alberta singing "Can't Help Lovin' Dat Man" to Paul Robeson, her finest moment in *Showboat*.

THEATRE ROYAL
DRURY LANE

Managing Director .. .. ALFRED BUTT

EVENINGS at 8.15 Precisely

Matinees :
WEDNESDAY and SATURDAY at 2.30 Precisely

SHOW BOAT

The Cast includes :

EDITH DAY

| CEDRIC HARDWICKE | MARIE BURKE |

| DOROTHY LENA | LESLIE SARONY |

| PAUL ROBESON | HOWETT WORSTER |

| VIOLA COMPTON | ALBERTA HUNTER |

Alberta in "Vive Paris!" at the Casino de Paris in 1933.

ABOVE: With special friends in London, 1928 (from left to right): Ivan Harold Browning, Marian Anderson, John Payne, Haroldine Browning, Alberta.

RIGHT: Lady Cook, "Mother" to the boarders at John Payne's house in London.

Alberta in the Thirties. (*Schomburg Center*)

ABOVE: With friends Mabel Mercer and Jimmy Donahue at Bricktop's in Paris.

BELOW: Her first airplane trip, between Paris and London, 1933.

Alberta at the Casino de Paris.

CHAPTER FIVE

Commuting Between Prejudice and Pride

Alberta returned from Europe in 1929 feeling very good about herself. A glimmer of a British accent complemented the fine English tweeds she wore. Her name had lit up the marquees of some of Europe's most important theaters. She had been a welcomed guest in homes of the nobility. She spoke French fairly well. And she could describe Fontainebleau room by room.

She arrived in America to find that sophistication was not an admired trait for black performers. Two of the most popular entertainers at the time were two white men, Freeman Gosden and Charles Correll, portraying bungling black characters, Amos and Andy, who were incapable of correctly pronouncing most words of more than two syllables. (In 1966 reruns of the radio program, which had been among the nation's most popular for more than two decades, were taken off the air in Chicago as a result of charges by the NAACP that it was a "gross libel on the Negro.")

Alberta's scrapbook testified to her status as a singer in Europe. She showed the photographs and press clippings to journalists and booking agents, but no glamorous job offers came her way. She was just another "little colored gal," a little older and far too refined for most club owners in the United States.

Alberta took what work was available to her. She recorded two songs for Columbia, "Gimme All the Love You Got" and "My Particular Man." And she went back on the Keith circuit, opening at the State Theater in Jersey City along with the four Marx Brothers' film *The Cocoanuts*. At least this time she was on the top of the vaudeville bill as "Queenie of the London Ziegfeld 'Show Boat Co.' " She put together an act with two dancers—Papoose and Johnny—and hired pianist Pearl Wright, who often accompanied Ethel Waters.

In September 1929 she was at the Regent Theater in New York with Rudy Vallee and his Connecticut Yankees and Jolly Joyce, "The Fat Boy of Joy." Early that fall she played other Keith theaters close to home in Yonkers, Brooklyn, and Paterson, New Jersey.

One of her performances at the Bushwick Theater attracted the attention of a critic at the *New York Times* (November 17, 1929), who wrote: "There is real class to this girl. She has been on the stage for some time. You can tell that by her personality. Among the songs she offers are 'Second Hand Man of Mine,' 'Keep Your Daddy Home' and 'There Ain't No Love.' She takes encores."

Even on the vaudeville circuit work was becoming more scarce. The emergence of talking films and the October 29, 1929, crash on Wall Street cut the demand for star performers such as Alberta. Luckily she had enough cash and jewelry stashed away to weather the depression that ensued.

There were always requests to perform for free at benefits. Alberta did her share, singing for the Harlem Children's Fresh Air Fund at the Lafayette Theater with Edith Wilson and for the NAACP at the Forrest Theater on West Forty-ninth Street. The latter was a gala affair, also featuring Duke Ellington and his Cotton Club Orchestra, Libby Holman, and Helen Morgan. The benefits gave Alberta the chance to show off one of her Paris-designed gowns and to sing in French a song like "I Kiss Your Hand, Madame."

Right after Christmas she went "home" to Chicago for a six-week engagement at the swank Grand Terrace Café with Earl Hines and his Orchestra. The Grand Terrace was sometimes compared to Harlem's Cotton Club because of its fabulous floor shows. It differed importantly, however, in that it welcomed black patrons.

The gala opening night crowd received Alberta warmly. "A five minute ovation greeted her after she made 22 bows and sang several encores," the Chicago *Whip* (January 4, 1930, p. 6) reported. "She was overcome with emotion and hurried to her dressing room." The *Whip* applauded her singing in French as "remarkably sweet of volume and rhythm" and said she "sings with the grace and ease that is hers and Ethel Waters."

The regular crowd that came to the Grand Terrace during the rest of Alberta's stay weren't so enthusiastic about her classy airs and singing in French, according to Kid Thompson, Florence Mills's widower, who was in Chicago at the time. "Alberta was all in lace and satin," he said. "The people of Chicago didn't know her as an aristocrat. They wanted her to sing like she did before, in a lusty voice, snapping her fingers and carrying on." According to Thompson, the manager of the Grand Terrace told Earl Hines, "Just tell her she's got to go back and sing those old songs like she used to." Alberta ignored the order and, as a result, had to endure lukewarm audiences.

She returned to New York and concentrated for a while on settling her mother at the apartment Alberta owned on West 138th Street. Miss Laura had been married in Chicago to Jim Fields, brother of Cham Fields, who owned a saloon and restaurant there. Now that Jim Fields was dead, Alberta thought it was time she provided financially for her mother.

She wasn't ready to live with her mother, but she wanted her nearby. Alberta was again sharing an apartment with Lottie, always a friend in spite of the fact that their lives kept taking different directions. Lottie seemed more settled, having received one-third of the small estate Bert Williams had left his widow, Lottie's aunt, who died in 1929. Keeping up with Lottie wasn't especially settling for Alberta. They moved from one place to another in the next few years.

Alberta sang at Small's Paradise in Harlem for a week in February 1930. But she was upstaged by the big band and glittery floor shows and the nimble waiters, who deftly balanced loaded trays on fingertips while dancing the Charleston on their way to and from the kitchen.

Two months later, yearning for an appreciative audience, she applied for a new passport, telling the State Department she planned to return to Europe at once. At the last minute she decided to accept a part in *Change Your Luck*, a new musical comedy being presented by Cleon Throckmorton. Garland Howard wrote the book for the play; J. C. Johnson, the music and lyrics. The plot had something to do, although critics weren't sure just what, with the attempts of Ebenezer Smart (played by Hamtree Harrington) to avoid Prohibition agents. A female boxing act in the second act was a special distraction. Alberta, as Mary Jane, sang "Waisting Away" and the title song. The sets were "miles ahead of anything that a colored show has ever had before," the *New Yorker* magazine observed (June 21, 1930, p. 30).

Unfortunately the heat inside the theater on opening night, June 6, 1930, was stifling. That may have made the critics who sweltered through the evening less generous. Few of them were hot about what they saw. "Displaying a commendable indifference to the temperature, a group of energetic and obligin [sic], if misled, Negroes took over the stage of the George M. Cohan Theatre last night there, literally under the torrid glare of the Broadway electric lights, alternately ran and crawled through the first performance of a new musical comedy, 'Change Your Luck,' " said the *New York Times* (June 7, 1930, p. 10). "Needless to say, it was when they ran, or, to be precise, danced, that they were, in the manner of Negro musical show entertainers, at their best."

Variety reported that the play "opened cold," was poorly cast, and had too many ballads and too little comedy (June 11, 1930, p. 54). It did praise Harrington and Alberta for their comic routines but predicted correctly that they would not be able to save the production. It folded. Alberta's fate onstage in musical comedies continued to be nothing but bum luck.

Her fortune was no better when she opened at the Lafayette Theater in the fall of 1930. She was appearing in a revue called *This Way Out* with Jazzlips Richardson, Margaret Sims, and Sammy Stewart's Band. The entertainment accompanied a film with Corinne Griffith and Grant Withers entitled *Back Pay*.

Before the first curtain went up, Alberta, aware that Frank Schiffman, the theater's white manager, had previously hired artists at one salary, then lowered it because of poor audience reaction on opening night, asked for a copy of her contract. Schiffman had defended himself by saying a clause in the contracts gave him the right to cancel an engagement after the first show if he so desired. However, he didn't always submit the contract for the artist's prior approval of that condition or any other.

Alberta sensed that her request offended Schiffman and that a showdown was in the offing. Sure enough, after her first performance he sent word backstage that unless she accepted a cut of $100 off the $250 weekly salary originally agreed to, she was not to continue in the show. She refused. She followed the advice of her lawyer, Ralph Warrick, to report nonetheless for every show.

Schiffman then called her into his office and told her that her hanging around and talking with other performers was disrupting the show. He reportedly told her that she was "not the only singer in Harlem and that he could drag them in off the streets" (*New York Age*, October 18, 1930, p. 6). When she told him she would fight him in court, he threw her out of his office and barred her from entering the theater. There is no evidence that she sued or that she received any of her salary for that week.

Geraldyn Dismond, then writing for the *Afro-American*, blasted Schiffman in one of her columns because of this incident. "His crassness, high-handed methods and chicanery have made him deservedly disliked by members of the theatrical profession and those who unfortunately had to come in contact with him," she wrote (October 18, 1930, p. 9). She accused him of similar actions toward performers Johnny Hudgins, Moiret and Fredi, Trixie Smith, and George Dewey Washington.

That was Alberta's last invitation to sing at the Lafayette Theater. After a short stint at the Blossom Health Club on Seventy-seventh Street in New York she appeared in Philadelphia at the Pearl Theater and at the Olympia Gardens, which was celebrating the installation of an indoor miniature golf course.

By late November Alberta was again in New York for one week at Harlem's fashionable Alhambra Theater. On December 7 she performed at the NAACP benefit at the Waldorf Theater on West Fiftieth Street with a cast that included Libby Holman, Helen Morgan, Ethel Waters, Adelaide Hall, Duke Ellington and his Cotton Club Orchestra, J. Rosamond Johnson, Bojangles Robinson, and Molly Picon.

By year's end Alberta's frustration in not finding more work was so great that she complained to the press about her difficulties in this country, compared to the "kindness, consideration, appreciation," and bookings she received in Europe. "Of course I prefer Europe," she told a reporter from the *Pittsburgh Courier* (December 20, 1930, p. 3). "What Negro with sense doesn't?" She criticized the "unkind and brusque" manner in which booking agents were treating her in New York. "They do not want refinement and finesse in a Negro performer. All they want is niggerism, a whole lot of foot-stamping and shouting." She said the only time she knew she was "colored" in Europe was when she came in contact "with certain types of white Americans." Prejudices against her as a black entertainer were common in America, she said.

"The white agents here . . . tell Negroes that a European reputation amounts to nothing but they will pay a white performer twice the salary he formerly received after he comes back from abroad. Many of these white performers I have myself seen hissed off the stage in Paris and London."

She said she was going back to Europe as soon as she could. "Why, when I was steaming up the harbor here, I actually cried when I saw the Statue of Liberty again," she said, recalling her return from Paris the year before.

The *Courier*'s reporter wrote in the same article that during the course of the above interview Alberta politely excused herself twice to answer the telephone. He noted with what class she greeted callers, no matter who they were. In this case one was a "stage door Johnny from Chicago." The other was Adelaide Hall, one of the most popular black singers on both sides of the Atlantic and a protégée of Alberta's.

Adelaide was very fond of Alberta and looked up to her as a big sister. In 1925, before marrying a Trinidadian seaman, Bert Hicks, she asked for Alberta's opinion of him. Adelaide said she thought at first that he was "a little too much" because he wore spats, wing collars, and a handkerchief up his sleeve. "I knew Alberta could size up a person in a minute and judge his character," she said.

Adelaide wasn't as keen in sizing up Alberta's nature. She said she never knew Alberta was a lesbian—"funny," as she put it—until someone suggested it to her sixty years later. Alberta's only concern about the marriage, said Adelaide, who was very pretty and talented, was that Bert Hicks might try to discourage her from her budding career as an entertainer. "Alberta was very proud of what I had done with myself," she said.

Alberta was even more proud of her when at the end of the summer of 1932 Adelaide bought and moved into a house in the fashionable white town of Larchmont, in Westchester County, just north of New York. Adelaide held her own against the hostile protest of neighbors. She challenged the best of the bluebloods among the whites there to match their lineage with hers to see who had the most legitimate right to be in that area. After all, she said, she was a descendant of an Indian tribe that lived there long before Christopher Columbus was even in knee breeches.

Adelaide did marry and went right on entertaining into the 1980s, to the delight of audiences in Europe and America. She and Bert Hicks ran a club on the Rue Pigalle in Montmartre from 1935 to 1938 called the Big Apple (she claimed ownership of the name before it became a nickname for New York City). From Paris the couple returned to London to buy and run a private dinner club in Mayfair, the Florida Club. After the war they owned another place on Regent Street called the Calypso Club.

Adelaide had a great deal of professional respect for Alberta, whose path she crossed often in those years. "She was really an outstanding artist," she said. "No one could sing a song like she did." Remarkable, too, was the way Alberta overcame her "biggest obstacle in not being pretty."

Actually an even greater barrier to success was Alberta's unwillingness to "play the game, to go to bed with the guys controlling the shows," said Doll Thomas, the electrician and projectionist at the Alhambra from 1927 to 1934 and from then until now at the uptown Apollo Theater. "She wanted to be respected as the talented individual she was without all the bullshit associated with show business," he said. "And that was awfully hard to do in those days. It was just part of the deal."

Alberta did manage to get back to the Alhambra two more times in 1931, solely on the basis of her talent. She played in a revue beginning the week of January 12 called *Laugh Land*, with Amon Davis, Ola Wright, and Ray Moore. She was there again the week of May 2 with top billing as "International Singing Star and Queen of Entertainers" appearing with Ray Parker and his Stompers.

Geraldyn Dismond gave a glowing review of that show (in an unidentified article in Alberta's scrapbook): "Miss Hunter, internationally famous for her ability to stand still and sell her lyrics, her resonant and colorful contralto voice, her elegant clothes and magnetic personality, is the idol of Alhambra fans. From box to gallery the house is hers, and never do they want her to leave the stage. This week, dressed in the latest formal egg shell satin pajamas with cerise jacket and slippers, she rocks the house singing, 'There Ain't No Love,' 'On Revival Day,' 'Find Out What They Like and How They Like It,' and 'He May Be Your Man.' "

After appearing at Philadelphia's Pearl Theater in May, Alberta went shopping for extra furniture for her apartment in preparation for moving in with her mother. She bought several large armchairs "for her friends to sit in when they came by to visit" and where she could read until midnight, as was her habit. She stopped following her gypsy friend Lottie in her constant change of apartments and lovers. At one point Lottie married a man named Davis, a waiter at one of the clubs in New York, but they didn't live together long, Alberta said.

Alberta also did some flirting with a man, Dr. Wiley M. Wilson, former husband of millionairess A'Lelia Walker. "I used to see him on the sly," she said. "But his last wife, Inez Wilson, found out about it. She couldn't stand me, but she had to take it. He used to think I had the nicest figure of any woman on earth. Poor me," said Alberta. "I liked him as a sweetheart." Asked how serious it was, she said, "Very serious."

But it was Miss Laura who was to become Alberta's constant focus of attention until she died twenty-three years later. As always, she was easy to get along with and to please. She never had a complaint. She wasn't any great shakes in the kitchen although she made good spaghetti, more than her daughter could do. "She could keep starvation away," Alberta said. She even made her daughter's bed. "Oh, darling, you'll just get in the way," she said if Alberta lifted a finger around the house.

"My mother was a lone wolf," said Alberta. The only friends she had were Jimmy Daniels's mother and a woman named Carrie Paine. "My mother wouldn't go out to visit anyone," Alberta said. "I'm exactly like my mother. She didn't visit, and she didn't talk much." Her two friends always came to see her. Mrs. Paine could never stay for long because she always had something on the stove for her ever-hungry husband, who was a redcap.

Rose McClendon, an actress who lived downstairs until her death in 1936, came upstairs every day to check on Miss Laura when Alberta was traveling. "But Alberta's mother wouldn't open the door for her," said Harry Watkins, "because Rose was bawdy and would shout, 'Fields, open this damn door.' "

Miss Laura read a lot and asked that anyone coming into her house bring her a newspaper. She devoured the black newspapers and the *New York Times*, down to the classified ads. "She knew every politician and everything he had refused to do to help you," Alberta said.

She was very formal, even with Harry, who showered attention on her and paid her bills and brought groceries when he was in town and Alberta was traveling. She always called him Mr. Harry.

Miss Laura, who dressed like a Quaker, always sat straight as a broomstick, held out her hand to the rare newcomer, and said, very correctly and distinctly, "How do you do, Mr. or Miss so-and-so?" Both women were extremely secretive except when they disapproved of someone. "If I don't like you, it's period," Alberta said.

Mother and daughter became closer than ever. "My mother would do anything for me," Alberta said, "and I showed my love for her by any little thing that I thought would please her. I knew she didn't like lamb, so I wouldn't come near her with it. She was crazy about beer and cabbage. I would always try to come in with something and hand it to her to see the smile on her face. She was a good woman."

Before Alberta traveled, she bought enormous stocks of canned food and supplies, which she stacked in a back room of the apartment, originally designed as the maid's room, so her mother would not want for anything. "It looked like a grocery store," said Harry

Watkins. Some of those cans were there so long, he said, that they would pop open from time to time with loud bangs.

When Alberta was in New York, she'd occasionally go to a movie with a friend. Mae Barnes went with her in June of that year to see the first black-produced talkie film, *The Exile*, at the Lafayette Theater. The movie had been barred recently in Pittsburgh because it portrays the love of a black man for a "near white girl" (one-tenth of one percent black). Alberta and Mae sat in one of the front rows. The film was more than a bit stupid, according to Mae. At one point a man kills a woman, then holds up his gun and says, as if talking to the audience, "I've got one bullet left. What am I gonna do with it?"

Alberta shouted, "Take it and shoot me in the head for coming into this goddamned theater." Alberta got up and walked out. The audience doubled over in laughter. "That's the way she was," said Mae. "Kind of sassy."

Alberta was in a bickering state the rest of the year. Twice it was reported that she quit her job at the Hot Feet Club. She was there once more in December 1931 since on the night of the sixth she had a motorcycle escort take her from the club to a benefit at the Hotel Astor.

Alberta played a few more Keith houses, including those in Philadelphia and Washington, in the first months in 1932. Maestro Ralph Cooper brought her to the Harlem Opera House late in February for a week's engagement.

In May she teamed up with her old friend Lil Armstrong, who was divorced from her husband, Louis, that year after a long separation. They played the Lafayette with Cora La Redd and her Red Peppers Band and Sunshine Sammy and his Pals before the showing of the "gripping melodrama" entitled *Disorderly Conduct* with Spencer Tracy. The *Interstate Tattler* described Alberta as being "resplendent in white satin." She "gave the girls a sizzling formula for keeping the good man home," with her ever-popular rendition of the song "If You Want to Keep Your Daddy at Home" (May 19, 1932, p. 8).

("Banjo") Ikey Robinson said he played for that show. He wasn't particularly impressed with Alberta. "I was into jazz," he said. "She did mostly risqué numbers that I thought were better for a cabaret."

He swore she sang a song called "If I Can't Sell It, I'm Gonna Keep Sitting on It"—"nothing smutty," he clarified. "You took your pick of which way you wanted to see it." Alberta indignantly declared she never sang anything so naughty-sounding. However, in 1926 she recorded a song she called "Gimme Some of What You're Sitting On."

Whatever she was singing, she was doing it again with Lil during a week's engagement that summer in Baltimore. In the fall Alberta introduced several "scorchy" tunes Lil wrote with Ralph Matthews: "I Don't Want No Damaged Goods" and "Send Me a Man."

Toward the end of the year she put on a tall top hat to match the one worn by Gladys Bentley, a male impersonator whose double entendre songs competed with her own in their joint act to draw a crowd of white celebrities to the Clam House on 133d Street.

White women could even come alone to places like that or Jock's and "never be bothered," Alberta said. "They were well protected, honey. Those huck men would kill a snake if they caught somebody trying to bother those women. Negroes in Harlem, men and women, wouldn't let anybody bother you all up there. Harlem was packed all the time with white and colored men and women. I guess that's the reason you all liked us so. We were crazy about you, and we protected you."

For someone as apt as she in getting press for herself, Alberta's name disappeared completely from newspaper entertainment pages during the first half of 1933, indicating that she was having a hard time finding jobs. Lillian Alpert, who worked for Marty Forkins's agency in managing black stars like Bojangles Robinson, said Alberta often came in those days to her office in the Palace Theater Building, hoping to find work. Forkins wasn't able to place Alberta since he worked mostly in placing bands that had their own singers, she said. Then, fingering the diamond ring Bojangles had left her, Lillian reflected and said sadly, "It's too bad they didn't see her talent when she was young. She wasn't recognized then because she wasn't pretty."

It's not surprising then that Alberta sailed for France in late May 1933. She went to work this time in Fred Payne's Bar at 14 Rue Pigalle. Payne, a white American expatriate, advertised "afternoon bridge, cabaret all night long" and drew a fashionable clientele for both activities.

After her own shows Alberta frequently went to Bricktop's, where Mabel Mercer was performing. Mabel had been in Paris since after World War I, singing among other places at Chez Florence and Le Grand Duc. Alberta loved Mabel's elegant singing style.

After a month in Paris Alberta accepted an invitation to appear on a program at King's Hall, Bournemouth, England, with John Stein and his Tzigane Orchestra and the King's Hall Ambassadeurs Band. Throughout her life she disliked airplanes. But just to say she had been on one, she flew to England, making sure to document the historic event with a photo for her scrapbook.

As usual, she had her choice of offers to sing in Europe. After performing for several weeks at the La Gaîté Cabaret in Amsterdam, she returned to Paris, where on October 1 she began appearing in *Vive Paris!*, a show at the Casino de Paris on the stage where slinky Josephine Baker had pranced and pounced for several years before. Cécile Sorel was the star of the extravagant production.

Alberta's big number was in front of a gigantic birdcage filled with leggy, plumed dancers on swings. The theater program explained the theme: "These Negro dancers, lost in the great heart of Paris, sometimes on dark winter evenings dream like caged birds of the isles of their sunlit islands bathed by the azure sea."

One of the dancers, or *claquettes* as they were called, was Gustav Wally, a white man and grandson of the king of Denmark, according to Alberta. "He couldn't dance a lick," she said, but the producers let him dance because he was who he was. She thought he was very nice, and that was all that mattered to her.

The economic depression was now affecting Europe and emptying the tables at many a night spot in the Montmartre section of Paris. Jimmy Daniels, who had been the host and the toast of Jean Cocteau's le Boeuf sur le Toit, returned to New York in October. Two months later Bricktop went bankrupt on Pigalle and packed her bags for Cannes, where, with her typical optimism, she decided she would have better luck. "As long as I wear a dress, my chances are good as any," she was quoted as saying (*Chicago Defender*, January 13, 1934, p. 5).

Alberta spent most of the winter, a time when Paris so often exudes the grimness of wet slate, singing to the tropical birds in the cage. By spring 1934 she was ready to fly free herself. Gustav Wally told Alberta to write a friend of his, Inge Lise Bock, artistic director of the National Scala Theater in Copenhagen, if she ever wanted to go to Denmark to perform. Alberta did write her and was delightfully surprised by the response. "She sent me a contract without seeing me, saying good morning, nothing, just through his word," Alberta said. The first date was set for the month of May 1934.

Alberta loved the Danes, and they adored her. "I was one of the first black women they had seen walking down the street," she said. Journalist Sven Rye recalled the day Alberta came to the house at Hostrup's Have in Copenhagen that he shared with Svend Aage ("Jesper") Jespersen, assistant to Bock. "We invited Miss Hunter for lunch, and I remember that we had forgotten to tell our housekeeper that our luncheon guest was black, so when Alberta Hunter rang the doorbell, the housekeeper almost screamed: 'There is a black woman at the door!' We felt embarrassed; but Alberta Hunter took it with a smile, and we spent some wonderful hours together at our apartment."

Alberta felt very special in Copenhagen. The theater assigned a woman, Thilda Olsen, to be her maid. "She was the sweetest thing in the world," Alberta said. "Every time I arrived back in Copenhagen by train, she would be there at the train station, waiting for me." Alberta especially liked being invited for tea by the Danes because of the food they served with it. "Talk about cold cuts!" she said. "The best eggs and cheese. And such a welcome!"

She opened on May Day at the Scala, a grand vaudeville theater with a restaurant and separate bar. Roy de Coverley, a correspondent for the local newspaper *Berlingske Tidende*, whom she had met earlier in New York, found her rehearsing that day at the piano in the bar. She was dressed in a Molyneux ensemble, "topped with a ridiculous little hat," he wrote in an article he sent to the *Chicago Defender* (August 11, 1934, p. 9). "Her nails flashed ruby as she beat time for a not-too-skillful pianist with her little brown hands." She was nervous that evening, fearful the pianist might botch up her opening.

But as usual, she was in control, according to Coverley's description of her first number, which she sang in the bar:

"Two Tickets to Georgia." Dark brown voice with velvet over-tones. Rhythm. Brown eyes flashing, dark red mouth smiling. White satin body swaying to the beat. Jazz as I have never before heard it sung in Copenhagen rippling out into the mellow lighted room. White faces, critical at first, then softening in appreciation as the magic of a singing Negro girl and Negro music take pos-session of them. Applause. She had done it.

Then later in another part of the place with a band. Full of confidence now, Alberta walks out on the stage sensuous in red velvet. The band, which is really good as Danish bands go, swings into her introduction. She begins slow, throbbingly.

An unsigned review in the *Berlingske Tidende* (May 3, 1934) called Alberta a "blues Marian Anderson." The critic said: "There was no shadow of Negro worshipping in the enthusiasm about Marian An-derson, and there is neither about Alberta Hunter. But there is a lot of enthusiasm for Negroes' fantastic rhythm-sense and their musical voices." When Alberta sang "a modern banal 'Schlager' as 'Lazy-bones,' " the review continued, there were "strange transitions . . . queer jumps in rhythm and melody, jumps that are always successful and astonishing and which give new impressions.

"Alberta will be pampered in Copenhagen, and not without rea-son." She was indeed. Roy de Coverley introduced Alberta to a set of his chic friends, including "a charming woman lawyer" he didn't name. He did say Alberta went with him and an attaché (his girl-friend) from the Polish legation in Copenhagen to the woman's house in the little town of Hillerd for the Whitsuntide holiday. He gave the impression that the weekend and the company agreed with her. He described Alberta "curled on a sofa," reading D. H. Lawrence.

In spite of the sophisticated environment Alberta found herself in, she felt she could let her hair down with the Danes; that was why she always loved them. Harry Watkins remembered being in Copenhagen once to sing at the Tivoli Gardens near the Scala and going to hear her perform. When she spotted her tall, dashing friend, she let out a yelp, stopped singing, and went over to greet him.

No one else, except a rude person, could ever make her interrupt her performance like that. But Harry was different. He knew her as no one else knew her. He represented home to her—her ties to it and to her mother. As good as Europe was to her as a performer and as a person, home was still home, and she missed it.

Nostalgia, however, was not to deter her in her pursuit of fame. Alberta remained for a second month in Denmark by popular demand and left only on July 2 for London.

Soon after her arrival there she looked up Harry A. Steinberg at the Southern Music Publishing Company. R. S. Peer, the company's president in New York, was very fond of Alberta and had asked his associate in London to introduce her around since she had not been in England for five years. Steinberg did a splendid job. Within a few days she was the special guest on a BBC International broadcast with Henry Hall and his Orchestra.

The *Amsterdam News* called it a coup (August 11, 1934, p. 6). "Leading artists from all over the world bend every effort to get a chance to broadcast with Hall's band, as it is a real publicity stunt for them," the account said.

Alberta restricted her repertoire to popular ballads. Some of her blues songs might have been questioned under the standards of the BBC Variety Department, which strictly prohibited artists from mentioning such subjects as religion, public personalities, marital infidelity, effeminacy in men, immorality of any kind, and physical infirmities; unnecessary emphasis on drunkenness; or reference to blacks as "niggers" and to Chinese as "chinks."

About mid-July Alberta started on the vaudeville circuit in Scotland and England, playing successive weeks at the Theatre Royal in Edinburgh, Tivoli Theater in Aberdeen, Pavilion Theater in Glascow, Shakespeare Theater of Varieties in Liverpool, and the Hippodrome in Brighton.

She was lucky to be in England at all because the Ministry of Labor was denying work permits to most foreign entertainers in a move to protect local performers. The last outside group to be approved was Lew Leslie's *Blackbirds of 1934*, which was billed as "A Harlem Rhapsody" and "The Fastest Show on Earth" and played at the London Coliseum. Edith Wilson was in that show, as was Valaida

Snow, the singer and trumpet player who had recently been acquitted in a New York court on charges of bigamy.

Leslie's permit had to be renewed each month and was granted on the condition that all members of his troupe enter, perform, and leave England as a group and that the orchestra play on the stage, not in the pit. Duke Ellington and his Orchestra, on the contrary, were not permitted to perform that year in England.

Alberta's good fortune continued into September. Jack Jackson, a hot jazz trumpeter whose band was the rage at London's new and very exclusive Hotel Dorchester on Park Lane, across from Hyde Park, heard her and asked her to sing with his group and to join his radio broadcast every Thursday night. Jackson admired women who had good figures, his sprightly widow, Eve Jackson, said. He remarked to her that "Alberta didn't even have good tits."

"Her ugliness was fascinating," Eve Jackson said. "And she was so keen on what she was doing that she didn't pay much attention to that." Alberta did have a "great, great presence," she said, "as if to say, 'I'm here.' And such a friendly smile. And as a black she was a novelty.

"Jack fell for her totally," Mrs. Jackson continued. "He loved her rhythm. And although her voice was thin, she had great phrasing. You understood every word she said."

The *Amsterdam News* repeated a column from London's *Melody Maker* (November 17, 1934, p. 10): "Her singing on the air with Jack Jackson's band brought in great numbers of letters of appreciation from all over Europe, even from Russia."

Alberta fulfilled her commitments on the vaudeville circuit in mid-October. Shortly before that date she began recording twelve songs with Jackson's band on the His Master's Voice label. The first session was on September 24. She sang "Two Cigarettes in the Dark" and "Miss Otis Regrets (She's Unable to Lunch Today)."

Alberta's greatest satisfaction was in being able to perform at The Restaurant (now called The Terrace Room) at the Dorchester. Evening clothes were de rigueur in The Restaurant. One also had to be judged suitable by the maître d'hôtel to gain entrance and rub elbows socially with royalty.

At the time visiting maharajas rented out entire floors of the hotel for themselves and their entourages. They and their women, bedecked in emeralds, sapphires, and rubies, sat late into many a night below the domed ceiling of The Restaurant as Alberta sang.

Mrs. Wallis Warfield Simpson, then a socialite from Baltimore, was often there also with all her girlfriends and her future husband, the prince of Wales, who "made the most colossal demands on singers," according to Eve Jackson. One night he wanted to hear the music of *Stop Press*, a C. B. Cochran show. The show hadn't opened yet, so no one was allowed to play the music. The prince insisted, however. Jackson played it and later had to pay a stiff fine for doing so.

In spite of his demanding nature, Alberta remembered the prince of Wales as being very dignified. One day a waiter spilled a pot of tea on his royal shoulder. "He never even budged," Alberta said. "Shows you what refinement will do to you."

The prince, too, was smitten with Alberta. "He'd dance right up to where I was, and he'd stand there and listen to me sing. He was crazy about 'Time on My Hands.' I'd always sing it for him."

Noel Coward was another regular at the Dorchester. She thought Coward wrote a song especially for her, "I Travel Alone." Soon after writing it, he asked her to make a demonstration recording that he could take to the United States. The words applied as much to her life as to his:

> *The world is wide, and when my day is done*
> *I shall at least have travelled free*
> *Led by this wanderlust*
> *That turns my eyes to far horizons*
> *Though time and tide won't wait for anyone*
> *There's one illusion left for me*
> *And that's the happiness I've known—alone.*
>
> *I travel alone*
> *Sometimes I'm East*
> *Sometimes I'm West*
> *No chains can ever bind me*
> *No remembered love can ever find me.*
> *I travel alone*

Fair though the faces and places I've known
When the dream is ended and passion has
*   flown*
I travel alone.
Free from love's illusion, my heart is my own;
*I travel alone.**

Jackson liked the song so much he also asked Alberta to record it as part of the series they did together that fall. While Alberta performed at the Dorchester, she became a film personality as well. British International Pictures gave her a role in that country's first color film, *Radio Parade of 1935*, directed by Arthur Woods. British radio, stage, and screen stars, including Clifford Mollison, Helen Chandler, Nellie Wallace, and Will Hay, also participated.

The film was a spoof on the broadcasting business. Mollison played the part of the complaints director of the fictional National Broadcasting Group, an autocratically run company where new ideas are discouraged. One day the bright young man confides his imaginative programming ideas, without knowing it, to the director general, whom no one knows. Immediately he is put in charge of new programs.

He mounts a gala variety show only to have the Theater Trust tell him at the last minute that the cast, under its contract, is not available. So he recruits replacements from the station's staff and broadcasts the show over enormous screens placed in Trafalgar Square.

Alberta's scene, the only one in color, was the grand finale. Young, scantily clad black dancers in feather headdresses writhe languorously atop huge kettledrums. In the forefront, feet planted firmly on the stage, is Alberta with a choir behind her singing "Dark Shadows."

The film received pitiful notices. "It goes on for a very, very long time and ends with a burst of colour which does not quite come off," said a reviewer for the *Times* of London (December 24, 1934, p. 8).

Soon after a year's end broadcast for the BBC at the Dorchester with Jack Jackson, Alberta joined the cast of a revue called *Robinson Crusoe* at the Hippodrome Theater in Lewisham. Her old friend John

Payne played the cannibal king of Bangaloo, a South Sea Island. Alberta was a fair princess. The English critics seemed more appreciative of the performances of blacks than did their contemporaries in New York, at least if the *Kentish Times* (January 4, 1935) is any indication. It's review said: "All coloured pantomime (this is the first England has ever had) is certainly a good idea. There is something about a coloured artist that lends originality to whatever he does. If he acts, it is comedy with a strong flavour of humanity. If he sings, it is singing saturated with emotion."

The reviewer found Payne was a "splendid" cannibal king and "a genial soul, who might easily pop you into a cauldron with a few carrots and turnips and cheer you on your last journey with one of his rumbling bass chuckles.

"Another artist whose work is typical of the show's atmosphere is Alberta Hunter, well-known singer of film and radio repute. She has a voice you could call contralto until you realised to what vibrant depths it really went. You might say she was a torch-singer, but no torch-singer ever put such energy into her work. The best way in which to describe her performance is to say that she sang 'The Isle of Capri' and made it sound like a new song. And that is saying a lot."

That was Alberta's swan song to England. The Ministry of Labor, which had been extending her visa every few weeks for the past six months, refused to renew it after January 12, 1935. Out she went.

Alberta had offers to sing in Sweden and Denmark, but she went instead to Paris for a few weeks, then sailed for New York on the *Île de France*. She told friends she was confident British authorities would allow her back in England in April and that she would return at that time.

In New York Alberta blamed her hasty departure on the misconduct of some black performers in England. "The actions of a number of prominent Negro entertainers in breaking contracts, jumping hotel bills and deporting themselves in questionable manner have been responsible for a rising prejudice against colored performers," she told the *Amsterdam News* (February 9, 1935, p. 1). One London hotel had recently refused to accommodate the Mills Brothers, she said, because of the "disgraceful experience" it had just had with a noted black entertainer. For that reason the British government was not renewing any work permits, including her own.

She warned of more serious prejudice against blacks in Germany under Adolf Hitler's control. She told fellow entertainers to stay away from that country. In Hamburg, en route to Denmark the year before, she said children had chased her down streets shouting "nigger" at her. Officials were very rude to blacks in Germany, she said, and had even expelled Joe Cork, who had a contract to perform in Berlin.

France was no longer a haven either, but for other reasons. Alberta claimed that the "impoliteness" of the French had discouraged tourism there to the point that a number of clubs were having to close. Many performers were stranded there now, she said, having to sing for their supper.

America wasn't that much better—not Harlem anyway. The *New York Times* printed an article suggesting that Harlem was still "vibrant" and "joyous" in spite of having been the area within New York that was hardest hit by the Depression (*New York Times Magazine*, May 19, 1935, p. 4). The article went on to talk about the resentment of blacks in Harlem toward the whites who were invading it for entertainment, adding that Harlemites were showing "admirable restraint" in reacting to this situation.

It spoke of the "blatantly unfair" refusal of white merchants in Harlem to "employ colored help," mentioning that a boycott against such merchants had brought some results. Worse was the fact that the percentage of Harlem real estate controlled by whites rose from sixty-five percent in 1929 to ninety-five percent in 1935.

". . . spokesmen have seized on these figures to argue that the housing evil might not be so disgraceful if Negroes had more of a hand in the administering of the property," the writer said. "Another factor that piques thoughtful Negroes has been the maintenance, practically at full blast through the depression, of the so-called white man's Harlem. Nightly, expensively dressed women and their escorts visit the various 'hot spots,' the night clubs and 'atmosphere' bars."

One of the photos accompanying this article showed white patrons on the dance floor of an unnamed Harlem nightclub. "Harlem resentment is two-fold. Not only is there the flagrant contrast between the patrons of the resorts and the unfortunates on the streets (which, after all, may be observed dramatically on Broadway); the more sardonic fact is that the places that reap a good profit, even at necessarily reduced rates, are almost all run by whites."

The *Pittsburgh Courier* expanded on this article, talking about the humiliation blacks faced in being turned away from the doors of the clubs in question and the unfortunate "glorification" of the nightclub scene that gave young blacks the idea that entertaining the white race, often by spoofing their own, was a better aspiration than education and professional development (June 1, 1935, p. 2). About all Harlem did get out of the intrusion was the distribution at Christmas to its poorest residents of free food baskets. But even those, the *Courier* noted, were partly paid for by the black employees in the clubs.

Alberta was not successful in either living or working in this kind of environment. For the American Record Company she recorded four songs ("Driftin' Tide," "You Can't Tell the Difference After Dark," "Second Hand Man," and "Send Me a Man"), none of which was ever issued. Then, on April 21, she opened in *Connie's Hot Chocolates for 1935* at the new Connie's Inn at Broadway and Forty-eighth Street. The *Pittsburgh Courier* (April 20, 1935, section 2, p. 8) said: "For the first time in ten years—with one exception which failed— an entirely all-colored revue will appear in a Broadway Night Club."

Hot Chocolates became the second exception that failed. The cast, stated the publicity, was "headed by that charming international star Alberta Hunter." She sang in the finale: "That's What Harlem Is to Me, Tell Me What It Is to You." The score of the show was written by Andy Razaf, who with Fats Waller also wrote "Ain't Misbehavin' " and "Honeysuckle Rose." (Andy Razaf, nephew of Queen Ranavalona III of Madagascar, was a shortened version of Andreamentania Paul Razafinkeriefo.) Others on the bill were Pete, Peaches and Duke; Edna Harris; Muriel Rahn; Timmie and Freddie; and Teddy Hale—not a cast that would compare in its quality of talent with some of the other revues in the past years.

Alberta had the brief pleasure of seeing her name in lights on Broadway. But the public wasn't impressed, and the show bombed.

Enough was enough. Alberta returned to Europe, arriving in Cherbourg on the *Aquitania* on June 14. Harry Steinberg sent a letter to her at the Hôtel de Paris which she often used as a base in Europe, suggesting that she go to London. The Danes wanted her back right away. And there was an offer to sing in Egypt.

"Miss Hunter is so swamped with offers for her services that, instead of singing the blues as most vocalists are doing, she is singing 'I Wish I Were Twins,' " the *Chicago Defender* said (July 6, 1935, p. 8). She decided to stay put in Paris at her old familiar haunt, Fred Payne's Bar. Alberta continued to be able to make and save great sums of money when few other entertainers could.

Bricktop was back in Paris, going broke by night and clacking around Pigalle by day in her copper shoes and housecoat, shouting raucously from the street up to the windows of friends, "Hey, you bitches, whatcha doing?" and "Kiss my ass," if someone like Alberta didn't respond.

"Brick was very loud," Alberta said disapprovingly.

She far preferred the quiet demeanor of Mabel Mercer, who was living on the same street. Mabel Mercer, born in England of a black American father and a white English vaudeville star, often sang at Bricktop's. Mabel taught Brick how to walk and bow elegantly in good company, but she couldn't keep her from causing a ruckus when she wanted to.

"Mabel was a fine person," according to Alberta, even if she did call cookies biscuits. "She would say," Alberta said, mimicking Mabel's English accent, " 'Come and get some biscuits and a cup of tea.' Now you talk about a lady. Ooh, Lord," said Alberta. "And talk about dignity!

"Every day of my life she would invite me, but I wouldn't go," Alberta said. "Honey, I am not coming up there drinking that strong tea," Alberta told Mabel repeatedly. She went there at least once, though, because she could describe Mabel's cat. "Old, snobbish cat," Alberta said, raising her head to a stately pose. "Cat took on her habits. I never saw such a swellheaded cat in all my life. All black. A beautiful cat. But he was a snob if there ever was one."

Come fall 1935, everyone seemed to head out of Paris. Bricktop folded again and went to Biarritz. Mabel went to work at Frisco's, a fashionable cellar nightclub in London's Soho. And Alberta went to Copenhagen for another two-month stint at the National Scala. She also made a few radio broadcasts with Eli Donde's band at the Old Lorry Theater in Copenhagen. Alberta said they were so impressed with her singing "My Old Kentucky Home" that it was set to chimes and played regularly there.

As the cold Scandinavian winter set in, Alberta decided to head for the sun and lands that were yet a mystery to her. She and the pianist who accompanied her in Denmark, Norma Payne Davies, sailed for Alexandria on November 8. The headlines in the *Paris Herald Tribune* on the increased warfare between Benito Mussolini's Italian troops and those led by Haile Selassie in Ethiopia just to the south of Egypt did not dissuade them from crossing the Mediterranean. They opened at the Casino Excelsior in Alexandria on the fifteenth.

A clipping she saved from a French-language newspaper called *La Réforme* called Alberta *Reine du* [Queen of the] *Blues* and a *grande et magnifique artiste*. "She doesn't only spell out her songs, she lives them," the review said. "She attains with the blues a sincere emotion, a sentimentality that is common to Negro people that she intensifies even more." The critic encouraged readers to go see her. "She has a face that talks, rouses, enchants, ravishes."

Alberta was a tourist at heart. She bought postcards and took photographs of everything that caught her eye, from the inscrutable Great Sphinx in the desert to a row of men with their heads down on a boardwalk, their rear ends sticking up in air, and their bare feet poking out from their robes as they prayed to Mecca.

On January 26, 1936, Alberta wrote about Egypt to her friend Dorothy West, a writer then living in Boston. "Dot! darling. Egypt is very picturesque but the natives are the dirtiest people I've ever seen [;] after seeing conditions in Egypt I realize that America is the best place for *poor* blacks." Alberta explained an enclosed photo of her atop a camel: "Four of us hired camels one day and crossed the Sahara Desert a few days later we went out to see the Sphinx and Pyramids, my! what a sight I shall never forget." She said she would be returning soon to Europe, if not the United States, "for the war clouds are slowly but surely rising and it wouldn't be wise to be caught down this way. The feeling is so intense that it makes one uneasy."

Alberta left Egypt in early March 1936, after having played for nearly two months at the Continental Cabaret in Cairo. She and Norma went first to Istanbul to work at the Garden Petits-Champs and then to Athens for an engagement at the Femina Music Hall. Alberta wrote the *Chicago Defender* how impressed she was with an Easter procession in Athens with thousands of people carrying candles and walking up a hill toward a church at night.

In early May the two travelers were in Paris and again at Fred Payne's Bar. Alberta did a show with her old friend Garland Wilson at Le Hot Club de France on July 3, then embarked on a two-week trip to England.

In August 1936 she rejoiced with all blacks at the news that their sensational track star Jesse Owens had won four gold medals for the American athletic team at the Olympic Games in Berlin. His prowess so infuriated Adolf Hitler, defender of the superiority of the "Aryan" race, that the Führer reportedly left the stadium rather than pay tribute to a black man.

Alberta enjoyed being in Copenhagen the month of September 1936, all the more because of the warm hospitality the Danes gave her and other blacks.

For the next six months she commuted between London, where she did broadcasts for the BBC, and Paris, where she sang at Fred Payne's Bar. On February 17, 1937, a BBC television crew filmed her singing only for the cameras at Alexandra Palace. On the twentieth and twenty-second of that month she made two radio broadcasts following the recommendations of the BBC's Bryan Michie. "I suggest for this you might care to include your more sophisticated numbers with, of course, one or two popular numbers," he wrote her on February 5, 1937.

That same month she warned black American newspapers that the American Consulate in Paris was advising "race" performers not to accept contracts to appear in Italy. Il Duce had put a ban on performances by such so-called undesirables. Several groups that had traveled to Italy after the ban had been enacted were left stranded, she wrote. The American government assumed no responsibility for them. So a word to the wise, she said.

One of a select group of international stars asked to give television and variety performances under contract to the BBC during Coronation Week, celebrating the crowning of King George VI on May 12, 1937, Alberta was back in England. Her invitation, said one newspaper article in her scrapbook, was partly due to the fact that she had "never been connected with any incident of a rowdy or questionable nature." Another put it more graciously: "I can't think of a more thoroughly liked entertainer and one more generally pleasing to English audiences than Alberta Hunter."

From England she went to Ireland to appear at the Theatre Royal in Dublin and the Savoy in Limerick. The latter engagement was a bit of a letdown in that Alberta had to compete for the audience's attention with Miss Louise and Co., the company being a bunch of dogs that danced and did somersaults at the nudging of their mistress. That, admittedly, was a discouraging contrast with the regal event she had helped commemorate in London a few weeks before.

NBC asked her to do a special short-wave broadcast from Paris to America, a novelty at the time and therefore a feather in her bonnet. This invitation resulted from a meeting with Edward G. Robinson at Fred Payne's Bar in Paris the year before. The actor, who had been in England filming *Bullets or Ballots*, was in Paris adding to his substantial art collection with some purchases from the Wildenstein Gallery. He was so impressed with Alberta's singing one night that he went back another evening, this time accompanied by John Royal, vice president in charge of programs for NBC, and an associate of his in London, Fred Bate, so that they could hear her.

"Mr. Royal told me anytime I was ready to come back to New York to just let him know," Alberta said. "Well, I thought it was a little talk. You know how people promise you things."

When Bate asked her to do a special broadcast with Leslie Hutchinson live from London in 1937, she figured NBC was doing it to see how she sounded on the air before offering her anything on a regular basis. She wired her mother, who had still never heard her sing, and friends in New York to make sure they all would be listening at the appointed hour. "I said hello to America and then hello to my mother," she said. "It was the first time she had ever heard me perform. She just sat by the radio and cried."

The broadcast was a success. NBC asked her to come to New

York at once. Alberta wanted to return home. Her mother had not been well, and she worried about her. However, she couldn't resist an offer that came just then from a representative of New York's prestigious William Morris Agency to fill in for a month for a singer who had suddenly left the *Cotton Club Revue of* 1937, a show that the agency had sent to Europe. The group had performed in Paris first in June and was to open on July 26 at the London Palladium. NBC would just have to wait. Besides, a few more good credits in her portfolio would make her that more attractive to it, she thought.

Some of the critics found the *Revue* a bit noisy. The *London Star* (July 27, 1937) was astonished by the sound of "supercharged jazz served at breathtaking speed.

"When Teddy Hill's 1,000-volt band came into action some of us wished we had some cotton-wool [to plug their ears]. A lovely band, but oh! those trumpets." However, it praised Alberta as "a singer with a big, dark voice" in her rendition of "September in the Rain."

A reviewer for the *Pittsburgh Courier* (September 4, 1937, p. 21) called her the "Apostle of Gaiety": "The manner in which she puts over her numbers at the Palladium each night sends a stir of interest through the most lethargic imagination of English people. Alberta has an extraordinary range of facial expression and uncannily 'speaking' hands, which are the concord of her personality and appeal."

Again, her public behavior drew attention. "Alberta has proved herself a model of propriety and has therefore gained a mark of public esteem in London and Paris."

Alberta wanted always to be around people she considered ladies and gentlemen. When she spotted that quality in young people, she put them under her wing and nurtured them. She found such a protégée in Margot of the talented ballroom team Margot and Norton in that show at the Palladium. Margot was the daughter of George Mitchell Smith, one of the members of James Reese Europe's famous band. Having grown up in a convent and being very quiet, she was putty in Alberta's hands. "She kept telling me that's what she liked about me, that I was a lady," said Margot. "I was too dumb to be anything else. I was very naïve."

Alberta also sympathized with Margot and Norton for being as talented and good-looking as they were yet not being able to find work in American clubs, hotels, or films with the style of dancing they were doing. "Blacks were not supposed to dress up in evening clothes and dance as we were doing," Margot said.

New York agents told Margot they couldn't perform in ballrooms there for another reason. "Norton might make a pass at a white woman," they were told. That was highly improbable, Margot said. "He wasn't in the least bit interested."

Alberta invited Margot to stay rent-free at an apartment she had at the time at 43 Trinity Court on Gray's Inn Road, rented from a Swedish woman. Alberta offered plenty of free advice, too, especially on saving money.

"But she never took me out to dinner," said Margot. Alberta did take her on Sunday afternoons to tea parties at the home of a prominent woman in London. Margot didn't remember the woman's name, but it was probably Lady Ascot, whose home Alberta was known to frequent.

Alberta, with her very expensive flat shoes and equally dear tweed suits, looked right at home among all these proper Englishwomen. None of them was associated with the entertainment world, but they didn't seem the least stuffy. They sat on pillows on the floor and listened to poetry readings. Margot at the time found their form of entertainment "very boring." But she was impressed that Alberta knew all these well-heeled people and was able to carry her own so well in conversation with them.

There was no indication that the women in the group had anything but poetry and platonic relationships with one another on their mind, Margot said. "It was all on the up-and-up," she said. But in retrospect the thought did cross her mind that "whatever relationship Alberta was having over there," it was with a white person.

Whomever Alberta saw that summer, she was most discreet about it. "I never saw her with anybody, and she wasn't living with anybody," Margot said. "She was always very serious and quiet."

Alberta opened other doors to Margot and Norton that meant much more to them. She gave them the names and addresses of all the agents and theater managers she knew from Cairo to Copenhagen. She told Margot how to approach these people, what to say to them, where to have her gowns made, how to get together a portfolio of photographs, who should do their musical arrangements. She also told them where to buy diamonds in Romania; how to get their money out of Warsaw and Prague, should they play there; and where to stay cheaply throughout Europe.

In no time the young team was booked at the Club Harlem in Paris, where Alberta entertained from time to time, and on the Italian Riviera, all because of Alberta's good name and reputation with the people she had them contact. They were also booked for an engagement in Berlin. That was their last stop in Europe. Hitler packed them onto a boat and paid their way nonstop back to America. After a few frustrating years at home they gave up dancing. Norton joined the police force, and Margot became a schoolteacher.

Alberta returned to the United States to take NBC up on its offer. Before leaving Paris, she had a blood test. The results, postmarked September 30 in Paris and sent to her New York address, relieved her. All the reactions, including one to the Wassermann test, were negative. It was the only medical report she ever saved.

Alberta booked passage on the *Normandie* to New York. The liner confirmed her reservation, then advised her that it was giving her another accommodation, of lesser quality than the one she had booked. She discovered that an American white woman had booked the other berth in the cabin to which Alberta had been assigned. The white woman created such a fuss upon learning that she was to travel with a black woman that the company bumped Alberta down to an inferior cabin.

Alberta lodged a complaint with the American Embassy, which wasn't known for its responsiveness to such problems, especially when reported by blacks. Then she threatened legal action. The only American newspaper that apparently reported the incident was black (*Chicago Defender*, October 9, 1937, p. 11). The company, perhaps fearing more negative publicity in France, booked Alberta in a better room. The whole unfortunate mess only reminded her that she was going home.

On board on September 29 she received a radiotelegram from Fred Bate in London, whom she had advised of her travel plans. PLEASE CONTACT WILLIAM RAINEY RADIO CITY GOOD LUCK BON VOYAGE—BATE, the message read.

Since it was John Royal who had personally extended the invitation a year earlier for her to look him up, she went to see him first, rather than Rainey. She received an icy glare from Royal's secretary, one of those formidable, if not downright nasty, guardians of important people. "Mr. Royal?" the secretary queried. "Yeah!" Alberta said. "Surprised?" Alberta reported: "She looked at me 'cause I looked like a buzzard. She couldn't get over the fact that a little huck like me had nerve enough to come and ask for a man like John Royal. When she announced me—it killed her to do it—he came to the door and, when he saw me, threw his arms around me." That reaction and the ten-week contract he had drawn up immediately for her to sign put Madam Secretary in her place. Under the agreement, beginning on October 15, Alberta would sing for five minutes in the early evening on station WEAF with none other than Norman Cloutier and his sixteen-piece *all-white* orchestra. She did so well initially that the time period was expanded to fifteen minutes. On Fridays her program was broadcast nationally; on Mondays she sang for an international hookup—Alberta Hunter, singing to the world.

"They played for me," she said. "I knew nothing about arrangements. I would just say play so-and-so in E flat. I didn't even know what I was saying about the key. But I had heard other musicians say something like that—'Play it in B or E flat.' "

She saved three fan letters, perhaps her first, all written in October and November 1937 on postcards to her, care of WEAF, either seeking her photograph or asking, "Why can't we hear more of Miss Alberta Hunter?" That last one, signed C. Payne and without a return address, arouses the suspicion that her mother's friend Carrie Paine sent it.

Ben Gross of the *New York Daily News* (November 27, 1937, p. 27) added kudos: "I liked the singing of Alberta Hunter. . . . Her tones are sweet and tinged with emotion."

Neither her success with her own radio program on NBC nor her mother's health was enough to keep Alberta at home. She booked passage to return to Europe days after the December 24 termination of her contract. She had to cancel those plans when NBC exercised its option to extend the contract for a few more weeks. The NBC people certainly would have tried to keep Alberta active for a longer period, but they saw how eager she was to get back to Europe.

James Mahoney, an NBC official, wrote her shortly after she departed, saying, "I may say right now that I enjoyed working with you more than any other artist with whom I have come in contact in recent years, not only because of your ability but because of your disposition. May I take this opportunity to wish you every success in your future work and to express the hope that should the occasion arise wherein I may be of any service to you that you will not fail to call upon me."

Alberta performed during February 1938 at the Dancing Tabaris in The Hague, then settled back in at Fred Payne's in Paris for the rest of the winter and spring.

She commuted monthly to London for radio broadcasts. In April she applied for a visa to Morocco, Syria, and Lebanon, then canceled any plans she had to travel there. Instead, she went to Hamburg in late May for a few days and on to Copenhagen for the month of June for her now traditional performances at the Scala and Lorry. In July she was in Stockholm playing at the Odeon and in Oslo at the Rode Molle.

Alberta returned to Paris the last week of July in time to greet her journalist friend Geraldyn Dismond, who arrived from New York for a visit with her aunt and two Chicago friends, Pauline Reed and Marie Moore. (Marie was wife of Federal District Court Judge Herman E. Moore, who had been Willard Townsend's attorney in his divorce suit against one Alberta Hunter. None of the women was aware of that connection.)

Pauline recorded in her travel log that the group went sightseeing around Paris with Alberta and Enid Raphael, a singer who was living with Alberta at the time, cooking for her and washing her hair. ("There weren't any hairdressers in Paris then who knew how to do our hair," Alberta said.)

On the evening of August 4 they all went to see Bricktop, who was running the Big Apple now that Adelaide and Bert Hall had returned to London. It was an intimate club, Alberta remembered, decorated in dull red and mahogany with a huge, luscious apple painted on one wall and a golden brown-skinned girl wearing a sunbonnet on the opposite wall.

"A gal who is a gal," Pauline wrote of Bricktop in her diary. "With hair in a knot. She ordered champagne and sent it back. Asked for an older year. Big names rolled off her tongue as if she were saying biscuits and butter—Aly Khan, Barbara Hutton, Duke of Windsor."

Bricktop was successful as a hostess because she treated everyone like a celebrity. Harry Watkins said of her, "She could be talking to fifty people at once and you thought that she was talking only to you."

The group of visitors, wanting to see all the varieties of nightlife for which Paris was notorious, moved on that night to some more colorful establishments, such as the lesbian theater across from the Big Apple. Pauline described Lulu, the owner of the place, as having a "striking masculine build." Alberta, she said, "fitted in anywhere, in bars in an old prison to [a bar] where waitresses picked up coins with their vaginas. When in Paris she took on the flavor of Paris."

All that would have to be left behind. On September 28, 1938, the American Embassy sent a sobering letter to all registered Americans in Paris. Alberta's arrived at the Hôtel de Paris. It read: "In view of the complicated situation prevailing in Europe, it is considered advisable to recommend that American citizens who have no compelling reason to continue their sojourn here arrange to return to the U.S."

Alberta wrote immediately to Messrs. Royal, Rainey, and Phillips Carlin at NBC in New York, saying she was returning and would like to work for them again. Carlin wrote her at her New York address, telling her to contact him after her arrival.

Before she left, Alberta renewed her French identity card, thinking that would facilitate her early return, sang "We'll Meet Again" a last time at Fred Payne's Bar, and said good-bye to Bricktop, who was hanging on to the bitter end. She sailed for New York on October 19 on the *Île de France*.

Once in New York she signed up for a series of broadcasts on

NBC's station WJZ. But she also wrote Inge Bock at the National Scala in Copenhagen that she'd love to sing there in April or May 1939. Bock replied on November 18 from Denmark that the Scala was booked up until autumn of the next year. Also, the hundred-krone salary Alberta wanted was too high, she said, "as you are here so often, but we are sure, we shall agree about that."

Obviously it wasn't going to be easy to get back to Europe right away. So Alberta put her mind instead to finding engagements in New York. The first in November was at the El Morocco Club, where she was said to bring down the house singing "Find Out What They Like and How They Like It." Then she went to Tony's, a spot patronized by show people, on West Fifty-second Street. Fats Waller and Maxine Sullivan, a young singer who had become a sensation in the past six months, were singing at other clubs on the same street.

Alberta clipped a column of Dorothy Kilgallen's in the *New York Journal* of November 30 which said about Maxine: "When she skyrocketed to fame and popularity as an off-hand singer of hot and classical ballads, Maxine Sullivan's salary hopped from $40 to $700 a week. But she has so many agents and managers—so many people have a 'piece' of her—that she doesn't get much more than $40 a week now." That simply confirmed Alberta's bias against ever having such a coterie of "helpers." She would continue to help herself, thank you.

Alberta was the talk of the town in most of the black gossip columns at the time. The word was being passed from Harlem to Chicago, from Pittsburgh to Baltimore, that Alberta was in love with an Englishman of Danish descent by the name of Baron Sommery Gade. She supposedly had met him two years before at Fred Payne's Bar in Paris, just before she left Paris for club dates in other countries.

"I heard from friends, however, that the baron kept coming back looking for me," she told the *Amsterdam News* (November 5, 1938, p. 21). "But I didn't pay much attention to it thinking I was only being kidded." She didn't see him again, she said, until that summer of 1938, when she was back performing at Fred Payne's. "He walked in the door while I was singing and gave out one shriek and said, 'Oh, there you are.'

" 'Yes, here I am,' I answered, taken aback at the outburst. Later he asked me to have a drink and expressed surprise, as do most Europeans, when I told him that I don't drink. Finally, I had a Coca-Cola with him."

"When I finished working that night, he asked me to have breakfast with him and to drive me home, but I refused. However, the next night, he drove me home and made an appointment for lunch." Since then, said the newspaper, he had been "her most persistent suitor."

"He's so grand," she said when she was asked to describe him. "He is one of the handsomest men I have ever seen, in a big, outdoor sort of way. He has dark hair and each temple is gray." According to her story, he owned an estate in Isle Adam, a little place outside Paris, and had several yachts on the Mediterranean.

She coyly refused to answer questions about her intention to marry him. "Maybe yes, maybe no," she told the same newspaper later (November 26, 1938, p. 21). "But those in the know will tell you that the baron wants to marry the little brown thrush." This was the caption to a photo of Alberta on a phone, supposedly hearing sweet words from her baron on his daily telephone call.

No one close to Alberta who is still alive has ever heard of this person. Alberta never mentioned him. What she did leave as a trace were several letters from someone who sounded to the manner born but perhaps a bit on the down-and-out side of the good life. One such letter, sent to her in New York on November 18, 1938, came with a return address (but no name of sender) at the Hôtel de la Mairie in Isle Adam. It read:

Dearest Alberta,

I am so pleased you wrote me. I thought I should never find out where you were.

I got back from Spain about three weeks ago and found you had left. You didn't hear from me for sometime because I rather had back luck in Spain and [it] was impossible to get any mail out of the place, but believe me I never forgot you for a moment.

I am here for a few days and then go back to my little pub in Isle Adam, do write me dear, how long will you be in the states.

I should love to join you if you could only find me something to
do out there.
Shall certainly try and listen in about 1.15 Europe time to WJZ.
Hope your mother is quite well now,
Lots of love dear,
Flicka.

A second was sent on January 27, 1939, from the Hotel Splendide
in Piccadilly, London, saying, ". . . as soon as I am well I shall leave
for Paris. I prefer it to London and it's cheaper to live there." It closed
"My love dear."

A third and last letter from the Hôtel Astoria, Paris, on April 5,
1939, thanked her for her "sweet letter received at Fred's bar. I was
so surprised when it was handed to me. Dear you can always reach
me by mail at the following address: Fouquet's Bar, Avenue des
Champs Élysées. I don't quite know my plans . . . but of course I
shall endeavour to be here on your arrival."

All three letters were signed "Flicka," a word that means "girl"
in Swedish. The name was apparently a cover at a time when important people had to be cautious about maintaining certain relationships, certainly homosexual ones.

A postcard "Flicka" sent Alberta from Le Lavandou on the French
Riviera on August 25, 1938, suggests this was the case. She wrote,
"Hope to be back next week—please forgive for not writing more
often but hate the performance. The business I think will be alright
[sic]." It was signed "Much Love. F."

Alberta kept the mythical baron alive until 1941. In 1940 she denied there would be a wedding. "The Baron is sweet, but European
men are too dominating," she told the *Afro-American* (February 17,
1940, p. 13). "They expect their wives to stay at home and do as they
are told, without thinking for themselves, and I am too independent
for that, so I don't think we'll marry."

But on January 1, 1941, *Down Beat* (p. 13) in Chicago announced
she was engaged to the baron: "Their marriage has been delayed
due to the war blockade, but the baron is now in Tangiers where he
has purchased a beautiful estate as a bridal gift for his bride to be."

As prominent as the baron was supposed to be, his name never appeared in any other book except this one, including the registries of the English peerage. Alberta never mentioned the name again to anyone, and the press, conveniently or out of consideration, forgot to bring up the romance after that date.

At the end of 1938 Alberta was asked to join the cast of Dorothy and DuBose Heyward's *Mamba's Daughters*, which opened on January 3, 1939. Asked how she got the part, she said, "I just walked into producer Guthrie McClintic's office, read the role, and was signed. Simple as that."

The play created many firsts. It was the first important black show on Broadway since 1930 when *Green Pastures* opened. It was the first black company to play the Empire Theater in New York, as it was the first to perform the next year at Washington's National Theater. And Perry Watkins, who created its sets, became the first black designer to work on a major Broadway production.

Alberta found herself on stage on Catfish Row in Charleston, South Carolina (where the Heywards set the action for their earlier libretto for a play called *Porgy* that later added *and Bess* to its name and a Gershwin score). In *Mamba's Daughters* Ethel Waters as Hagar tries to give her daughter Lissa, played by Fredi Washington, all the opportunities she didn't have when growing up. When Gilly Bluton (Willie Bryant), a gambler Hagar befriended years earlier, tries to blackmail Lissa and threatens her successful singing career, Hagar strangles him to death. She hears Lissa sing on the radio, then kills herself.

Alberta, as Ned's wife, Dolly, is responsible for much of the violence in the first act. She winks once too often at her boyfriend, provoking her husband to pull out a razor and slash the cheeks of her young suitor.

Also in the cast were Georgette Harvey as Mamba (Hagar's mother), Maude Russell, and José Ferrer.

Rosetta Le Noire, director of the black AMAS Theater in New York, was there for the opening. "I'll never forget that night," she said. "They took I don't know how many curtain calls. Finally Ethel Waters just stood there with the company all bowing their heads and the tears came down their faces. Then the house went wild."

The play itself was not warmly received. *Time* magazine (January

16, 1939, p. 41) said the playwrights, "using an old sucked orange of a plot, have squashed the pulp all over the stage."

However, Ethel Waters's performance in her first dramatic role was heralded as everything from brilliant and beautiful to magnificent and moving. Only Brooks Atkinson of the *New York Times* panned both the play and Waters's performance in it. He said she "does not go very deep inside her part. . . . [H]er limp, plodding style, which she seems unable to vary, results in a performance rather than in the expression of a character."

Enraged by that review, Carl Van Vechten and several friends, including Judith Anderson, Tallulah Bankhead, Dorothy Gish, and Oscar Hammerstein II, bought an ad in the *Times* (January 6, 1940, p. 24) to rebuke Atkinson. It read: "We the undersigned feel that Ethel Waters' superb performance in *Mamba's Daughters* . . . is a profound emotional experience which any playgoer would be the poorer for missing. It seems to be such a magnificent example of great acting, simple, deeply felt, moving on a plane of complete reality that we are glad to pay for the privilege of saying so."

Atkinson, not known for ever retracting his views, went back to see the play and changed his mind about it and Waters. In an article in the *New York Times* (January 15, 1940, section 9, p. 1) he said the first time he saw the play he had the grippe, which explained his "lugubrious" review. He didn't, however, sound too much more enthusiastic. He wrote of Waters's "giving a valiant performance in a play that may be clumsily put together."

About the only newspaper that acknowledged in the text of the review the presence of Alberta Hunter was the *Bronx Home News*.

The press was doing a better job reporting on an audacious novelty in Greenwich Village in the hands of Barney Josephson, the man who changed Alberta's life almost forty years later. Barney, a former shoe salesman in New Jersey, grew up angry at the way he saw whites treat black people. Channeling his love of black music, he opened a little club called Café Society at 2 Sheridan Square in the Village the same week that *Mamba's Daughters* opened. The bands, the performers, and the clientele were all mixed. Black couples and white couples couldn't help touching elbows on the small dance floor.

Anyone who made a racial slur was immediately told to leave. "I was having a ball," said Barney.

It was a gutsy thing to do in those days, but it paid off for him, the audiences, and the many performers who became stars once they had appeared there. That cold winter's night of the opening a little lady stepped forward. She was not well known outside Harlem or prison. Her name was Billie Holiday. Also on the bill were Joe Turner and stand-up comic Jack Gilford.

On another entertainment front a step forward was made. Hattie McDaniel became the first black to win an Academy Award. She received the Oscar for 1939 as best supporting actress for her subservient role as Mammy in the film *Gone with the Wind*.

As fitting was the tribute to McDaniel, it really didn't signify a new era of opportunity for blacks on screen. "Hollywood is the bunk it seems, in so far as the American Negro is concerned," Ivan H. Browning wrote in the *Pittsburgh Courier* (March 16, 1940, p. 21). "Hollywood seems to appreciate Negroes less than any place in the world. Hollywood doesn't give the Negro artist his just deserts due to his talent nor appreciates the tremendous box-office patronage of the American Negro."

Radio was no better, he said. "It puzzles me why the American Negro continues to buy products like Lucky Strike cigarettes, Philip Morris cigarettes, Campbell's soup and many others when they will not give the Negro artists a chance on their radio programs."

Even in the nation's capital the door was slammed shut to one of the greatest black singers ever. Early in 1939 the Daughters of the American Revolution refused to let Marian Anderson give a concert in Constitution Hall, which the DAR owned. The nation's first lady, Eleanor Roosevelt, a great defender of blacks, resigned from the organization and persuaded Secretary of the Interior Harold Ickes to make the site in front of the Lincoln Memorial available for the concert. On a chilly Easter Sunday in 1939 Secretary Ickes presented the noted singer to a crowd that included Supreme Court Justice Hugo Black, Senate Majority Leader Alben Barkley, and Secretary of the Treasury Henry Morgenthau, Jr. "There are those, even in this great capital of our democratic Republic, who are either too timid or too indifferent to lift up the light that Jefferson and Lincoln carried aloft," Ickes said. "In this great auditorium under the sky, all of us are free."

Marian Anderson belted out "America" to seventy-five thousand Americans, black and white, gathered at her feet in adulation and pride. She also sang the aria "O Mio Fernando" from Donizetti's *La Favorita*, Schubert's "Ave Maria," "Gospel Train" by Harry T. Burleigh, and "Trampin' " by Edward Boatner. Her closing number spoke for her race. It was "Nobody Knows the Trouble I've Seen."

The world-famous contralto could sing all she wanted to out-doors. She could also sing indoors on June 8, 1939, at the White House for King George and Queen Elizabeth of England and at the World's Fair in New York soon after to impress other foreign visitors. But it would take her another sixteen years before she was invited to sing at home for America where she belonged, in the Metropolitan Opera House.

Alberta, more than most other black performers, knew what that deprivation was all about. Her friend's dignity in suffering that humiliation and eventually getting to the top made Alberta feel joyously united with her.

Alberta also had to wait for any further recognition at home. Rarely was her name even mentioned by the press during all the months she was with *Mamba's Daughters*. To make matters worse, Ethel Waters treated her as she did everyone else who she feared might in any way compete with her—like trash.

And Alberta did stand out on a stage, no matter who else was on it, said Rosetta Le Noire. "Everybody in the business used to say, 'I don't know if I want to be on the same stage with Bert. Who's going to look at me? They're going to look at Bert.' She has a knack of being able, even if she's whispering, to hold your attention. I don't think she's ever been trained in drama. But she can throw away a line and make you break up."

"Everybody had to like Alberta or be jealous of her and the way she handled an audience and got applause," said Revella Hughes, who added that Ethel Waters, "who never had anything good to say about anyone," naturally considered Alberta's talent a threat. "And she envied Alberta's sincerity, the person she was."

"Ethel gave me a bad time," Alberta said in understatement. "She treated me like a dog. Fine artist, but, oh, she was so mean. I would sing that song at the end, 'Time's Drawing Nigh,' and people would come backstage asking for me, not for Ethel. She called me every name in the book and wanted to hit me. I wouldn't answer back. I'd just look at her and turn my head and walk away. And that killed her. 'Cause she wanted me to let myself down to her level. But I didn't do it."

Ethel was a sinner one minute and a saint the next, according to Maude Russell. "She was the kind who would cuss out the whole cast with the foulest language you ever heard and then get sanctimonious and say, 'Oh, Lord, they're mistreating me.' "

"Later she wrote me a letter asking my forgiveness," Alberta said. "She knew she was wrong. She couldn't help it. That was just her disposition. It was professional jealousy. I don't think she meant any harm. She didn't hate me as a person."

The play closed for the summer on May 20, 1939, in preparation for a fall tour. During that spring Alberta broadcast every Wednesday evening on NBC's radio station WJZ in New York. But not one to miss any opportunity, she registered at the New York State Department of Labor and went every Thursday from May 25 to September 25 to collect unemployment benefits.

In June and July she obtained visas for France and England respectively, thinking wrongly that she could set up some appearances there during the summer. About the only blacks going anywhere at that time were scores of young men shipping out to army camps for training.

In August Alberta recorded six songs for Decca, for the bargain-basement price of twenty-five dollars each, with Lil Armstrong on piano: "Someday, Sweetheart," "Fine and Mellow," and four of her own—"I'll See You Go," "Chirpin' the Blues," "Yelpin' the Blues," and "Down Hearted Blues." The last, her 1922 composition, was popular again. Teddy Grace and Mildred Bailey also made recordings of it in 1939.

Obviously she was not aware yet of J. Mayo Williams's antics because on August 25, 1939, she signed an agreement with him, transferring all her rights to two of her songs on the Decca recording ("I'll See You Go" and "Yelpin' the Blues"). He signed for the Decca Distributing Corporation in Chicago.

Alberta was feeling spunky on August 11, when she took out an insurance policy with the Empire City Savings Bank for a thousand dollars with her mother as beneficiary. On the application she gave the year of her birth as 1913. Being eighteen years younger than she really was meant she paid a lower monthly premium.

Having no other good options, Alberta joined the road show of *Mamba's Daughters* with Ethel Waters and most of the original cast. Maude Russell kept right on as the understudy for Ethel Waters, not realizing that Ethel would rather die than let such an attractive and talented young lady take her place onstage.

They opened on October 2 at Chicago's Grand Opera House. Chicago papers remembered that Alberta had gotten her start there but paid no attention to her performance in this play. They did mention that the Domestic Workers Union of Chicago threw a tea in her honor. For some reason Alberta, sticking out from under a little pillbox hat, posed for the event with a cigarette, although she never smoked.

She also gained some notoriety by giving an interview to the *Daily Worker* (November 3, 1939), a Communist newspaper, about a racist incident that occurred to her. One day at a restaurant near the opera house in Chicago the management refused to serve her a sandwich and a cup of coffee. As was her style, she defied them by plopping herself down at a table and saying she wouldn't move until she was served and would be more than happy to sue them if they persisted with their bad manners. She was served.

She went on to tell the newspaper she was opposed to black men fighting in the war. "So long as one Negro is denied the right to vote in Texas for lack of [money to pay] a poll tax, no other Negro should feel any obligation to fight for a 'cause' which takes his life and gives him no liberty."

This was the first and last time Alberta let the *Daily Worker* interview her. Once she found the newspaper was in the hands of the Communists, she refused to talk to them. She didn't like a group she considered "foreign" panning *her* government, as many mistakes as she thought it made. She also felt, wisely, that the best way to survive in the entertainment business was to keep one's politics to oneself.

The cast moved on in November to St. Louis, Columbus, Cleveland, Indianapolis, and Cincinnati. In December the show played in Detroit and Boston; in January, Philadelphia, Washington's National Theater, and Baltimore's Ford Theater; in February, New Haven and Toronto; in March, Buffalo, Louisville, and Milwaukee.

In many of those cities Maude and Alberta were roommates. Alberta, who shared a room only because she wanted to save money, retreated into a cocoon. "She was very peculiar," said Maude. "She didn't have four words to say." She wouldn't want to go out to eat or drink with the cast. And if she were with them, she'd try to get someone in the group to plunk a coin in the jukebox to play one of her songs. She kept her money to herself, often up to eight hundred dollars in a money belt she wore all the time, and managed to save almost all her weekly pay. She lived off a loaf of bread and a pound of bologna, stored on the ledge of the window in their room.

Alberta was happier getting back to her mother's spaghetti in New York on March 23, 1940, when the play reopened, this time at the Broadway Theater, at Broadway and Fifty-third Street.

The play survived only two weeks in spite of rave reviews. Alberta said the producer closed it because of Ethel's "meanness." The *New York Age* (April 20, 1940, p. 4) attributed the short rerun to labor difficulties. It seems the union was requiring the maintenance of eight stagehands, as needed for a traveling company, although only half that number normally was employed on a New York production at the time.

Alberta desperately wanted to return to Europe. In March 1939 she had acquired a contract from the National Scala in Copenhagen for May 1940. The fact that additional American performers had been kicked out of Europe months before didn't discourage her. Bricktop was one of the last, coming back in late October 1939, shortly after Great Britain and France declared war on Germany. Lady Mendl and the duchess of Windsor chipped in to pay her way home because she was penniless.

Alberta's passport had expired on March 31, 1940. She had to have it revalidated in order to leave the country. She wrote a personal letter to Secretary of State Cordell Hull on May 1, 1940:

Dear Mr. Hull:
I am a colored American girl but have been in Europe for about fourteen years. I have been in twenty-five different countries—having sung in each.
I played opposite Paul Robeson in "Show Boat" at Drury Lane in London; I have been brought to America at different intervals by the National Broadcasting Co. for a series of broadcasts. I have just closed with the show "Mamba's Daughters" that played the National Theatre in Washington not so long ago but since the show closed I have been unable to get work.
I do not want anyone to give me anything. I am too proud for that, but I am turned down on every hand because of my "*race.*" I have my passport and my English visa is still good. In fact it will be for another month. Will you please let me go back to Europe where I am accepted as a fine artist and where my color is not a *curse*?
I speak, read and write French fluently. I sing in French, Danish, Italian, Viennese. I sing any type song but classics. Still I cannot get work in my own country. They say I'm *too refine* [sic].
I was born in Memphis, Tenn. I am the only support that my mother has. If I do not work my mother cannot eat. I own or should say am buying a cooperative apartment at the above address but to date I owe four months rent and I am about crazy.
Please excuse the liberty that I am taking in writing you, but I must work, Mr. Hull.
I do not want charity in any form for I have my health and strength.
Dear Mr. Hull, please answer this letter at once. Excuse mistakes, please, as I am very nerveous [sic] at the moment.
Awaiting your reply,
Yours very truly,
Alberta Hunter.

The Department of State in its bureaucratic way clocked in Alberta's letter on May 2 at 1:08 P.M. On May 8 the "Department" replied in the name of (Mrs.) R. B. Shipley, chief, Passport Division, whose name was typed and then stamped with a block in print letters. It said: "Madam: The Department has received your letter of May 1, 1940, concerning your desire to proceed to Europe, and has given careful and sympathetic consideration to your case. However, the Department greatly regrets that it is impossible to grant you a validation of your passport to enable you to travel to Europe at this time." The letter asked that Alberta return her passport to the State Department, where it was to be retained, uncanceled, in accord with existing regulations, since it was potentially valid until March 31, 1942.

Alberta was home to stay, for a while at least.

CHAPTER SIX

Jumping and Jiving
with the U.S.A.

If Alberta had to stay put in the United States, she would make the best of it. She wasn't alone. Large numbers of black entertainers had returned from Europe on their own by the fall of 1940, when the Nazis banned Josephine Baker and all persons of African descent from Paris. Many of them came to New York in search of work. Few of them found jobs as performers.

Many night spots were going out of business for lack of customers. The Cotton Club, which six years before had moved from Harlem to midtown, put up a FOR LEASE sign. Even world-renowned Bricktop put a CLOSED sign on her club in Manhattan.

A new crop of younger performers was competing with the old-timers for what jobs there were. They were very talented people like Lena Horne, whom Alberta adored, and Ella Fitzgerald, who Alberta thought "had the truest voice I've ever heard." Ironically, Alberta served as a judge at the W. C. Handy Stars of Tomorrow concert, a benefit for the New York Urban League at Town Hall on September 29, 1940, and helped salute and select some of the newcomers who were moving up fast to replace her and her contemporaries.

But Alberta wasn't going to throw in the towel without a struggle. She composed and recorded four new songs: "I Won't Let You Down," "Boogie-Woogie Swing," "My Castle's Rockin'," and "The Love I

Have for You," the most beautiful love song she ever wrote. She signed contracts to sing weekly on the Mutual Network on WOR and with NBC on WJZ. And for several months until 4:00 A.M. each night she was billed as the "dusty songstress" at the Times Square Grill, where she sang with Bob Howard and the Profit Trio. She even sang at the New York World's Fair during "Negro Week," sponsored by Sears, Roebuck.

At the end of 1940, after a short stint at Jimmie Williams's Pioneer Lounge on East Fifty-first Street in New York, she went looking for new opportunity on the road. She played Chicago for a few weeks and then opened in Detroit in a show produced by bandleader Jive Cadillac.

Marvin Welt, an agent in Chicago, wrote Tom Rooney, an agent in Hollywood, on February 5, 1941, recommending Alberta for club engagements. He attached a photo of Alberta dressed as Queenie for *Show Boat:*

> Don't allow that Mammy part in Show Boat fool you regarding her size as she is quite small and I don't imagine weighs over one hundred and fifteen pounds.
>
> Miss Hunter wants to come to the coast for two reasons. First she has never been there and second she feels if she is working out there she may be fortunate to get into a musical movie.
>
> The finer [the] white place she works in the better she will do. She has a very fine education and really knows how to converse with real people.

Nothing came of the introduction. Alberta stayed in Cleveland at the Cedar Gardens for the month of February 1941 and at the Gourmet Club in March and April. Winsor French, a writer for the *Cleveland Press*, recommended her highly (February 26, 1941): "Miss Hunter is not to be passed over lightly. With Ethel Waters, Adelaide Hall and Paul Robeson, she ranks among the most distinguished colored entertainers we have today, and if her name is somewhat unfamiliar in America it has long since been a byword abroad. . . . [S]he still has her voice and her artistry and my suggestion is that you go study it." Elsa Maxwell and Cole Porter were her early fans in Paris, and they "know a good thing when they see it," French said.

Another review said Alberta made "all the microphone huggers sound silly." She used no mike and belted out her songs, and "her notes are as soft and exciting as black velvet" (*Cleveland Press*, March 20, 1941).

She was in Chicago at the Sherman Hotel, with Paul Jordan's Orchestra, on April 28, the date of an article she saved from the *Nashville Banner* reporting the Supreme Court's ruling that blacks were "entitled to equal pullman facilities." But as all blacks knew, what they were entitled to and what they got in those days were two different things. At least, the law and certain prominent whites were beginning to recognize the need for greater racial justice.

Author Pearl Buck joined their ranks in criticizing unfair treatment of blacks. In a column in the *New York Times* (November 15, 1941, p. 16) she wrote at length about the subject:

> The reason why colored Americans are compelled to live in ghettos, where they are helpless against high rents and miserable housing, is the segregation to which race prejudice compels them. Race prejudice compels colored people to take what work they can get because there are so many jobs Negroes cannot get. Race prejudice makes and keeps Negroes' wages low because some labor unions will not admit colored labor on the same basis as white labor. Race prejudice and race prejudice alone is the root of the plight of people in greater and lesser Harlems all over the country.

In closing, she asked, "Is democracy right or is it wrong? If it is right then let us dare to make it true."

Another articulate combatant of racism at the time was Willard Townsend, Alberta's ex-husband. In May 1942 he addressed a meeting of labor leaders (*Chicago Defender*, May, 30, 1942, p. 8): "We of the United Transport Service Employees of America are here to lend every effort towards winning the war. But in this fight, surely one or two things must be sacrificed by those in control in America. Either they must give up their freedom or they must sacrifice their prejudice, and if they think more of their prejudice than freedom, then surely we will lose our freedom."

Although discrimination was often most blatant in the South, Alberta found she could make a good living there. In May 1941 she ventured below the Mason-Dixon Line with a brief stop at the Club Plantation in Nashville, followed by a four-month stay at Abe and Pappy's nightclub in Dallas.

Traveling to the South was a hassle since blacks were herded into Jim Crow cars as soon as trains from the North crossed into southern states. Alberta normally managed to occupy the same seat all the way.

On one of her trips south an "Uncle Tom" redcap, trying to nudge her into an inferior car, told her, "Please, miss, don't make trouble. I've had this job fifteen years."

"Yeah," she replied. "And you're gonna have it fifteen more." She refused to move. "He knew I meant business, so he told the others I had been hired by a gangster, so they better leave me alone. Baby, I rode first class all the way."

Another time she let the black porter know that she worked for a big, bad Texan with a rough reputation. The word got around quickly that she was "one niggah not to be messed around with."

When she was mistreated, Alberta went to the trouble of writing a complaint to railroad authorities. J. F. Gaffney, Jr., general passenger agent of the Nashville, Chattanooga & St. Louis Railway, answered such a letter from Nashville on February 7, 1942: "Dear Miss Hunter," he wrote. "Your letter, February 4, with reference to your experience while traveling on our Train No. 3 from Memphis to Nashville, last Monday, February 2, has just been received. Can assure you a thorough investigation will be made. Thanking you for bringing this matter to our attention, I am, Yours Truly." That's the last she ever heard of the "investigation."

There must have been some racial trouble in Dallas that made Alberta put on her editorial hat and lecture the locals on the situation. She saved a letter dated August 15, 1941, from Lynn Landrum of the editorial department of the *Dallas Morning News* that read: "Dear Alberta, Let us hope that the bad things which exist in our racial relations in Dallas will get better and that the good people of your race and of mine will find a way which will let us all live in peace and decency and happiness. I have hopes that this may be brought to pass, at least in some degree. With kindest regards. Yours sincerely."

As unhappy as Alberta may have been with racial discrimination in the South, she made herself at home there. "The South is ripe with 'berries,' " the *Chicago Defender* (October 11, 1941, p. 20) quoted her as saying. "She'll remain down there and cash in for awhile." In Texas they threw silver dollars by the handful on the stage to show their appreciation. Not one to stoop for her tips, she hired a boy to scoop up all the money on the floor.

Alberta was never as critical of whites in the South as were most of the members of her race. "You can say what you want to say about the [white] southerner, but when a southerner likes you, baby, you're liked. He doesn't let anybody bother you. He'll go to hell for you. He's all right. You know how you stand with a southerner. If he doesn't like you, he's not two-faced. He lets you know he doesn't like you, so you stay out of his way."

She encouraged other black performers to come South. "There is a lot of work here for good colored artists," she wrote (*Afro-American*, October 25, 1941, p. 13). "But they must be okay because these people are critical." You have to give them what they want to hear, she said, or they simply start shouting for it.

Alberta was not so enamored of the South that she did not criticize it for wrongdoings. In the same article, for instance, she took a swipe at radio stations in the South, if not elsewhere, for not letting black performers participate in the advertisements they aired: "When the radio chains say that they cannot give colored artists work, and especially on commercials, it seems a bit exaggerated for all the clubs I am working in here are white. If they enjoy our work so much in the cabarets and on stage, it does not make sense that they do not want to listen to us on the air."

The Club Plantation tried to get Alberta back to Nashville in October 1941, but she couldn't resist the charm and silver dollars of Texans who insisted she stay with them. Only the following February 1942, after singing at the 400 Club in Fort Worth, did she go back to Nashville.

Apparently she did well in Texas. The *Afro-American* (February 28, 1942, p. 13) ran a photo of Alberta and casually suggested in the caption that readers not miss noticing the three chunky diamonds all on one of her fingers, a display of wealth that was not typical of Alberta.

Her hands were clean again the next month when the *Chicago Defender* (March 7, 1942, p. 21) pictured "patriotic" Alberta Hunter at the time she was reported to have bought a hundred dollars' worth of war bonds, the first of many she bought throughout the war.

Alberta wanted to help any way she could with the war effort. Since the 1930s she had saved articles about the growing persecution of the Jews in Europe. She also clipped an item from the *Chicago Defender* (October 19, 1940, pp. 1–2) telling how the Nazis in Rheims, France, had destroyed a monument erected in 1922 in appreciation of the role black U.S. soldiers played in World War I.

From her personal experiences in Germany she knew the lot of blacks would be no better if Hitler were victorious. She knew what was going on in Europe because she corresponded with friends in England, France, and Scandinavia. (For years after the war she sent them personal "care" packages.)

She wrote often to George V. Keeling, chairman of Keelavite Rotary Pumps & Motors Ltd., Coventry, England, a man she had met in Paris at Fred Payne's Bar. He wrote her on October 28, 1940, and asked her to send some of her records to be played in the bomb shelter, where people were spending hours at a time, and on a local radio station to "give the boys a message" that would encourage them.

He answered her letter of March 11, 1941, referring to his countrymen's determination to survive the continued German blitzkrieg. "If Hitler thinks bombing is going to beat us, he's mistaken," he wrote on April 7, 1941. "He's got to kill us all or none of us. We shall never give in." He then praised America's entry into the war. "There is over here heartfelt gratitude for the help the U.S.A. are [sic] giving us. We shall never forget it. It is almost as if the war is worth while if it brings the two great English speaking countries together."

Billie Warner, a friend who called Russia home and had helped Alberta find bookings in England in earlier years, also kept in touch with her. On November 8, 1941, she wrote asking Alberta to return the brooch she had given her as security for a one-pound loan. It seems Alberta ran a minipawnshop in earlier days, making sure she had something of value from those few people to whom she lent money. Billie didn't enclose the money, so she didn't get her brooch back. On March 3, 1942, she tried again, saying she would refund the money owed after receiving the "wee brooch." She tried to ingratiate herself by passing on news of mutual friends. Some of it was good. Harry of Harry's New York Bar was at the Ritz Hotel doing well, and Leslie ("Hutch") Hutchinson was in a very good show at the Prince of Wales Theater. But she had bad news in that a friend of hers, Rai, and Fred Payne's friend, Freda, both were "interned" by the Germans.

Alberta later learned that Fred Payne and musician Arthur Briggs also were put in a concentration camp for the rest of the war, that her good friend John Payne was well and living outside London with Lady Cook and her son Sir Francis, and that Turner Layton's home had been bombed in London.

So much information did Alberta seem to have about who was doing what and where that she decided to put it to journalistic use. She convinced the *Afro-American* to let her do a regular column called "Alberta Hunter's Little Notebook." She started writing in late May 1942 and stuck with it on a regular basis until August 1943. In her first column she said that she had just closed in Nashville, spent two days resting with her mother in New York, then traveled to Boston, where she opened the first of a series of summer engagements that would take her to places like the Laurier Club in Lowell and RKO Theater in Springfield, Massachusetts, and Walsh's Theater Restaurant in Pawtucket and Snow Street Cabaret in Providence, Rhode Island.

Alberta's column, which she always signed "Cheerio, Alberta," followed her style of correspondence to newspapers in the 1920s. She wrote little of herself. Her writing remained distinctive. She no longer treated her readers to her unique travelogues. But she did stand apart from most journalists in the messages she delivered.

At a time when most other writers of entertainment news were concentrating on the newer and younger stars, Alberta reminded her readers about the older performers who were still around, whether in or out of show business. She wrote about Lil Armstrong's "doing her stuff," "Old Maude" Russell's making a hit one place or another, and Cora La Redd's driving a taxi.

She called "Brother" Harry Watkins the "boy with one of the sweetest voices I've ever heard" and advised that he was performing at "one of the smart mountain hotels" (September 26, 1942, p. 10). Later she promoted him to the "sepia son of song" (December 5, 1942, p. 10).

She wrote repeatedly about some of her favorite spots down South. "You talk about money," she wrote on August 1, 1942 (p. 11). "The Club Plantation [in Nashville] reminds me of the Dreamland in Chicago for the artists who worked in the Deamland made pl-en-ty of dough—and they do just that at the Club Plantation."

She wrote often of people performing there and at her favorite clubs in Texas. Either she felt genuinely indebted to them, or she put them in debt to her, monetarily or otherwise, for all the free publicity she gave them, sometimes even announcing when one of them needed a musician. For instance, in her column dated December 5, 1942, (p. 10), she wrote: "Mrs. Davenport [at the Club Plantation] wants a good tenor saxman and a knockout trumpet player. Do not apply if about to be inducted."

She also used her column to box the ears of a few friends she respected but who she thought were losing control of their lives. "A word to Una Mae Carlisle you are too fine an artist to let anything spoil your colorful career," she wrote on May 22, 1943. Then, on August 14, 1943: "Una Mae Carlisle opened at Elmer's [in Chicago] but stayed only a few days. Una, why don't you pull yourself together?"

She praised black performers who were opening doors for others in typically white establishments and chastised those whose behavior she thought was unprofessional and likely to wreck the chances for their colleagues. Avis Andrews "has done something that was thought impossible," she wrote on October 31, 1942 (p. 10). "Not only is she the first colored artist to perform at the swanky Versailles Restaurant at 151 E. 15th Street [New York], but she is sensational.

"It is gratifying that the first colored artist to be engaged here is one of Miss Andrews' calibre for only too often have some of the reefer smokers and liquor heads opened at smart spots to close with the management swearing never to engage another colored artist." She sermonized in July: "The artists with poise, experience and above all things, good character, are the ones who survive" (July 25, 1942, p. 10).

The following week Alberta was in New York for four days, accompanying Mrs. Davenport to see black shows and to shop for talent for her club in Nashville. Alberta couldn't resist criticizing some of the young people she saw onstage. "Saw several revues in Harlem and believe me, the sooner the principal women, particularly the singers, pay more attention to their wardrobe than they do to posing so close to the mike that you cannot see their faces or understand one word they say, the more money they can go [sic] on a job" (August 1, 1942, p. 11).

And finally, as an "exclusive," she reported that Victoria Spivey and Billy Adams were a flop in Nashville (June 12, 1943). "One reason, dirty costumes. Another, hoary material."

The fall of 1942 Alberta was back in New York. On September 15 she and her pianist, Garland Wilson, participated in a broadcast sponsored by the Office of British War Relief from the garden of the Connecticut home of the noted columnist Dorothy Thompson. Joining in the program were performers Peggy Woods, Greer Garson, Charles Laughton, and Douglas Fairbanks, Jr.

On October 3, 1942, Alberta was in Washington, D.C., at the invitation of the Red Cross to discuss a possible assignment abroad. She told a reporter at the *Afro-American* (October 10, 1942, p. 10) she was "very disappointed over not being able to accept foreign service with the Red Cross."

For the first time Alberta admitted publicly that she might not be able to remain an entertainer all her life. She encouraged her readers to take advantage of the free courses related to defense work being offered during wartime. "I intend sticking to my theatrical work, but in my spare time I'm going to take a course that I think will enable me to qualify to make an independent living when my theatrical sun starts going down," she said in her column (October 24, 1942, p. 10).

She didn't follow her own advice. Instead, she took a month's engagement at $150 a week opening on November 13 in Utica, New

York, at Tommy Joys's Ace of Clubs with Arthur Gibbs at the piano. She was in New York for Christmas and to see Jimmy Daniels, who had recently been drafted and was on his way to boot camp.

She also called her former husband. A cryptic notation in an address book reads: "I called Willard Townsend . . . said he got divorce." It's not apparent why she wanted that information. It's interesting that she didn't know twenty years after the fact that she had been legally divorced.

The conversation was not congenial. Alberta penned a letter to Willard that same day asking him for proof of the divorce. She saved his formal reply. "Dear Miss Hunter," he began a letter dated December 30. It was on letterhead stationery of the office of the International President, United Transport Service Employees of America.

> I have your letter dated December 28, 1942, registery [*sic*] number 442240 in which you seek affirmation concerning divorce proceedings. In reply thereto I wish to state that the decree was granted in March of 1921 by Judge Hurley in the Superior Court, Cook County, Chicago, Illinois. [The correct year was 1923.] The attorney for the plaintiff is the present federal judge, Herman Moore.
>
> I would suggest that for further information, which might be fully attested by the County of Cook, you write them. Very truly yours,
>
> Willard S. Townsend.

In spite of this cryptic exchange between Willard and Alberta, she said they were close. She said she went to dinner with him or dropped by his office whenever she was in Chicago. "I was crazy about Willard," she said. "We were just good platonic friends."

That winter was a lean one for job offers, so in February 1943 Alberta and three hundred other people went to City Hall to be sworn in by Mayor Fiorello La Guardia as civilian defense volunteers. Marie Moore, whose husband, Herman, was federal district court judge in the Virgin Islands, was in New York at the time supervising the volunteers at Harlem Hospital. Dr. Binga Desmond, who had been married to journalist Gerri Majors, had talked to Alberta and interested her in doing volunteer work.

Mrs. Moore assigned Alberta to work as assistant laboratory technician at Harlem Hospital in the pneumonia laboratory under supervision of Dr. Jesse Bullova, professor of internal medicine at New York University. Part of her duties required learning to operate an electroencephalograph, the machine used to record electrical activity in the brain.

Not only was Alberta the first black woman to work in that capacity, but it was the first time anyone other than a senior nurse was allowed to perform the tasks required. Dr. Bullova said he made an exception in her case because of Alberta's mathematical ability. Mrs. Moore said Alberta was an "extremely conscientious worker."

The honor didn't last long, for Alberta was back in Nashville at the Club Plantation by the end of that month. She returned to New York on May 7, 1943, but then only for a brief visit with her mother before she headed for Chicago to open May 22 at the Downbeat Room of the Garrick Lounge downtown. Dinah Washington was supposed to be appearing there, but as Alberta remembered it, she became ill. Joe Glaser, one of the country's top talent agents, asked Alberta to fill in.

Alberta stayed at the Garrick for a full year. During that time she saw many old friends who came through Chicago. In June the *Afro-American* reported that La Waters "blew into town for a hot minute" and that Ethel, Mac Stinnett of vaudeville fame, and Alberta "had a real get together" (June 19, 1943, p. 8).

She also received a surprise visit from a strapping twenty-three-year-old man named Sam Sharp, Jr., a basketball player for the Harlem Globetrotters, who was in Chicago for a game. Walking down the street that day, he saw the sign at the Garrick advertising the famous singer. He said excitedly to a buddy with him at the time, "That's my aunt." Sam was the son of La Tosca, Alberta's sister.

"Oh, man," his friend said with grave doubt. Sam left a message at the theater that he would be coming back that night.

Alberta Hunter. The name lit up his memory. His first recollection was of his being a little boy and his sister Jesse, about three years older, receiving in the mail from Aunt Alberta a gorgeous doll, complete with bed and a sumptuous wardrobe of doll clothes. "Jesse was the envy of the neighborhood," Sam said. The doll was white with long blond hair. "They weren't making colored dolls then," he added. Sam's mother, La Tosca, had left home, and his father had brought the children up. Sam never knew that his mother had any other name than Dump, he said, until he went to school and the teacher insisted that he write his mother's real name.

La Tosca's first husband, Bernard Gray, left her to join the army when she was fifteen years old. After the service he played for Fletcher Henderson's band. They had one son, Bernard Gray, Jr. When La Tosca left her second husband, Sam Sharp, she went to live in Indiana for several years with her aunt Mary. She returned to Denver years later alone and driving a Model T Ford. At one point she lived next door to her husband and children, but she never moved back in with them.

La Tosca was a fairly carefree person, always laughing and singing, always dressed in stylish clothes. She got in trouble with her second husband early on when she cut her hair in the "Roaring Twenties style, with bangs," Sam said. "My father almost flipped. He saw to it that she grew it back the way it was.

"Ma got by because she had a nice personality," Sam said. She was six feet tall and very attractive. "Gosh, she was nice-looking. And she was crazy about Alberta. Ma liked her drive.

"Alberta wasn't too good a letter writer. She liked to receive them. If she went overseas, she would send a card, maybe, 'Just to let you know I'm here.' Bam!" She was better about sending money to her sister's family.

That night in Chicago Alberta took one look at her nephew and could see La Tosca and herself in the handsome young man before her. "I was so proud of him," she said. "He had such a wonderful smile of kindness."

Alberta hugged him, in a rare display of emotion for her. Sam sensed she was strained showing her feelings, in contrast with his mother, "who was kissing and hugging us all the time." Sam said: "I got a thrill out of seeing Auntie sing. I couldn't believe it." He had heard her on the Victrola at home in one of her early recordings with King Oliver's band. "But the records in those days didn't sound anything like they do now. Everything was high [pitched]." He was stunned when he heard her live in Chicago. "That little lady with a big voice knocked me out. I sent a special delivery letter home saying that I saw Auntie."

Sam was even more impressed by some of the "high-powered people" who were clapping their hands for his aunt. She introduced him to the owners of the White Sox and Cubs baseball teams. "She knew them all," he said. "And they told me then pretty soon there were going to be blacks in baseball. I came back home and told the guys that, and they almost laughed me out of town." After all, it was about that time (April 1944) that Joe Louis and Sugar Ray Robinson, both army sergeants, were jailed at Camp Silbert, Alabama, because they refused to obey Jim Crow regulations on army property.

"They asked me if I knew any good ballplayers." As it turned out, a lieutenant in the army stationed with him in Louisiana at the end of the war would be the first black to get into the big leagues; his name was Jackie Robinson.

Sam didn't see his aunt again for many years. They both went off to the war. He didn't see much action, landing in Japan soon after the atom bombs had been dropped. Alberta, however, after a brief engagement at Paris Qui Chante on West Forty-eighth Street in New York, joined the USO and got in the thick of battle. She knew she would enjoy entertaining the troops after participating in a show on July 26, 1944, for seven thousand men at Camp Kilmer, New Jersey. She was especially impressed by their "spirit of brotherhood."

In June 1943, several months after the USO started sending entertainment groups overseas, Noble Sissle recommended it hire entertainer Dick Campbell to recruit artists of his race for assignments abroad. "He didn't say what I was," said Campbell, a handsome man who could easily pass as a white. "They took me only because they thought I was white."

Alberta said that Campbell called her and asked her to take a USO unit overseas. "I did it because I wanted to help my country," she said. "After all, it was my country. I wanted to try to help my boys come home."

Her motivation for wanting to be a part of the USO was sincere. But it actually was she who approached Campbell and asked to be selected. "I was hesitant about giving her a job," Campbell said. "She was still a name, but she wasn't doing very well. I was afraid she wouldn't do very well with the soldiers. She had no sex appeal. And that's what they were looking for. But I knew she was a good solid performer and could belt out a song and wouldn't cause any conflicts with other performers. To tell you the truth, I was sorry for her because I knew her in Chicago when she was a big star." (Campbell had been a singer with Dave Payton's orchestra at the Regal Theater in Chicago in 1930 when Alberta was at the Grand Terrace.)

Campbell offset Alberta's "mannish" appearance by assigning to her unit Mae Myrtle Gaddy, a young singer with Cab Calloway's band who, he said, "flaunted sexuality."

He knew Alberta was "tough," so he put her in charge of a unit of blacks going to the China-Burma-India theater of operations.

"I felt very safe making Alberta the manager of the unit because I knew she'd keep people in line," he said. "She was a stickler for the regulations. And she had definite opinions about how people in show business should behave themselves."

Mae Gaddy's mother also had confidence in Alberta. She came to New York from her home in South Carolina to see off her sixteen-year-old daughter. (Mae lied about her age to get into the USO.) "Just talking with Alberta you knew she knew the ropes. Alberta was a person in charge," Mae said.

The unit (342), established in early August 1944, included a trio from Chicago called the Rhythm Rascals with Ollie Crawford on guitar, Leonard ("Baby Doo") Caston on piano, and Alfred ("Al") Elkins on base. The other member of the group was Marion Joseph ("Taps") Miller, a dancer and trumpeter. For almost two months the members of the unit spent their time filling out government forms, getting passports and necessary visas, taking inoculations, being fitted for uniforms, rehearsing their show, and just getting to know one another.

Baby Doo was a little out of place at first. He felt uncomfortable around what he called "big peoples." As he put it, "Peoples know when you have had the background and training. They can tell when you've had that college experience." Growing up in a little sawmill town in Mississippi, Baby Doo had walked six miles to a one-room schoolhouse where there was one teacher for seven grades. Much of his learning came at home from the records his mother played of Bessie Smith, Ma Rainey, and Blind Lemon Jefferson. "It was always in my mind that I wanted to make it big like them," he said. At age four he started playing on a ukulele he made out of a cigar box and a broomstick handle. By the time he was eight a cousin bought him a banjo-uke from a mail-order house.

But even after years of living and playing with the band in Chicago, using the "concert guitar" his mother bought him, he still felt "as green as grass." Alberta gave him pointers on how to act, how to sit at the table and eat, how to dress. She'd say, "Okay, honey, straighten your tie. Make sure your shoes are shined. Don't put your cap on straight. Put it a little over to the side of your head. Look dignified. You're an artist. You have to have standards. You're not like these other people out there. You got to look the part."

They left New York on October 15, 1944, and landed in Casablanca for a twenty-four-hour layover. Alberta immediately marched her weary troupe off to see a sultan's palace. She was determined that the youngsters under her command were going to see the world, not just a bunch of army camps. After stopovers in Cairo and Karachi they arrived in Calcutta. Using that teeming city as a base, they traveled by every means of transportation to out-of-the-way campsites. On one trip, said Baby Doo, they sat in seats installed in a boxcar pockmarked with bullet holes. On another they were in a caboose filled with cockroaches. Alberta refused to ride in it again. "I'm an artist," she told the transportation officer responsible for their unit.

Much of the time they donned parachutes and strapped themselves into the bucket seats of cargo planes. They almost lost Ollie out of one plane. On takeoff his guitar started sliding across the floor toward the door, which had been left open for a supply drop. Baby Doo caught Ollie by his suspenders as he went scrambling after it. Someone else caught the beloved guitar.

Each member of the group wore a jacket with an American flag on the back along with a message in the native languages telling any locals who might find him or her whom to contact. A reward was promised.

And were the troops ever happy to see them arrive deep in the jungle with a piano and generators on the back of a truck and a banner that read, "The show we are about to present is sent to you by your folks at home." And was it a show!

"Honey, when Mae sang the first words, them soldiers would scream so loud you could hear them from here to Berlin," Alberta said. "What a woman. What a voice. She was a killer. Now she's got about nine thousand children."

Alberta did her part, too, according to Baby Doo. "She had a way of just walking out on a stage and snapping her fingers and attracting everyone's attention," he said. "She taught me how to sell a show. It was the way you put yourself and your songs across."

Alberta would sing a song like "If I Could Be with You" and have the men "hollering," as she put it. Then she would holler back at them, "Suffer, you dogs," and they would take it in great fun.

The *Yankee Doodler*, a military newspaper (January 27, 1945), said Alberta "had the hardest time of getting away from the audience of any performer to appear" before the 305th Air Service Group. "When Alberta finally had to leave, due to early sunrise here at this time of the year, the boys were still clamoring for her to sing their particular favorites."

"She was worth waiting for as she cajoled 'Talk to me boys,'" said the *Slip Stream* newspaper (February 24, 1945) of Alberta's performance in Agra, India. "For thirty minutes she sang, strutted and talked as GI's tore up the benches and yelled for more. Her final number, 'Basin Street,' had every man in the Bowl hanging limply on the ropes as the show closed."

Wherever they went, the soldiers built special quarters for their guests to stay in, with their visitors' names on a post outside their doors; they even built a hot shower for them, an unusual convenience in those parts.

When they weren't performing, Mae was always with the soldiers. "These guys were so charged up," she said. "They hadn't had any entertainment in years. They waited so long for us to arrive. And man, they couldn't wait to get a seat. They had so many questions about the States, about where they came from, home talk. You couldn't push them aside." In between shows Mae served doughnuts and coffee in the canteen. She worked in the Red Cross quarters and helped the men write home. "Some of them knew how to write, but when you're in a war zone, it's hard to sit down and concentrate."

USO entertainers carried the rank of captain and, therefore, had the right to eat in the officers' mess. On a few occasions on this and successive trips abroad that privilege wasn't extended to Alberta's troupe because they were blacks. Once when they were told to eat in a kitchen, Alberta refused to eat. Her musicians didn't follow her example. "You know how men get hungry," she said. "They don't care."

Alberta saved her metal food tray for the rest of her life as a reminder of that discrimination. "This was a U.S. Army vessel, and in some places I was refused food to go in it," she said, still in disbelief twenty-five years later.

Mae ate with the soldiers every chance she had. "They saved their rations for us," she said. "We were there for them." After the shows she would dance with them, too.

Alberta kept to herself on most of these trips. "She never liked to mingle with people before a show or very little afterward," Mae said. "That made her more important. She was the star. When the audience finally got to see her, she was more special."

Baby Doo had another explanation for Alberta's behavior: "She didn't socialize because there's always a guy who's going to get fresh, and Miss Hunter didn't want to leave herself open to no insults from no generals, no majors, no captains, nobody. She always kept herself at a distance. That was Alberta."

Unless, of course, she was in the presence of someone who was also a star and who she felt was on her level or above, someone like Melvyn Douglas, who served as the special services officer in Calcutta and was responsible for all USO units that came to India. "She was very outgoing with him," Mae said.

There were moments when the war came very close, like the time they were caught in an air raid in Burma. In the middle of the night the sirens wailed. Everyone grabbed a helmet, which in calmer moments doubled as a wash basin, and scrambled for a foxhole outside the tents. Someone yelled at Mae to go wake up Ollie in the tent next to hers. He was known for sleeping through anything. Mae was able to rouse him but found she couldn't utter a word to him. "I was hysterical," she said. "You don't know what you're going to do when you're in a situation like that." She stood at the door of Ollie's tent and couldn't do anything but point at him. He got the idea soon enough when the first bullets flew by.

Baby Doo ran out of his tent with the mosquito netting from his bed entangled in his feet. He dived into a lone foxhole. When he came to his senses after the raid, he realized there was a boa constrictor down the hatch with him, sharing his state of shock. They parted company hastily and amicably as soon as the all-clear sounded.

Alberta had her own difficulties that evening. She jumped into the first foxhole she found outside her tent. It wasn't deep enough to suit her fancy, so she scurried to a bigger one and burrowed in. No one was wounded on that raid, but the enemy did manage to blow up the mess hall.

After that experience Alberta learned to watch the Indians or Burmese among them. "They would hear the sound of those planes coming long before we heard the sirens," she said. "So when we saw them running, we'd throw our wash pans or anything else on our heads and start running with them." This way they had time to find the deepest foxholes around before the action started.

Their USO unit, being small, could get into isolated spots that larger groups could not reach. One of those places was Hill 60 in Burma. The area was so dangerous that they had to perform at night on the back end of a covered truck with a few soldiers on the ground pointing their flashlights up at them.

In places like that, Mae said, you would see handkerchiefs come out of pockets during the show. "The guys would be missing their parents or their girlfriends." Afterward the men came up to them to touch them and say thanks for risking their lives to entertain them.

For the troupe, too, the hardships were real. "I can remember nights I wanted to cry to come home," Mae said. "Alberta would talk to me. She was like my mother. She would say, 'Everything is going to be all right. Look what you're doing. It's a great experience you couldn't pay for.' "

Often Mae thought it would be better to pay *not* to have it. It was bad enough having to shut windows and doors (if they had any) to keep wild animals out. And even though they slept with mosquito nets tucked in around their mattresses, they were instructed to turn over very gently in bed during the night so as not to startle snakes or other creatures that might have crawled in with them. But the worst was having to step over dead bodies of air-raid victims along the Ledo Road in Burma.

Alberta took it all in stride. She wrote back often to the *Afro-American* with the names and home states of the soldiers she met in the jungles of Burma. She said they asked her to tell their families they were well and in good spirits but lonesome for home. "You will never know how much a letter means until you are where it takes mail a long time to reach, so impress it upon everyone to keep the letters coming," she wrote in a dispatch from "Somewhere in Assam" (published by the *Afro-American*, March 3, 1945, p. 8).

Alberta also wrote Dick Campbell in New York and kept him posted of their progress and needs. He wrote her on February 6, 1945, saying in part, "I have always known that you were a top-notch showman and able to take care of yourself under any circumstances and that is one reason why I placed you in charge of the unit. I know you would deliver." He also appreciated the fact that she was able to keep her troupe in shape. That task called for tactics as varied as those used by a field commander on the front line.

With someone like Baby Doo she acted like a stern mother. One day he went out drinking and smoking marijuana with Taps Miller. When he walked out onstage that evening for their show, he said, "I felt if I made a step, I'd leap like a frog." Finally seated at the piano, he saw the keys go "this way and that away." When he woke up the next morning, there was Alberta in his room, waiting for him.

"Leonard," she said, "you really embarrassed everybody in the show last night. You're the only piano player we've got. I was kind of depending on you. You appeared to be such a nice fellow. I know you didn't do this on your own," she added.

Baby Doo apologized and said, "Miss Hunter, if you give me one more chance, I won't pull this no more." She gave him his chance. The lesson was learned.

Taps was another story. He was a hopeless case as far as Alberta was concerned. Baby Doo said Taps had made a lot of money quickly in the United States and that "success had gone to his head." He wasn't about to take orders from Alberta. According to Baby Doo, one day Taps got so angry at her in a Calcutta hotel room that he threw a whiskey bottle at her. Fortunately he missed.

Alberta thought he was too much the womanizer and had influenced Mae Gaddy to do a bump-and-grind dance onstage that was "promiscuous." After all, her written list of instructions from the USO emphasized the point that she was to keep the show "clean." Alberta wouldn't describe what was so bad about Mae's act, other than to say, "When she was dancing, she did things she shouldn't do. She just sneaked that shake in there. Jiving. I didn't want to work on that stage with Mae doing all those vulgar things. I didn't want my unit to be tapped as a sporting house routine."

Mae's comment was: "It was a jazz boogie number. I had to move. I drove 'em crazy." She said Alberta didn't like her being able to "knock the audience dead" with a number that got more attention than she received. "It was jealousy," said Mae.

Alberta must have lost control of the situation near the end of the tour because she wired Campbell in New York and complained about Mae and Taps. On February 21, 1945, just as they were leaving New Delhi, she received a telegram from Dick Campbell: "Inform Mae Gaddy to cut shake routine dance and tell Taps Miller to take orders from you or else." Alberta never mentioned the telegram, said Mae, who had nothing but praise for Alberta, even after learning in 1985 about her official complaint. "This woman was really show business, a great entertainer. I learned a lot from her. Being with her in those crucial times really toughened me up."

Its tour of duty over, the unit landed in New York on March 31, 1945, after a monthlong stopover in Casablanca. Alberta packed away her souvenirs: the metal tray, the knife, fork and spoon she ate with, and a denim jacket she had worn, which had been signed by many of her GI fans on one of the world's worst battlefronts.

Poet and playwright Countee Cullen heard Alberta was home and tried to convince her that she would make a wonderful Lila in his new musical *St. Louis Woman*. She didn't want to wait around to find out. She signed up for her next USO tour, this one with Unit 556, also called the Rhythm Rascals, bound for Europe.

Germany surrendered on May 7, 1945, but there were still a lot of soldiers to entertain away from home. The same performers from Alberta's first group were in this unit, with the exception of Taps Miller, who was replaced by a five-foot-tall female trumpet player, Geneva Taylor Scott, whose artistic name was Jean Starr. They sailed for Le Havre on May 24, 1945.

The troupe went immediately to a small town outside Paris, called Chatou. It was there that a white soldier made some wisecracks in French to a Frenchman on the base about the black performers. Alberta, after overhearing most of the conversation, in French asked the Frenchman to repeat the soldier's comments. He replied that he hadn't understood what the soldier was saying.

"You're a damn liar," Alberta told him. Then she repeated word for word in French what she had heard the soldier say. She reported him to his commanding officer. After that incident word that nobody was to mess around with Alberta in any language got around. "She wouldn't tolerate that at all," said Baby Doo. "She spoke out and said what she had to say, and that was it. They always gave her respect: all of them."

The unit performed in the Paris area for about a week. Mickey Rooney, who was there with another USO unit, started palling around with Ollie, who was about his size, whenever they both were free. Baby Doo remembered the two of them jamming all the time. Rooney would play the piano, he said, and try to sing like Nat ("King") Cole.

Late in the evening of June 9, 1945, shortly after the group had arrived in Nancy, France, Alberta awakened her unit and told them to pack their things and be ready for immediate departure to Frankfurt am Main, Germany. They were off on a high-level secret mission.

Alberta said, " 'Chilluns,'—that's what she called us," Baby Doo said. " 'Y'all get ready 'cause we're going to entertain Mr. Eisenhower.' " In spite of the nearby presence of all sorts of popular white entertainers, like Mickey Rooney, Jack Benny, Sonja Henie, and Marlene Dietrich, General Dwight D. Eisenhower wanted them.

"Alberta had a reputation all over Europe," said Baby Doo as a justification for their selection. "Maybe he wanted to prove the point that we had black artists in the United States who could perform as well as anybody else."

Alberta on the set for the first British film in color, *Radio Parade of 1935*.

ABOVE: Alberta, her pianist Norma Payne Davies, and gentlemen friends pose on camels in Egypt in 1936 before their "ride across the Sahara."

BELOW: Broadcasting with Eli Donde (on violin) and members of his band in Copenhagen, 1935.

With her pianist seeing
the sights of Istanbul in
1936. Black tourists were
uncommon in those days.

—#—

Margot Webb, a protégée,
and Alberta shared an
apartment in London during
the summer of 1937.

—#—

Ethel Waters (far left) lets Alberta (center) have a small scene in *Mamba's Daughters* in 1939.

=//=

Alberta lends her voice to the war bond campaign in 1944.

=//=

LEFT: Alberta at the piano of the Rode Molle in Oslo, 1938.

BELOW: Broadcasting with her own show for NBC radio, 1937.

TOP: With her first USO group, bound for India and Burma (from left to right): Alberta, Alfred Elkins, Ollie Crawford, Leonard "Baby Doo" Caston, Mae Gaddy, and Marion Joseph "Taps" Miller.

LEFT: Alberta's USO ID.

BELOW: Alberta with a favorite, Melvyn Douglas, a Special Services officer, 1944.

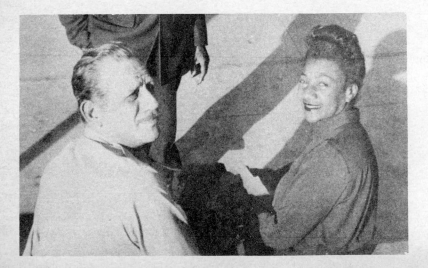

Strapped to her parachute, she flies with the USO to England, 1952.

Japanese women and children surround the black lady in pants, 1947.

Entertaining the troops in Korea in 1952.

Posed for the early 1950s and the end of her first career.

Graduation day at the Harlem
YWCA nursing school, August
14, 1956.

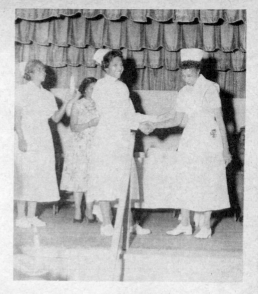

Lovie Austin (left) and Alberta
get together again to record the
"Down Hearted Blues" and
other old favorites in 1961.

"Having a good time" with Gerald Cook, her pianist, musical director, and friend. (*Linda Alaniz*)

Alberta discusses a problem with her trusted manager and friend, Barney
Josephson. (*Susan Kuklin—New York*)

LEFT: When they celebrated each other's birthdays she sang to Eubie Blake his song "Memories of You." (New York Post, *Joan K. Rosen.*)

BELOW: Preaching a lifetime of living to her "children" in the audience.

LEFT: Alberta and Yul Brynner celebrate Lena Horne's birthday. (*David LeShay*)

BELOW: The greatest night of her life, singing for "her" President Carter at the White House. (*The White House—Washington, D.C.*)

Never happier than when she was alone to think, think, think.
(*Hans Harzheim—Düsseldorf*)

Alberta sings the blues again from 1977 to 1984. (*Susan Kuklin—New York*)

Reminiscing with "Brother" Harry Watkins a month before her death.
(*Stuart Goldman—New York*)

At their destination the entertainers were ushered into a large room where Eisenhower was seated with several dignitaries. The unit was placed in the open end of conference tables arranged in a V and asked to perform.

The *New York Herald Tribune* (June 11, 1945, p. 4) described the events of the previous day: "The wine, the liqueurs, the filet-mignon, the petits-fours, and everything else which General Dwight D. Eisenhower served at his headquarters here today for Soviet Marshal Georgi K. Zhukov went over well, but it took a Negro sextet from the United States to put the party in the groove."

Russian Vice Commissar for Foreign Affairs Andrei Y. Vishinsky and Britain's Field Marshal Bernard Montgomery were also present for a celebration of their victory over the Germans. Zhukov took advantage of the meeting to give the Soviet Union's diamond and ruby star of the Order of Victory to Eisenhower and Montgomery.

"The generals, who for so long had measured their actions by artillery barrages, bombardments and troop movements, beat time to the jive of 'The Three Rhythm Rascals,' from Chicago, and three Negro vocalists from New York," the newspaper report said.

Alberta might have gone into that room thinking she knew what she was going to sing, but she soon found out who was boss. Eisenhower was calling the shots. First he wanted everybody to sing "Swing Low, Sweet Chariot." Then it was "Oh! Susannah." Alberta didn't know the words to that one but picked them up as fast as she heard them the first time around. This obviously was no place for some of her risqué lyrics.

"Eisenhower knew the words to every one of those songs," Alberta said. "He's a wonderful man. One can readily understand how he brought the various nations together." He even harmonized with their rendition of "Deep in the Heart of Texas."

When Baby Doo started pounding out "Caldonia, Caldonia, What Makes Your Big Head So Hard?" on the keyboard of the nine-foot grand piano in the room, the entire piano started rocking back and forth in rhythm with the music. The generals nudged each other and strained their necks to see what was making all that weight jump up and down.

One of the drivers for the unit had seen Baby Doo pull this trick before, raising his left knee under the piano and making it sway. When he saw the size of the concert piano that day, he said, "I bet you twenty-five bucks you won't rock this one."

"I knew I was going to have a problem with that one, so I put both knees up under it," said Baby Doo, who now sports a diamond stickpin in his tie, wears sharkskin suits, and drives a snazzy yellow Cadillac between his playing engagements in Minneapolis, where he lives. "I had sore legs for a long time after that, but I won that twenty-five dollars."

Reporters from the *New York Times* and other major newspapers waited impatiently outside the meeting room. "When we came out, they asked us, 'What are they talking about now?' " said Mae. All the correspondents heard was little Jean Starr saying, "Whew! This is really wonderful."

"But oh, how nerve-racking!" Mae told them. Alberta, who was so excited she asked all the top brass for their autographs, responded, typically, in a more formal tone about the great honor it was for their unit to be chosen for the performance. She added her disappointment that she hadn't had some advance notice that Russians would be in the audience so that she could have sung something in their language.

The Russians apparently didn't leave with any such regrets, according to the *Herald Tribune* account. "They shuffled out of the dining room to the tune of 'Roll Out the Barrel' and they were still swinging and swaying when their big planes with the red stars took off in the late afternoon."

Alberta's unit went on to Germany and Austria to entertain and see the sights. In Vienna she learned to sing several songs in the dialect spoken there. On August 15 she wrote on the back of a photo from "the home of Franz Liszt [*sic*] writer of the famous 'Merry Widow Waltz.' We were here when the Japs surrendered. The people went wild."

The same month they visited a palatial house that Hermann Göring had occupied in Zell-am-See. She reported that the house had satin instead of common wallpaper on the walls and a table made out of pure silver in the dining room. She found it interesting that many of the paintings on the walls were of religious subjects (*Afro-American*, September 15, 1945, p. 10).

The unit also visited Berchtesgaden in Bavaria to see Hitler's mountain house, the Eagle's Nest. They went by small truck through tunnels to about three thousand feet in altitude, then had to walk up another three thousand feet to the top of the mountain, which was camouflaged in green netting. Inside Hitler's hideout Alberta took out her pocketknife and carved her initials along with many others on a table, then had a photo snapped of herself sitting on top of it.

The group was back to work in early September in Rheims, France, performing at the Municipal Theater on the same bill with the Rockettes from New York's Radio City Music Hall. "Believe me when I say we have 'em hanging from the chandeliers," Alberta wrote back to the *Afro-American* (September 22, 1945, p. 10).

Rheims was the site of a happy reunion with her old friend Sergeant Jimmy Daniels. But it was also the scene of another racial incident. She didn't give any details because she was far more impressed with the way the commanding officer, Colonel Floyd W. Brown, handled it.

As she told the story to the *Amsterdam News* (December 8, 1945, p. 16), Colonel Brown told the special services officer in Rheims that he would tolerate "no foolishness or alibis. We are all in this war together, and these people [blacks] will be treated courteously and with respect. . . ."

The grand, and free, tour of the Continent came to an end. The Rhythm Rascals returned to New York on November 13, 1945.

Several European agents who had booked Alberta before the war were anxious to sign her up again for engagements in London and Paris. She told them no, thanks. She wanted to stay home.

Shortly after her arrival she answered a reporter's questions about her future plans, saying, "I'm going to be with Uncle Sam till he takes this uniform off me. I've never been so satisfied and had so much protection in my life. If you're with the USA, everything jumps" (*Amsterdam News*, December 8, 1945, p. 16).

CHAPTER SEVEN

Making Her "Show"
Go On . . . and On

Alberta had to trade her military uniform for a slinky gown because no more USO tour assignments awaited her. She opened in January 1946 at the Club Bali in Washington, D.C. She was still there at the end of the month, when she received word that her sister, La Tosca, had died in Denver. Alberta told the *Chicago Defender* that she wouldn't be able to attend her sister's funeral "because of professional commitments" (February 9, 1946, p. 16).

It wasn't that her employer was hardhearted and wouldn't give her time off to attend her sister's funeral. She simply didn't want to go. She never went to funerals. "When you're dead, you're dead," Alberta said. She resented people making funerals a big social event and measuring a person's worth by the money spent on the affair.

Moreover, she showed no sign of sentiment toward her sister or regrets that their relationship hadn't been better, even upon La Tosca's death. "She never visited," Alberta said. "I never visited her. Period. She just took sick and died. So we were just a family of hello, good-bye, see you later."

Alberta did admit as much as to say that La Tosca led a Christian life, sang in the choir of her church, and was "a very nice woman." Even that doesn't sound like a loving tribute.

Three months later Alberta was performing at the Music Hall

Supper Club in Portland, Oregon, when she received a telegram advising her that she was to be one of forty recipients of the Asiatic-Pacific Campaign Ribbon for "outstanding service." For that she could disengage herself from a professional commitment and travel all the way back across the country. Alberta, all spit and polish in her camp shows uniform, accepted the award, as did Mae, Baby Doo, Ollie, and Al of her group. Among others decorated that day were Paulette Goddard, Lily Pons, Keenan Wynn, Paul G. Waner, William Gargan, and Henry Armstrong, a black who, Alberta noted, was the only boxer to hold three world championship titles at one time.

Alberta returned to Portland after the ceremony. She reported to the *Afro-American* (May 4, 1946, p. 6) that the city's YWCA, where she was staying, had no color line. (Alberta stayed there to save a buck, not because she was conducting a survey on color barriers.) She also praised the way Portland treated its black population. "There is a bit of prejudice and discrimination here, but there are many interracial groups doing a lot toward better understanding between the races." She noted that most of the churches had interracial choirs. . . Furthermore, the city had many recreational facilities so you didn't see teenagers hanging around on the streets, something that upset her about Harlem at that time.

From there Alberta went to Los Angeles, where she spent a few weeks as a houseguest of Ethel Waters. Ethel, who was in New York, sent a letter dated May 11, 1946, to Alberta, whom she always called Flossie. She was answering a note from Alberta asking what she could pay Ethel for staying at her home. "It's like this Pal," Ethel wrote. "I don't charge any thing for helping out a Pal until you can get located because I don't have any rooms to rent." The room Alberta was using, she said, was used by "any two women or two men who are close friends of mine that I personally ask to visit with me." Ethel clarified that a man, whom she referred to as 29, who was also staying at her house, was not her boyfriend, although "he wants to be." Finally, she said, "the weather and the niggers here are just the same . . ." She signed the letter "Your buddy—Waters."

Alberta could well afford to pay Ethel for her room because she received the tidy sum (for her in those days) of $875 for entertaining one week at the Strand Theater in Long Beach. She also reported to the *Afro-American* (July 6, 1946, p. 6) that she had dinner with Flo Mills's widower, Kid Thompson, who had just purchased a ten-unit property in "one of the most beautiful neighborhoods of Los Angeles—a lulu." Alberta contacted Melvyn Douglas, her friend from USO days in India, who was now back in Hollywood. She hoped he might help her arrange an engagement in Los Angeles. But by the time he could get back to her, she had already returned to the East Coast. He wrote on July 9, 1946:

> About a week ago I tried to telephone to let you know that I had been successful in contacting Sammy Lewis at Slapsy Maxie's for you.
>
> Mr. Lewis knows you and suggested that you get in touch with him for an audition and a talk. You can do whatever you think best about this, in view of the fact that you have returned to New York. Up to last week, I was not successful in getting in touch with Frank Bruni at the Florentine Gardens, and shall do nothing further on it of course unless you return here and want me to do what I can.
>
> I am very sorry to know your mother is ill and trust she is much improved by now. Sincerely, Melvyn Douglas.

Alberta settled back in New York, telling her friends she wanted to stay at home for a while. Often during that summer she went over to Jock's Music Room in Harlem, where Maxine Sullivan and Jimmy Daniels were appearing. She noted in a diary a couple of one-night club engagements: one on September 10 at the Republic in Brooklyn for a pittance of twenty-five dollars and another December 31 at Larchmont for thirty-five dollars.

She recorded more of her songs for the Juke Box Record Company: "He's Got a Punch Like Joe Louis," "Take Your Big Hands Off," "Don't Want No Man That's Lazy," and "Your Bread May Be Good, but It Ain't as Good as Mine."

The *Afro-American* called on Alberta to write for its November 2, 1946, edition the obituary of Mamie Smith, who had died on October 23. Alberta wrote that Mamie was the last of the five blues-singing

Smiths (none of whom was related): Mamie, Laura, Clara, Trixie, and Bessie, who had died in 1937. "Mamie was a boon to the early day [G]raphophone business," Alberta noted. "When she made her first record, 'Crazy Blues,' written by Perry Bradford, the first for any colored female singer, there was a rush for the horned instrument."

By now Alberta, at fifty-one years old, was outliving an era and the other entertainers of her generation who had stopped performing years before. Her own audience was becoming more restricted, as her return to the Harlem stage indicated.

She opened on December 6, 1946, for a week at the Apollo Theater on 125th Street with Eddie Heywood and, to her chagrin, Taps Miller and his Band. If she and Frank Schiffman had forgotten their earlier squabble at the Lafayette Theater in 1930, it was renewed that evening, now that he was managing the Apollo. This time she made sure she had in hand a written contract, the standard one used by the American Guild of Variety Artists, signed a month before the opening. It stipulated that she would be paid three hundred dollars for the week, less ten percent for the Gale Agency, which booked her, and it had no clause authorizing her dismissal if the show was unsuccessful.

But again, as at the Lafayette, she didn't make it through the first night. Alberta sang three songs but "did not go over well," said John Schiffman, son of Frank Schiffman (in a letter of September 6, 1985), referring to index cards his father kept on every performer at the Apollo. She was "closed out" and paid a hundred dollars, he said. Alberta may have been just as happy with that decision, for she was enraged at her rejection by the notoriously bad-mannered audience at the Apollo. Lena Horne had already had a similar experience at the Apollo; the audience drove her off the stage by throwing pennies at her. She left and refused ever to return to it.

Alberta didn't say a word in protest to the newspapers. It was her last attempt to perform at a Harlem theater. "But it broke her heart," said Harry Watkins.

She went on to sing to a more supportive and sophisticated audience at the 845 Club in the Bronx. Then, with the help of Prossie

Blue, a friend and agent in Chicago, she took bookings outside New York. She had to pay ten percent of her weekly salary to Prossie, but it was worth it to keep employed on a regular basis. She took what jobs came along regardless of an unevenness in the pay offered. For instance, for the week of January 27, 1947, she received $350 for appearing at the Exhibit Building in Columbus, Georgia. The following month at the Club Regal in Columbus, Ohio, she was paid only $125 a week, and as Alberta noted, "Social security [was] taken out [of that]."

That February the *Pittsburgh Courier* announced the results of its annual contest in which readers voted to pick the best black musicians and vocalists for the year. At the top of the list of seventeen female singers were Ella Fitzgerald, Billie Holiday, Thelma Carpenter, Lena Horne, Sarah Vaughan, and Pearl Bailey. Alberta never did appear on such popularity lists.

But that never bothered her. She was far more concerned about a different counting—of the battles her race was winning for equality. Entertainers still had to perform to segregated audiences in much of the country if they wanted engagements. So she was happy to see Nat ("King") Cole canceling two appearances in Kansas City that spring of 1947 because separate seating would be required for blacks. Actors' Equity won a victory that summer by agreeing with the League of New York Theaters as of August 1, 1947, to keep many plays out of Washington, D.C., theaters that banned blacks from attending.

Other important cracks were made in the nation's racist structure that year. In the spring Jackie Robinson joined the lineup of the Brooklyn Dodgers and became the first black to play for a major-league baseball team. He was named rookie of the year that year and the National League's most valuable player two years later.

P. L. Prattis, executive editor of the *Pittsburgh Courier*, gained membership in the Periodical Correspondents Association in 1947, thus being permitted to be the first journalist of his race to gain access to the press galleries in Congress. And Dr. Ralph Bunche, director of the UN Trusteeship Division, was appointed principal secretary of the Palestine Commission, which presided over the partition of the Holy Land, an effort that later won him the Nobel Peace Prize in 1950.

Then, on Labor Day 1947, Mae Gaddy became the first black to win on *Arthur Godfrey's Talent Scouts* radio show.

Unfortunately progress in race relations was achieved at an enormous cost. A wave of lynchings broke out in several states. White men, angered by their lack of control over social change, roamed the countryside, confident in the strength of a demented mob, and declared their manhood by strangling the life out of helpless victims.

Regardless of the turmoil, a performer's life had to go on. Alberta opened on March 17, 1947, for two weeks at the Café St. Michel in Montreal in an "all-star revue" called *Harlem's Funniest Moments*. There she received word that the USO was recruiting again for foreign tours, so she made a beeline for New York to talk her way into Unit 997, the Savoy Swingsters, managed by Herbie Cowen. Heading off with her were two comedy teams, Apus and Estrellita and Holmes and Jean, and the acrobatic dancers called The Three Poms.

The group was in the Far East from the end of May through September 1947. It must not have been an interesting or exciting tour because Alberta saved no notes, souvenirs, or clippings from the trip. All she wanted to keep was her passport. On their return to New York from Seattle on October 12 Herbie picked up the passport of each member, as was his duty. Alberta tried to talk him out of taking hers, but he wouldn't give in to her. So on October 20, 1947, back home, she wrote the State Department. She mentioned all the places she had served with the USO, including her trips during wartime, and made a patriotic plea for the return of that passport just to keep as a souvenir. "I cherish the thought that I went over during the hard fighting and did my bit towards bringing a bit of pleasure to our fighting men," she wrote. "My passport proves that fact. Now you can see why I would like to keep it."

Her old passport was returned. Since it was valid only for travel with the USO, she requested by separate letter on the same date and received a new tourist passport. She said she had offers to work at Fred Payne's bar in Paris as well as clubs where she had worked in Denmark, England, and Egypt. "I would like to take the first available ship so I can get settled before Xmas," she wrote. As it turned out, she never used the new passport during the two-year period for which it was valid.

On that last USO trip to the Far East her path crossed that of her former husband, Willard Townsend. President of the United Transport Service Employees, he had been appointed American member of and CIO representative to the World Federation of Trade Unions Commission. That group had been given the task of conducting an investigation into U.S. occupation policies as they affected social and economic conditions in the Far East. Its members visited Japan, China, Korea, the Philippines, and the Malay states.

By that time Willard carried a long list of distinguished credits. President Harry Truman included him as one of sixteen labor leaders to meet with an equal number of industrial chiefs at the end of the war for a labor-management conference. CIO President Philip Murray chose him to represent that organization at an international labor convention in Havana, Cuba, in 1945. He was on the board of trustees of Hampton Institute, the National Urban League, and the American Council of Race Relations. In 1947 he began writing a column called "The Other Side," which the *Chicago Defender* carried for years. He wrote about a wide range of subjects from trade unionism to race relations and the economy.

In August 1947 he became a subject of the news when he sued labor leader A. Philip Randolph and several of his colleagues for half a million dollars. The defendants, responsible for publishing *The Black Worker*, a monthly newspaper, were charged with falsely and maliciously injuring Willard's reputation. The complaint cited one passage in particular that referred to him as a "schizophrenic." The case was dismissed on February 23, 1950, at the request of the attorneys representing both parties.

Alberta was busy maintaining her own good reputation at the end of the 1940s. She was a leader in her own way, being the first black to perform at Boston's fashionable Stork Club in December 1947. After a short engagement at the Esquire in Montreal in January 1948, she hit the road in the United States with Unit 53 of the Veterans Hospital Camp Shows, managed by Tom Moseley. Noble Sissle produced their show, called *Jive Jamboree;* it had a cast of seventeen, including the Ebony Tones, a singing quartet; Herbie Cowen's Trio; pianist Jean Prater; The Three Poms, acrobatic dancers; Holmes and

Jean, comedy dancers; and Alston & Young, a singing and dancing duo.

On February 2, 1948, they entertained 1,150 patients at the VA hospital in Downey, Illinois, in two one-hour shows that afternoon and evening. The hospital filed an enthusiastic report with USO headquarters: "It is one of the snappiest, fast moving variety shows we have had and the performers did not spare themselves in making it top entertainment," it said.*

Bert Wishnew, a Camp Show producer, reviewed the work of several units, including Alberta's, and wrote† about their importance to the veterans they entertained: "These hospital audiences are as critical as any old time vaudeville audience used to be. They recognize and appreciate talent."

That's just what *Jive Jamboree* had, he said, having seen it in fast action at the Percy Jones Hospital Center in Battle Creek, Michigan. "I saw the unit perform in five wards Monday afternoon and, at night, drive 19 miles to the W. K. Kellog [sic] Convalescent Annex at Gull Lake, where they put on another show for veterans."†

In Battle Creek he witnessed an event that he said explained why USO performers like Alberta Hunter were so popular:

A nurse came over to me and said, "We have three amputees over here in a little room, all by themselves. They are too sick to be out in a ward. Could someone go in and just say, hello."

Well, the Ebony Tones and Alberta Hunter overheard the nurse and volunteered to visit the boys. They sang for them for 20 minutes. You should have seen those veterans' eyes when they said goodbye.

Another day, at the same hospital Alberta Hunter had just finished her number in a ward. A Negro boy came over and asked if he could put on her wrist a straw bracelet he had just made.

*National Archives Document RG 407, Records of the Adjutant General's Office, U.S. Department of the Army, Washington, D.C. Camp Shows, Inc., A-K-A, Records 1941–57, vol. V, p. 2442.

†Ibid., p. 2458.

†Ibid., p. 2461.

"I saw you in Japan and am very happy to hear you here now," he told her. "I hope you come back again."*

Entertaining the patients was a real joy for Alberta and her colleagues. But getting to them, especially in the South, made the job almost unbearable. "You can have it, I don't want it. It's too tough for me," she wrote from Jacksonville, Florida, in May 1948 to a journalist friend, E. B. Rea (*Afro-American*, May 29, 1948, p. 6).

"It's the first time I've ever heard Alberta complain and I've kept in contact with her almost throughout the world on tougher assignments than travelling through the U.S.," Rea wrote in his column.

Discrimination in the South against black entertainers, no matter what their mission, was still rampant. Dick Campbell said that for groups traveling in that region "eating in the kitchen was par for the course." But before they could get that far, they had to get to and inside the camps. Often a group of black entertainers, even on interstate buses, would be told to get off in some godforsaken place because otherwise there wouldn't be enough seats for whites. They would have to wait for hours until a truck from the base they were to visit came to pick them up.

If they did reach their destination on their own, the unit often would be barred from entering the army base. "We don't have no niggah shows here" might be the response from a surly white guard, who would deny them entrance regardless of what credentials or orders they had.

Time and again they would have to call New York and say, "Mr. Campbell, we got kicked out again." He would then call a general's office in Washington and wait patiently for word later from someone saying, "It's okay, they'll be there to pick up your unit."

And in spite of their rank of captain, the members of the unit would be required to stay in "sleazy, fleabitten black hotels and pay for their own rooms," Campbell said.

With all that hassle, Alberta was still able to concentrate on the positive when interviewed by a reporter in her hometown. "I regard entertainment of these poor souls in these hospitals one of the great-

*Ibid., pp. 2462–63.

est services that can be rendered," she said (*Memphis World*, June 4, 1948, p. 1). "It is amazing to what extent many of these men, broken in bodies, mentally affected by the shocks of war, still maintain such high spirit. All of us need to visit these hospitals at times just to see how well we are doing."

She also talked about how good it was to be back home. "I enjoyed being back in Memphis after so many years of roaming," she said. "It meant so much to me to see some of my childhood friends."

The newspaper commented: "These were the simple words that summed up the feeling of an outstanding stage and radio personality about the people of her home town.

" 'No wonder Alberta continues as one of the great artists of the day,' local admirers declared. 'She has never lost the common touch.' "

When the group went west, Alberta took advantage of a day or two off to take a "vacation" to cross the border and see a bullfight in Mexico. "Thrilling but cruel" was her only comment about that. She had more to say about the treatment of Indians in Arizona.

"Howdy, from the doggondest [*sic*] place you ever saw," she wrote from Phoenix in a column for the *Afro-American* (July 10, 1948, p. 6). Those words, she explained, were from a local tourist brochure, should anyone think for a moment she would talk like that. She quickly pointed out that there were notable differences between the virtues of Arizona, as described in the brochure, and the plight of the state's Indian inhabitants. "The white man should bow his head in shame and never raise it. I regret saying so, but I'm very bitter."

The discrimination extended to blacks as well. "We have been segregated on every turn. There have been places where we could not get a drink of water. Even the Mexicans refused to serve us— only in the kitchen.

"It goes without saying I did not eat. I would get something from the grocery store and eat it when I arrived at home."

She wrote her own guide for tourists, paraphrasing from the brochure given her: "A few of the desert creatures found in Arizona—all poisonous—are the rattlesnake, scorpion, gila monster, horned toad, black widow spider, and tarantula—other poisons are hatred and discrimination.

"Arizona has 'more tricks of nature's fancy than anywhere else in the world . . . all bathed in sunshine'—but the sweetest word I've been able to say here, was Adios."

Alberta was happier performing in Topeka, Kansas, and seeing how a number of blacks there were thriving. She wrote the *Afro-American* (September 4, 1948, p. 6) about Mr. and Mrs. Julius Moore, owners and operators of the Dunbar Hotel, the drugstore of Charles C. Lytles, a retired detective, and her meeting with Lutie Lytle Cowan, a former lawyer who for years had had an office on Broadway in New York City.

Alberta was in New York herself in September 1948 after this, her most arduous and longest Camp Show tour. She "rested" for a couple of days, then took herself to the road for a year, singing in places like San Jose, Sacramento, San Francisco and Oakland; Spokane and Seattle; Toronto and Montreal; and Baltimore.

In Baltimore E. B. Rea, the veteran journalist who knew Alberta, reported she'd been one of his favorite singers for two decades. Show business can be proud of her, he said, for she "has never been the clowning exhibitionist" (*Afro-American*, April 9, 1949, p. 6).

That summer she regained control of her copyright for "Down Hearted Blues" and contracted with Leeds Music to republish it. With that agreement she began to receive her first royalties for the song. She wrote Lovie Austin, who had written down the music for her back in 1922, telling her the good news and promising to send her a check for a hundred dollars. Lovie answered on August 2, 1949: "Sure you know I can always use the money, and whatever you do is okay with me. Just make sure you read carefully any paper you have to sign."

Regaining control of her earliest song stimulated Alberta to do more songwriting. At the beginning of 1950 she recorded for Regal Records four of those songs: "Midnight Blues," "I Got a Mind to Ramble," "Reckless Blues," and "The Man I Love Is Gone."

But composing and occasional club performances in New York weren't enough challenge to her energy. On January 23, 1950, she embarked on a three-month, twenty-eight-thousand-mile tour with the Swingin' Jamboree (Unit 86) Veterans Hospital Camp Show. It didn't matter that it paid a weekly salary of only $125. She could perform six out of every seven days for people who appreciated her, and that was just fine with her.

One of the recent past Camp Shows, with Mae Gaddy, had included both white and black performers. The mixture caused such problems with accommodations that the new group was limited again to only one race. In the group were comedians Glenn and Jenkins; The Three Poms dancing girls; tap dancer Leslie Gaines; and Herbie Cowen's Band.

The Camp Show circuit in the United States was as rigorous as the old TOBA circuit, which herded black entertainers for one-night stands from one small town to another. The tour started at the Army General Hospital in Asheville, North Carolina. The entertainers gave two or three shows a day, packed up after the last performance, climbed onto a bus, and traveled much of the night to the next town. And so Alberta lived for the next seven months, traveling to Texas, New Mexico, Arizona, California, Oregon, Washington, Idaho, Montana, Wyoming, North and South Dakota, Colorado, Kansas, Nebraska, Iowa, Missouri, Illinois, Wisconsin, and Minnesota.

She took a breather after the tour, singing at Sunnie Wilson's Bar in Detroit in late May 1950. Fred Payne tried to lure her back to Paris for the summer, but she said she didn't want to leave her mother at home by herself all that time. That reasoning, however, didn't stop her from spending the months of June and July at the King Cole Lounge in Denver, the Troast Lounge in Kansas City, Missouri, and the Esquire in Montreal. Back in New York in August she signed a contract with Pickwick Music for three more of her songs—"What's the Matter Baby," "Sun Up to Sun Down Blues" and "What Have I Done?"—and sang for a short while at Bill Martin's Club.

Only after another long tour around the country in the fall of 1950 with the comedy team of Freddie and Flo and with Eddie ("Mr. Cleanhead") Vinsons and after a return on her own to Toronto and Montreal did she settle down in the spring of 1951 to be with her mother for a long while.

For the next year she worked back and forth between the Bon Soir, a club on West Eighth Street where Jimmy Daniels was the host and main entertainer, and on West Fifty-second Street at La Commedia, known as the "rendezvous for the Park Avenue crowd."

The Bon Soir, with two pianos as its trademark, was a very popular club and the showcase for many new stars, including Barbra Streisand, Phyllis Diller, and Carol Burnett. But it was at La Commedia that Alberta really felt at home, according to S. W. Garlington, theatrical editor of the *Amsterdam News* (November 3, 1951, p. 16). "Miss Hunter has several dates waiting for her—but she is not too anxious to travel, since she found a local spot that appreciates her type of entertainment," he wrote. "It's the type of entertainment the sophisticated or semi-sophisticated best appreciate. In the correct nitery for her, she's sensational."

As always, her risqué songs were the greatest crowd pleasers. Those were the ones with what she called "suggestive" lyrics. "We didn't call them risqué," she said, although she admitted they were "naughty" enough that her mother, who had heard about them, didn't approve of them. "But I was singing them because I could make money from singing them," she said. Her personal experience simply confirmed the academic evidence for the popularity of risqué entertainment that she found in an article she saved from *Variety* (April 16, 1947, p. 46): "Sociologists claim that sex is on an upbeat during wartime and post-war periods, as witness the return of nudity to cafes and stiff fights put up by the varied societies for suppression of vice on an increasing number of issues. However, the risquee balladeers have been popular long before the war. . . ."

Alberta maintained a notebook of downright dirty songs with scintillating lyrics that left nothing to the imagination. Those songs were the ones she sang privately to individual tables that wanted that kind of material and were willing to pay well to hear it. After all, a buck was a buck, and Alberta was out to get every one of them she could.

To her way of thinking she was singing a song as it ought to be sung, she was helping other songwriters by promoting their work and making them money, and she was fattening her own till. But the risqué or "naughty" song, she said, "wasn't the type song that I really wanted to sing."

She prided herself more on the religious songs she had written and began to record in March 1952, songs such as "I Want to Thank

You Lord" and "You Got to Reap Just What You Sow." (The latter is similar to the title of the song by Alexander Robinson that she recorded in 1923. Alberta's version of the song is also known as "You Reap Just What You Sow," "You've Got to Reap Just What You Sow," and "You Gotta Reap Just What You Sow".) The contrasts in the type of material she sang made her work that much more interesting to those who bought her records, saw her perform, or reviewed her work.

Right across the street from La Commedia was the Onyx, where an old friend of Alberta's—Billie Holiday—was singing in her unique style. "She was just so unusual!" said Alberta. "She had a style that nobody will ever copy."

Lottie Tyler had first taken Alberta to hear Billie back in the early 1930s when she was already creating quite a stir in Harlem. She was singing at the Hotcha, a little club on 133d Street, famous for its chicken cacciatore, where Billie Daniels, Jimmy Daniels, and Garland Wilson also were performing.

"I was just so carried away with her work," Alberta said. "Billie was young and very, very pretty. I used to go in every night after work and ask her to sit down, and I'd talk to her." Alberta tipped Billie—the whole bill, none of that Chicago-style passing it out in halves—to sing favorite songs of hers. "I think Billie made a lot of money in there because people were crazy about her."

Now, two decades later, Alberta typically worked six days a week and late into the night, so she rarely had the chance or the energy to see a show by Billie or by any of the other singers she liked. She did get to a benefit for Josephine Baker at the Golden Gate Ballroom at 142d Street and Lenox Avenue on May 20, 1952. That was a Sunday, her day off. Even then she went only because she adored Josephine and rarely was ever in the same city with her. Alberta was also very proud of Josephine's having worked for the resistance against the German occupation of France during World War II, for which France awarded her the Croix de Guerre, a military decoration for bravery, and the Rosette de la Résistance. (That was more recognition than Josephine received in her own country. In 1951 New York's Stork Club refused to serve her.) La Baker was so happy to see Alberta in the audience she walked up to her after the show and planted a kiss on her cheek, a demonstration of affection that Alberta would allow few people to make.

Within a few weeks Alberta was receiving her own recognition from an audience that was equally fond of her. The prestigious American Society of Composers, Authors, and Publishers (ASCAP) elected her to its membership, a rare achievement for a female of any race in 1952. Other black women also were making their mark early in that decade. In 1950 Althea Gibson of Harlem became the first black to play in the national tennis championship at Forest Hills. (She won both the U.S. and English woman's singles championships in 1957 and 1958.) And Gwendolyn Brooks, a Chicago housewife, was the first black to win a Pulitzer Prize in poetry.

Not one to sit back and rest on her laurels, Alberta packed her duffel bag that same June and donned her USO uniform again. She sent her mother a postcard on July 2, saying succinctly, as usual (not even bothering to write "Dear Mother"): "Arrived here in Stevinsville [the correct spelling is Stephenville], Newfoundland enroute to Prestwick, Scotland, Love Alberta."

Alberta had joined the Swingin' Jamboree (Unit 1044), led by Snub Mosley, who played the slide saxophone, an instrument he created. In his band were Willard Brown and Albert ("Budd") Johnson, both on sax; John Brown, bass; Edward Cornelius, Jr., drums; Ken Bryan, accordion and piano; Frank ("Gabbs") Galbreath, trumpet; and Huey Long, Sr., guitar. Also in the group was Arrie ("Strut Flash") McKethan, a dancer.

Cornelius, who was about twenty years old, liked Alberta because she was one of the gang. "You didn't have to worry about taking care of her," he said. He also appreciated some of her interests outside music and was happy when she suggested the entire unit visit the home of the poet Robert Burns at Alloway on their way to Glasgow.

Alberta took Edward under her wing, as she did many young people she liked, and called him Junior. Their first night at a hotel in Prestwick he had to dress in coat and tie for dinner. Edward sat with Alberta at a table with what he called a "barrage of cutlery" on the side and in front of the plate before him. Luckily he had about the same meal as Alberta so he could watch her and see which fork and knife she used for what. Not to embarrass him with any instructions, she would whisper to him something like "Look at those people over there. They're using the butter knife for the fish knife."

Edward spoke a little French, so Alberta often spoke to him in that language to help him practice. "It came second nature to her," he said. It also helped distinguish her from the rest of the group. He enjoyed the special attention and the chance to learn from her. When they landed in France, she said to him grandly, "*Nous sommes ici* ["Here we are"]."

She also counseled her young charge when she saw the way he went about trying to attract the attention of young women in Paris. "If I were a woman your age," she told him, "I would more likely be attracted by a different approach." She encouraged him to be a bit more suave in manner.

"As old as she was, she was sensual . . . when she wanted to be," especially onstage, he said. "She would shake her bottom half as if she had known carnal pleasures somewhere along the way." And she could reduce all sorts of men, including him, to tears by singing songs about sweethearts straying or spirituals like "Yield Not to Temptation." "She knew what it took to evoke an emotion," Edward said.

The troupe performed at bases in Scotland and England. One of the places they stayed was Barbara Hutton's home, which Alberta said, the U.S. government had requisitioned for the billeting of troops. Unfortunately no satin sheets or down pillows were left out for them.

At the beginning of August 1952 they went to France, where they stayed overnight in places that Alberta noted for historical significance, like Orléans, "where Joan of Arc was burned to death," and La Rochelle, "where the Protestants burned churches of Catholics, then settled in New York."

After a brief stop in the Azores the group returned to Westover, Massachusetts, on August 26. On the last leg of a trip to entertain the troops in Newfoundland, they had a close call. A bum landing gear of their "Flying Boxcar" forced them to make an emergency landing in a field near the airstrip at St. John's. A few days later, on September 3, 1952, they were safely back in New York.

No simple dangers like that were going to discourage Alberta. She signed up for another unit—1076, the Dixieland Jamboree—also managed by Snub Mosley. This, her seventh and last tour, was bound for the Korean war front. She was proud of being the only woman on board. "They said they didn't have no place for no crybabies," she said. "So they sent me, because they said I had a lot of nerve." They didn't even take Strut Flash, the dancer, on this trip. Carl Pruitt replaced John Brown on bass, and Burnie Peacock replaced Budd Johnson on sax.

They left New York on October 20. Alberta put more effort into a letter she wrote her mother from Tokyo on October 26, in which, for the first time, she admitted the danger her work involved:

Hi baby—
Arrived here in Tokyo Thursday, had a wonderful trip a bit tiresome.

The Japanese people have certainly worked hard to build their country up and believe me everybody respects them.

We leave for the battle line in Korea tomorrow morning at 5 A.M. We have been allotted our army clothes and we must leave all our street clothes here in Tokyo. We'll be in full battle outfits. We have bags we sleep in and combat boots in fact this is it. If we're lucky we'll be back if not I for one died doing what I wanted to do. Do not be worried if you do not hear from me, for if anything is wrong the army will notify you. I will not be where I can write for a while.

Mother I am the first Negro girl to entertain the G.I.'s in Korea. No other Negro girl has been over. Isn't that swell. Call Jerry [Major] and tell her to tell Miss [Betty] Granger [a writer for the *Amsterdam News*] about my being the first Negro girl to go to Korea to entertain the G.I.'s.

Jerry's no at the Amsterdam [*News*] is AC2-7800.

Be sure to notice my new address at the top of this letter. Write it down so you will have it. Tear the other one up I gave you before I left, and use the one at the top of this letter or on the envelope.

Love your child
Alberta

To the battlefront they went, ducking in and out of air raids. On November 20 they were at Uijongbu, just south of the thirty-eighth parallel, while a "projectile battery" was blasting away. "The British were in trouble," Alberta wrote down on the back of their itinerary. "You have never heard anything like it." The unit passed through a valley, "where," she wrote, "some of the worst fighting took place—dead bodies still there." Amid all the commotion and carnage, Alberta was happy to report having met Major John Eisenhower, Ike's son, who ate at the same table with the unit and had his picture taken with them.

Pleasant diversions like that were rare. The soldiers they entertained—sometimes as many as fifteen thousand in one place—kept their rifles across their knees, resting nervously in wait for a nasty war to resume at any second. Alberta saw loneliness, weariness, and fear embedded on their brows. "Those boys are awful young, they're away from home and you've got to put all that terrible teardrop stuff into words for 'em," she told a reporter for the *Armed Forces News* (November 1952 edition, p. 11). You have to "sing 'em sweet, sing 'em hot, sing 'em melancholy. Give 'em the blues, the way-down-rusty-dusty-broken-hearted stuff, man.

"Maybe they're gonna be dead tomorrow. Sing for 'em as if it's the last song they're gonna hear sung. 'Cause maybe it is. Every time you stand in front of those boys you don't know: should you sing what makes 'em sad or makes 'em happy. Both, maybe."

The combination of the bitter and the sweet appealed to the troops. They were even more appreciative of the fact that Alberta, even in freezing weather—when the men in the band were clad in heavy coats, gloves, and caps with earmuffs—appeared in gowns not only with no coat but also with no underwear.

"You know that those soldiers got so tired of looking at nothing but men in soldier clothes. I knew they didn't want to see no woman come out there with no jeans and pants and things on," she said. "So I had—well, I was supposed to look pretty decent in a dress. You know how women are vain. So I had those slinky dresses, and I had nothing on but the dress, see? Not even my little shorts.

"Those fellows were very nice. They appreciated that I was making an effort." Some of the other female singers in subsequent USO tours complained that Alberta made it hard for them by appearing sexily clad. "That's me," she'd tell them. "I'm not making it hard on anyone. I'm using my own judgment. You use yours. To each his own."

But she admits it wasn't easy. "It got so cold I couldn't bend my fingers. I never suffered that much from anything I did trying to help people. When she was eighty-nine, she said: "It didn't hurt me. Look at me. I'm strong as leather." It was worth it, Alberta said, even though she attributed her arthritis in later years to her having performed so often without proper protection from the cold. She said Walter Winchell and Dorothy Kilgallen each wrote a "beautiful article" about her working in those thin dresses.

The unit spent fifty-seven days in Korea, crossing the thirty-eighth parallel in the north. They gave shows in spite of air raids at some of the camps and an incident at an evacuation hospital in which, as Alberta described it, "Nurse Sarah blew her top."

As was her wont, Alberta made light of the difficulties and spoke of the humorous moments. She said they got so close to the North Koreans at some times that she was sure they were listening to the show as well. "Instead of being up on a hill shooting at us, they would be up there dancing," she said. "Yeah, they had a ball, honest to God."

On December 18, 1952, the unit arrived in Tokyo, where they were wined and dined at the officers' club and given medals in appreciation of their work. Traveling in Japan didn't seem quite as hazardous as it had been in Korea. They went as far north as Hokkaido, which Alberta marked down as "northern most Japan near Siberia, Russia." That proximity impressed her. So did the air raids at Misawa on December 30 just as they were sitting down to eat at 11:45 A.M. and again later that evening. The worst of it for her, however, was a special services officer there. "Lousy S.S. told me to drink out of my hands," she wrote in her notes.

"Lousy" Americans never affected her impression of a country or its people. She liked the Japanese, especially the children, whom she found delicate and well mannered. Many of the photographs she brought back from that country show her posing with youngsters she met on the street. There was something about her that appealed to them as well, and it wasn't just her color. They didn't have the chance to hear her sing, unless they were working on U.S. bases. But there was an attitude about Alberta, a sensitivity, that they appreciated in person in the 1950s as they would love in her music decades later.

In January 1953 the Dixieland Jamboree toured Okinawa, Formosa, Guam, and the Philippines, where Alberta wrote a note to herself: "In Manila and the Philippines the work animal is the caribu [sic]. Principal products are: sugar cane, coconut oil, bananas. They live in little bamboo houses about four or five feet off the ground. Their animals live under the house."

Somewhere along the way Alberta received a letter from her mother mailed from New York on December 27, 1952. It was filled with the day-to-day activities of someone back home, unrelated to and isolated from the world Alberta was experiencing. Yet it represented the anchor that is home, and a mother in it. "Oh my dear sweet child what are you worried about when you know that I am no good in the world only to be here sporting on—you just having a fine time thank you and am so glad the good Lord keeps his arms around you and me ma just got your little letter out the mail box and was so glad to hear you are well and fine and so am I ha. ha. child ma did not write because Mr. Bernard called said he had nice letter from you and would tell you that I was well and fine and I told Mr. Harry [Watkins] to tell you in his that I was getting your mail."

She went on to thank Alberta for a package she sent and to explain the delay she had retrieving it from the post office because she rarely went down the flight of stairs in their building and didn't understand the instructions for getting the package.

She continued: "Ma have no knews [sic] only to say the more those people give me for you the less I have honey I hope the Rep [Republicans] will cut taxes so even if you are able to make money you can at least keep a few pennies of it ha. ha." She signed her letter, "lots and lots of love, ma."

Alberta was back in New York on February 6, 1953, after a week entertaining in Hawaii and seeing Dinah Washington perform at the Brown Derby there. Betty Granger, the writer for the *Amsterdam News*, commented on how well fifty-seven-year-old Alberta looked:

"You can keep young ducking those shells (February 21, 1953, p. 25).

Alberta's life resumed an old pattern. She went back to sing at the Bon Soir. However, this time—keeping a crowd-pleasing good thing going—she sang without her underwear. Jimmy Daniels loved to tell of her saying to him, "Now, Jimmy, if your mother falls, you let her stay on the floor 'cause I don't have anything on underneath."

Alberta also wrote more songs and saw to the necessary paperwork for renewing copyrights to old compositions and making contracts for new ones. But she had to wage a war to maintain rights to one of her songs. The problem started when she took a song she'd written in 1948 and published in 1950, entitled "Will the Day Ever Come When I Can Rest," to Bess Berman, at the Apollo Record Company. Alberta wanted her to ask Mahalia Jackson if she would record it. Alberta liked Mahalia, who was a devout woman and very shrewd in hanging on to her money. Like Alberta, Mahalia had left her home (in Louisiana) for Chicago before finishing primary school. She scrubbed floors there to earn enough money to open a beauty salon. After becoming a successful singer, she established a scholarship fund for young blacks.

Alberta spoke more harshly of Berman than of anyone else who ever tried to trick her: "She was a white woman, one of them thieves. Not because she was white. Some of my best friends . . . How would I have got where I am? My people didn't have it to give me. They didn't have the prestige to put me there. The white people put me there. But she . . . thought because I was a Negro she could treat me like a dog. Some people think all Negroes are crazy, you know."

Months later Alberta was visiting Doc Wheeler Morin, a neighbor in Harlem who was one of the first disc jockeys to specialize in the playing of records by blacks on the radio. He told Alberta that Mahalia had just made a great new record called "I Wonder If I Will Ever Rest." He sent Alberta to a shop right around the corner that he knew had the recording in stock. She wasn't one to buy other people's records, but this one she wanted. Sure enough, it was her song. Only the title had been altered. No credit for authorship was given on the label.

"I didn't say a word until it made some money," said Alberta.

Then she went to the Songwriters Protective Association for help. When the association approached Bess Berman about the song, she insisted that it was Mahalia's song. Finally Alberta threatened to sue.

"She kept on denying it and did everything she could until one Sunday somebody told me Mahalia was giving a concert in Brooklyn," Alberta said. She went and sat up front, close to the stage. Berman was there as well to hear Mahalia say to the audience, "My next song, ladies and gentlemen was written by this lady sitting right here, Alberta Hunter, a good friend of mine."

Alberta said: "And when she said that, what could Bess Berman do? So she had to give me my song back, and it came out in the newspapers." Apollo corrected its label on the record, naming Alberta as the songwriter, and paid her retroactive royalties on her song.

Doc Wheeler helped Alberta again, early in January 1954. Five days into the new year Alberta's mother fell seriously ill. Whatever excuses Alberta may have invented earlier about her mother's ill health to explain her own actions or inactions, she knew this was real. She wanted to take her mother to the hospital, but she couldn't get Miss Laura down the five flights of stairs in their building by herself. Alberta didn't call an ambulance. Whether that was a moment of stinginess or one in which she preferred a trusted friend, she called Doc Wheeler. He climbed the stairs, lifted Miss Laura in his arms, took her down to his car, and drove her to Harlem Hospital.

Twelve days later, at 7:25 P.M., seventy-seven years old, Miss Laura died.

Death had meant nothing to Alberta before this death. You die, you're dead, that's what she had thought of all the others she knew who had "passed on." But now, without "Ma," she hurt.

Levy and Delany, one of Harlem's most respectable undertakers, buried Miss Laura in Plot 1411 of the Elmwood section at Ferncliff Cemetery in Hartsdale, a prosperous suburb of New York City. Alberta paid seventy-five dollars to buy a space that would accommodate her mother's remains and eventually her own. They would be in good company there with such celebrities as Judy Garland, Ed Sullivan, Jerome Kern, Moss Hart, Elsa Maxwell, Béla Bartók, Paul Robeson, Joan Crawford, and Basil Rathbone.

Journalist Allan McMillan, who said he often called Miss Laura once a week when Alberta was on USO tours, just to see how she was doing, wrote of her (*New York Age*, January 30, 1954, p. 8): ". . . she was always so cheerful and eager to talk about events of the day. The fact that her daughter was doing something worthwhile for mankind gave her a sincere appreciation for people in show business."

Her mother's death made Alberta reflect on her own mortality. About that time several of her contemporaries in the theater, including Garland Wilson, J. Rosamond Johnson, and Hamtree Harrington also died. She also did some thinking about the distance she had long held between herself and the church. Her grandmother had worn herself out going to church in Memphis, she said. So Alberta rarely went back on her own after leaving home. "I am a firm believer in God," she often said. "I just don't believe in sitting in church all day. I go when I feel like it. There are some people who sit in church every time the church door opens but wouldn't give a hungry man a dime to buy a sandwich. When I want to go to church, I'll go and sit down in one of the seats where I think nobody's noticing me. And just sit there and rejoice. I always want to be alone. I can get closer to God by myself. I'm not one of those screaming, lurching, crazy church members."

But on April 4, 1954, she became a member of the Williams Institutional CME Church at 2225 Seventh Avenue, in the building of the old Lafayette Theater. She joined Williams, she said, because she liked the Reverend Louis S. White and his wife. "I thought they were good honest people, and I love honesty," she said. "And could he sing! Oh, honey, you talk about singing a song. When Reverend White got through singing a song, that song had been sung."

She also wanted to be sure that if anything happened to her, there would be someone to help her. "I knew that some of the church people are really sincere when it comes to looking after you and helping you when you need help. I knew if I associated myself with a wonderful group like that, I would be well taken care of."

The mid-fifties were a turning point for Alberta and for blacks in general. On May 17, 1954, the U.S. Supreme Court ruled in its landmark case *Brown* v. *Board of Education of Topeka* that separate educational facilities were "inherently unequal." Although the decision was considered the most important step toward equal rights since the Emancipation Proclamation of 1863, it didn't mean things were going to change very fast. That was proved by the fact that a courageous lady by the name of Rosa Parks was big news the following year, when she refused to give her seat on a bus in Montgomery, Alabama, to a white person.

Television sets across the nation in 1954 showed Senator Joseph R. McCarthy browbeating, among many others, a simple black woman in Washington, D.C., by the name of Annie Lee Moss. An undercover agent said she had seen that name, shared by several other people listed in the local telephone book, on a list of members of the Communist party. Senator Stuart Symington, convinced this was not the woman McCarthy said she was, spoke up bravely in her defense when it appeared she would lose her job as a clerk at the Pentagon. "Mrs. Moss," he said, "I believe you're telling the truth. If the Army won't take you back, you come around to see me, and I'll get you a job." (*Chicago Defender*, September 25, 1954, p. 2).

Other victims of McCarthyism weren't as fortunate. Barney Josephson, considered by some seditious because he invited the races to mingle at his Café Society, had to go out of business after his brother Leon told the press what he wouldn't say to McCarthy: that he (Leon) was a member of the Communist party. (Barney was always quick to point out, ironically, that Leon had been arrested in Copenhagen in the winter of 1934 for participating in a plot to assassinate Adolf Hitler.) Dorothy Kilgallen and other influential columnists condemned Barney by association with his brother, Barney said. As a result, his clientele dropped off, he had to shut his doors, and black talent lost one of its best showcases in New York.

From those days Alberta was an ardent supporter, morally and financially, of the NAACP, and she applauded in 1957 when the mass protests it helped organize led to the nation's first civil rights bill to guarantee the voting rights of blacks. Those were heady days with the promise of change.

She realized that her life, too, was at a crucial point. As Alberta told it, she gave up show business the day after her mother died because of her grief. That wasn't quite how it happened. (Alberta's friend Chris Albertson once asked her why she repeatedly told the story of her life with details that she knew were inaccurate. She told him that it was easier to repeat her version rather than hang herself by trying to go back to the facts. Let her biographer hang himself in the tangled web.)

There's no doubt that Alberta was deeply affected by her mother's death. But it's also true that she tried to keep making a living as she knew how to. She was back onstage that summer of 1954 in a road show of *Mamba's Daughters*, again in the role of Dolly, with Ethel Waters in the lead.

Then, on September 9, 1954, she reported for rehearsals of *Mrs. Patterson* at the Booth Theater in New York. Alberta expected to receive a major part in the play and was probably responsible for several press reports to that effect. As it turned out, she became an understudy for Helen Dowdy in the role of Bessie Bolt, a "blues-shouting" singer and gambling old lady who has sinned her life away in Chicago and whom the devil (Avon Long) has condemned to live in a tree.

The tree stands in the dusty yard of a ramshackle house in Kentucky, where a poor teenaged girl, Teddy Hicks, enacted by Eartha Kitt, yearns to grow up and live like her mother's elegant white employer, played by Enid Markey (the first Jane of Tarzan movies) with a gooey southern accent.

The play went to Detroit and Chicago for ten weeks of trials. The only press Alberta received that whole time was when the *Chicago Defender* carried a photo of her showing her scrapbook of yellowed newspaper clippings at a reunion with Floyd Cummings Edgerton ("Miss Florida"), the schoolteacher who had brought her as a child from Memphis to Chicago, and Helen Winston Phillips, the friend who had taken her in and arranged for her first job in a boarding-house. Alberta was certainly a long way from those days of peeling potatoes, but she knew the "climbing to higher ground" was now at an end.

She was again working at a job where she was told what to do, when. When the company packed its bags, she packed hers and watched quietly from the wings as the press and the audiences raved over a newborn star. She didn't even get to play the role of the woman up the tree because the actress she understudied for that part was never absent. In fact, Eartha Kitt doesn't even remember Alberta's ever having been associated with the play.

Mrs. Patterson opened in New York at the National Theater on West Forty-first Street on December 1, 1954. The play itself, by Charles Sebree and Greer Johnson, received poor reviews. " 'Mrs. Patterson' never really achieves the lift it aspires to," concluded the *New York Times* (December 2, 1954, p. 37). But, the reviewer said, as did most others, Eartha Kitt, making her debut onstage, "deserves a career in the theater."

"Miss Kitt seethes with a threatening energy, writhes, slithers and plunges abruptly across the stage like an animated warning of impending high winds," said the *New York Herald Tribune* (December 12, 1954, section 4, p. 1).

Vinie Burrows, who was in the cast, said of Alberta, "She was perfectly content just to collect her salary. She had already had a rich career. I don't know why she was even with the company." But no one felt sorry for her, Vinie said. "She didn't feel sorry for herself." Everyone liked her because she "always had a smile" and was "totally unassuming." She dressed "Salvation Army" style but would encourage the young women in the cast who were starting out to dress glamorously to promote both their careers and their marriages. "She loved to do things for people," Vinie said, whether it was getting someone a cup of coffee or giving a musician or stage doorman some change just to help him out.

The play closed in New York on February 26, 1955. The black newspapers said it was due to Eartha Kitt's having a kidney ailment. Ten days before the last performance *Variety* (February 16, 1955, p. 57) announced the play was doomed, saying it "has been playing to diminishing grosses for the past few weeks."

Vinie Burrows said Eartha wanted to see the engagement come to an end since it wasn't a success and would say to cast members, just before curtain time, "Let's get this abortion over with."

Alberta said *Mrs. Patterson* closed because Eartha Kitt wanted to be with someone she was crazy about in California. "I understood her. But it was dumb for her to close the show 'cause we all could use the money."

Eartha Kitt said she had to leave the show because she was indeed very ill at the time. Whatever happened, she was very much on her feet and in New York on April 21, 1955, the evening she opened at the Copacabana for a three-week engagement. There she was, the black press pointed out, in a new wardrobe of skintight gowns, singing in her sultry voice, "I Want to Be Evil."

Alberta thought Eartha was evil because she tried to establish the reputation of being the "first colored girl singing in languages." She said: "I'm not going to let her have it. Alberta Hunter is going to stop that jive. I'm the first. I'm the one. So put that down, hear? I went to Berlitz School so I could learn French correctly before Eartha Kitt was even born."

Alberta may have been the first black polyglot singer, but her languages didn't help her much that year getting jobs or publicity in the press. She applied for unemployment benefits as of March 1, 1955.

In January 1956 Alberta joined the company of a play titled *Debut*, written by Mary Drayton and based on Isabel Dunn's book *Maria and the Captain*. Inger Stevens, a beautiful blond Swedish-born television star, was cast as Maria Beraud, a southern belle who, on the night of her coming-out party, seduces a visiting Yankee newspaper correspondent by the name of Wyn Spaulding (played by British actor Tom Helmore). Alberta had the misfortune to be Mattie, a "happy Negro servant," who throughout the play remains offstage and sings a spiritual before each scene.

The company tried out in Princeton on February 1 (the day a black woman, Autherine Lucy, made history by enrolling at the University of Alabama) and for two weeks as of February 6 in Boston. On February 22, 1956, the play opened in New York at the Holiday Theater at Broadway and Forty-seventh Street. Five performances later, on Saturday night, February 26, the play closed.

Again Alberta had her own peculiar explanation of what happened. "It closed," she said, "because there was a little jealousy there between performers about their acting and billing."

It was "a mild, innocuous comedy of the South," with "Southern accents broader than the Jersey turnpike," said Whitney Bolton in his review for the *Morning Telegraph* (February 24, 1956), which probably best explains the production's real problem.

It finally occurred to Alberta that she was never going to be a star on Broadway or anywhere else. Furthermore, she simply had had enough of the entertainment world. As she said, "the music just left me." Besides, she added, thinking of the highlights of her career, "I did well the whole time I was in show business. Fortunately. I went as far as you could go. I played Broadway. I played the Drury Theater in London. I played the Casino de Paris and the National Scala in Copenhagen. People would come to me and want me to go in a show," she said of this period in the mid-fifties. "I didn't feel I could do justice to what they wanted me to do. I wasn't going to sing anymore because I didn't want to spoil what I had done. I wanted people to remember me as I was. On top."

So one day, with no fanfare, Alberta Hunter quit. Bam. As she did everything else. And there was no way of talking her out of her decision.

"No, baby."

CHAPTER EIGHT

Caring for the Sick
and the Poor

By the time that *Debut* closed, Alberta was already preparing her own coming out to an entirely different career.

Her mother's death had made her think about how she could "help humanity."

Although she had shown interest in doing volunteer work at Harlem Hospital in 1943, Alberta had not been especially fond of hospitals. "There was a time I couldn't go near a hospital," she said. "They were using that old medicine, that old, funny, stinking stuff."

Either the foul-smelling medicine was no longer in use, or her attitude had changed by 1955, when she became a volunteer worker at the Joint Diseases Hospital on Madison Avenue at 123d Street in Harlem. She became a permanent fixture at the hospital and dug into any task she was given. She was enthusiastic and sincerely interested in helping, said Elizabeth Styres, director of volunteers at the hospital. "And she was always smiling, a very warm smile, not a silly grin. Her heart was in everything she did. She was interested in learning everything."

Alberta even sat in on some nursing classes at the hospital. She saved pages of neatly written notes about everything from preparing a formula and bathing an infant to the delivery of a baby without a doctor. "I think she was trying to find out if she would really enjoy working as a nurse," said Styres.

Alberta liked working in a hospital even though she got in trouble with some of the nurses because she was so dedicated. "They started kicking on me," she said. "I used to go there and grab those babies and start working on them. They said they didn't have anything to do because I was doing all the work."

Alberta put in so many hours (1,958) in one twelve-month period that the hospital on May 24, 1956, named her Volunteer of the Year and gave her a pin and a carnation as thanks. Even more heartwarming to her was the name the children gave her: Hospital Mommy.

It became clear to her though that to do anything more than the most basic duties in a hospital, she would have to get some academic credentials. So, at the end of 1955, she boned up for and took the city's elementary school equivalency examination. She received an overall score of 88. (Her highest individual score on the test battery was a 94 in English.) On December 16, 1955, she received her diploma.

Armed with those good results and her youthful spirit, she approached the head of nurses at the hospital and asked if she could enter the training program. The woman in charge of the program interviewed her. She had her doubts about Alberta's physical stamina, so she asked a doctor to join her in examining her. She ran her hand down Alberta's spine. "She shook her head," said Alberta. "I saw her. She didn't know I saw her. And they refused me."

"She was quite hurt about that, especially after having put in all that time as a volunteer," said Elizabeth Styres.

"They turned me down because I was too old to start as a nurse," Alberta said. "But I never give up." So late one Friday afternoon early in 1956 she went to the YWCA school on 137th Street and asked to speak with the director, Phyllis Utz. "I tried to get her to make an appointment for a regular student interview, telling her that I was finished for the day," said Utz. "As I stood up and walked toward the door, she grabbed my arm. When I turned to her, she started to cry." Alberta's life onstage hadn't been wasted.

"I asked her what her name was, and she replied, 'Alberta Hunter.'

Unfortunately," said Phyllis Utz, "I had never heard the name before. When I questioned her as to why she was crying, she told me the story of her life in the show business world and said now she was too old to travel. Then she told me one of my former students had told her to come and see me."

Alberta asked to enroll in the course to train licensed practical nurses (LPNs). " 'But, Miss Hunter,' I said. 'You are too old to take this course. I have a license to protect.' I asked her for her birth certificate or her baptismal record, and then she cried and pleaded with me to please give her a chance."

Alberta told Utz that she didn't know how to do housework and couldn't think of "working, cleaning, cooking, and doing menial labor from sunup to sundown."

"She would not leave until I promised to think it over," Utz said. Alberta said she would come back on the following Monday for her answer. On Monday there was Alberta Hunter with one dozen yellow roses for Phyllis Utz. Alberta was not one to buy flowers for anyone. She hated flowers.

Alberta detected right away that it was going to take more than a bouquet to get her way. "Just give me a chance," she pleaded again. "I can't turn to anyone else. I like people. I think I can be a good nurse."

After an hour of more cajoling Utz agreed to accept Alberta. She gave her an application to fill out. "I put her age back," Phyllis Utz said (by twelve years), "so as to sneak her into the program." She didn't feel too guilty doing that because, as she pointed out, "There are so many people who don't want to try."

Alberta certainly didn't feel bad about the subterfuge. The year before, she had clipped a news article that said a woman was not required by law to give her age when applying for a job. So she wasn't doing anything illegal, not that this consideration had ever entered her mind in earlier years, when she fudged in reporting her age.

Alberta submitted three letters of recommendation: one from her minister, the Reverend Louis S. White; another from Harold C. Burton, the Republican district leader in Harlem; and a third from Lawrence Phillips, executive vice-president of USO-Camp Shows, Inc. In his covering letter to her, dated April 14, 1956, Phillips wrote, "I know of no one to whom I could give a letter of recommendation with more pleasure and sincerity of statement than to you."

Alberta enrolled with twenty-three other women in the next class, which met during the day. Most of her classmates were in their thirties and forties, worked at night, were either married or separated, and had families to support. Most of them knew nothing of Alberta's background. "She didn't want anybody to know of her past career for fear they might think she was given special attention," Phyllis Utz said.

Alberta's performance in school and later as an LPN didn't disappoint her sponsor. "In all my years in the nursing profession I have never met a more conscientious person," she said. Alberta was never late or absent from school.

Alberta bought every book recommended in class, including *Simplified Arithmetic for Nurses*. "Be sure to get this one," she wrote in her school notebook. Harry Watson said he had never seen her so serious, with textbooks scattered all over her apartment.

Her notes were as careful as her study habits. During a class on blue babies, taught on May 31, 1956, by Phyllis Utz, she wrote with very neat penmanship: "A collective term applied to infants having congenital heart defects which cause persistent cyanosis following birth. These defects cause insufficient oxygenation of the blood by either obstruction or bypassing pulmonary circulation." She also listed the qualities of a good nurse, among them: healthy state of mind and body, a sense of humor, a love of nursing and people, and "the ability to adjust to new situations, ask God's help at all times."

She didn't include neatness in appearance, but she took that for granted. She polished her white shoes every night and was immaculate every day with a freshly laundered and crisply ironed uniform. "She was as proud as a peacock in that uniform," said Utz. "The one thing she had was determination. She tried so hard. I spent more time tutoring her than anyone."

Alberta did very well on class exercises and easily passed the psychometric test, which, she liked to point out, several of the high school graduates in the course flunked. But she wasn't the smartest in the class, she said. "Some of these old girls had good heads on them, honey."

One of them was a little too smart. "When I'd go to make up the bed, my corners were bad," Alberta admitted. "She, and this old lady, the instructor, they'd get together on me. They hated me because they found out I had been in show business, and they got kind of envious and mean. They did everything they could to try to hurt me, but they didn't. That old man up there. He was behind me. When I had to solve those problems and put together different amounts of things, I wouldn't get no paper and pencil. What is so-and-so-and-so? And I'd say it right quick. I've always been a good mathematician. And I'd give 'em the answer."

The capping ceremony was on August 14, 1956. Phyllis Utz asked Alberta to lead the procession down the aisle of the school's auditorium and sing a song she had written several years earlier, "I Want to Thank You Lord." She sang the words as no one else ever did:

> *I want to thank you Lord for my blessings,*
> *For ev'rything you've done for me from day to day,*
> *I want to thank you again for the sunshine,*
> *That you sent along to roll the clouds away.*
> *Let me thank you again for understanding,*
> *And the will to always lend a helping hand.*
> *To some poor soul I chance to meet along life's highway,*
> *These are my humble thanks to you oh Lord, amen.*

Just remembering the emotion of that night, of the elation she'd felt when an official put the nurse's cap on her head, brought rare tears to her eyes nearly thirty years later. "That was the happiest night of my life," she said. "To think that I had been chosen to be a rescuer for my God."

All the graduates who wanted to pursue their training for licenses had to apply for six-month internships in basic nursing procedures. The city operated such a program under the coordination of Marion Cooper, director of the Central School, located at Goldwater Hospital on Welfare Island (renamed Roosevelt Island in 1973). Cooper accepted Alberta, but only by overruling some of her assistants, who thought that Alberta, whatever her real age, was too old to be considered. "I don't know this lady at all, but she seems a very serious person and a practical person," she told her staff. "I don't care if you recommend her or not. I'm going to give her a chance." Then, when Alberta did so well, she happily told the same doubting Thomases, "You see, you can't exclude someone just because of her age."

As an intern Alberta was assigned at different times to work at several hospitals, including Goldwater, Harlem, and Bellevue.

On April 23, 1957, at the conclusion of that stage, she received a certificate saying she had satisfactorily completed the practical nurse's training program. She was able to go to work on a temporary permit pending results of the state board examination that summer. Alberta passed the exam and received her license on August 7, 1957.

Marion Cooper asked her good friend Dolly Craven, director of nurses at Goldwater, to hire Alberta. She did, and on May 16, 1957, Alberta reported for work.

The hospital thought it had a fifty-year-old woman on its hands starting a career as an LPN, a rarity at that. Few of the staff knew she had been a famous entertainer, and no one guessed she was really sixty-two.

Alberta wanted no special treatment. So she moved to the nurses' residence near the hospital, occupying a Spartan room that was big enough for a small bed, a night table, and a desk. She kept pretty much to herself. Craven and Cooper had apartments on the top floor of the same building.

Dolly Craven liked music and knew of Alberta's former career. Through her, Marion Cooper came to know more of Alberta and of her past. "I thought she was such an unusual person," she said. "She was very gracious, courteous, kind, and sympathetic," in contrast with many of the students in her program, who "were young and giddy." Alberta worked as a nurse the same way Cooper heard she had sung, she said, "giving it everything she had."

Goldwater Hospital was not the kind of place most younger nurses wanted to work. The patients for the most part were elderly and suffering from chronic diseases. But Alberta preferred it to the other hospitals where she had worked briefly as an intern. "The atmosphere was a little different," she said. "The staff at Goldwater were more settled. They were family people. They were so kind, and they really cared about nursing. Not like some of those lazy chicks you see at other hospitals."

Alberta got along with everyone, which is not to say that she was close to everyone. One of the supervisors, a Miss Shorter, was "not to be fooled with," she said. "Talk about evil. She was a business-woman. If she asked, 'What is the blood pressure supposed to be?' you didn't say something like 'I think . . .' Don't you *think* with Miss Shorter. Nooo, baby. With her you had to know what you were talking about. Miss Shorter didn't take no tea for the fever. We loved her, but she was strict."

Alberta wasn't one to be fooled around with either, said Howard Garrison, associate director of nurses, a soft-spoken man who keeps a photo of Alberta on his office wall. "Everyone respected her and treated her in a more formal way because of the way she carried herself. She was not a person to play around or to joke." But she had an excellent rapport with the staff, he said, because "she would pitch in and do the work of nurse's aides."

More important was the way she got along with patients. "Nurses can all be proficient," Garrison said. "But what sets them apart is the caring they have and show for their patients. Alberta was very warm and very caring. She was as good a nurse as she was an entertainer. Maybe there's some parallel there, in that to do both well, you have to make people feel good. In bathing people and giving them food or medicine, it's the same process."

Few people knew how old she was. Anyone who found out couldn't believe it, said Garrison, "because she functioned at a level that was comparable to that of LPNs thirty-five or forty years old."

Alberta never let her own stubbornness interfere with her job. "She was strong-willed," said Margaret Weeks, associate director of nursing at Goldwater. "But once Alberta knew why certain policies had to be adhered to or why something couldn't be done a certain way, she understood it, and then she followed it. She was not one to go deliberately against policies."

She followed rules and regulations to the T, and not even a doctor was going to make her do otherwise. One day one of the many foreign doctors at Goldwater at the time called Marion Cooper to complain about Alberta. He had ordered Alberta to give some medication to a patient. Alberta said, "Nothing doing." Only a registered nurse was permitted to give it. "That's the type of individual she was," said Cooper. "She wouldn't break a rule for anybody. Most LPNs would have gone ahead and done it. Not Miss Hunter."

On another occasion a Haitian doctor gave her hell in French because she wouldn't do something irregular that he wanted her to. Was he ever surprised when she scolded him right back—in his own language!

Her shift on D Ward started every afternoon at three-thirty, but Alberta would show up at two-thirty and wait impatiently out in the hall to go on duty. "She liked her ward to be nice and straight when she took it over, and she left it the same way," said Mildred Crisp Littles, associate director of nursing at the time. She remembers meeting Alberta on a bus on Roosevelt Island and telling her how much she liked blues music. She told Alberta she'd grown up listening to Bessie Smith records played on a windup Victrola. Alberta then took something out of her pocketbook and showed it to her; it was a royalty check for "Down Hearted Blues."

Littles knew Bessie's version of that song with her "low-key, moaning" style. "Sometimes you get depressed after listening to Bessie," she said. She preferred Alberta's version of the song, once she heard it, because it was upbeat. "Alberta's blues make you feel elated and up," she said. "It has a jumping-type beat to it. It gives you an uplift. You don't feel down. It makes you want to dance."

Alberta's spirit at work was just as sprightly, she said. She became very familiar with all her patients and was as devoted to them as they were to her. She wasn't a clock watcher and never minded putting in overtime.

"I didn't care what time my time was up," Alberta said. Her shift ended at midnight. "If my patient was restless, I'd stay there and try to soothe my patient to sleep, no matter how long it took. Then, when they'd go to sleep, I'd go on home."

She treated all the patients well, but she had her favorites, all of them men. "Like old Steve. He was such a nice man. I'd say, 'Steve, how you feel?' I could see he was so uncomfortable. He had multiple sclerosis. I'd turn him over and change him as many times as I could and put nice clean clothes on him—just keeping my patients looking fine. I wouldn't go home unless they were all dry. I put myself in their place.

"When I came home, I'd sleep like a dog because I knew I had done my best. I knew I had brought some comfort to somebody else. That's the reason nursing meant so much to me."

Another of Alberta's pet patients was Louis Calamaras, better known at the hospital as Louie the Greek. She and he had a great deal in common. Both lived pretty much alone. Both were individualistic, inquisitive, sassy, and optimistic. She found her challenge in trying to keep him in line.

"She was a very, very strict nurse, what you'd call a disciplinarian," Calamaras said. "She used to try to put me to bed." He wouldn't stand for that, because either he didn't want to get in bed when she wanted him to, or as was also the case, he didn't want her to risk hurting herself trying to lift his weight.

She also tried to give extra food to her patients from a cart that was pushed around the ward periodically, but a supervisor stopped that, said Calamaras, "because it wasn't her duty."

Alberta would even come in to see her patients on her day off. Her presence would help quell impending rebellions. Nurses on her ward would hear patients say, "Miss Hunter doesn't do it that way," or "Miss Hunter doesn't do that." The "substitute" would respond: "Yeah, but this isn't Miss Hunter."

Now and then a supervisor would take Alberta off "her" ward to fill in for someone absent on another one. When that happened, Alberta would ask to be sent to the employees' health service unit, which would verify that she had high blood pressure at the time and shouldn't work that day anywhere.

Otherwise she was always in a good mood, Marion Cooper said. "She could laugh out of this world, even at herself. She would say, 'Wasn't I stupid to do that?' especially when she tried to cook something. One day she told me she tried to make greens by frying them in a pan with some bacon. I said, 'Oh, girl, you don't make greens that way. You need to cook them with a stick of lean.' "

More often Alberta was buying fresh strawberries and asparagus, liver and onions, pork chops or steaks and bringing them back to give Marion Cooper or Dolly Craven, people she always addressed by their last names. They had a maid who cooked for them. Alberta always declined invitations to share meals with them in their apartments in the nurses' residence. They would prepare a dish of food and send it down to Alberta's room. When they asked her once why she didn't accept their hospitality, she said she kept herself at a distance because she respected their being in positions of authority. That was true, but in addition, Alberta, as she grew older, liked to be by herself when she was eating—if not most of the time when she wasn't working.

She was much more content doing other little things for them. Marion Cooper was frequently at her desk late in the evenings and had little time for clothes shopping. Knowing that Alberta loved to go shopping, she often asked her to pick out a frilly blouse, a dress, or shoes for her. She paid for the purchases except when Alberta insisted that she wanted to give her something as a present. Alberta gave her a black pearl ring she had bought years earlier in Japan, and when Cooper had her twenty-fifth anniversary as an employee of the hospital, Alberta gave her a ring with a diamond bigger than a pea. When Cooper discovered her mother had mistakenly thrown out the diamond ring with some old rhinestone buckles, she told Alberta what had happened.

"Why, that's nothing," Alberta told her. "It doesn't matter."

All that really mattered to Alberta at that time was her new career. She became so involved with nursing that she severed most of her ties to the entertainment world and the people in it. Journalist Allan McMillan said she became a "recluse" and wouldn't answer his telephone calls to her. Maude Russell said Alberta "hibernated" for twenty years and wouldn't let anyone go to see her. Many people thought she had died. When Sheldon Harris contacted her in August 1975 to include her in a biographical dictionary of the world's blues singers, he said he had been trying to find her for years.

Alberta did stay in touch with a few friends. W. C. Handy wrote her and thanked her for her greetings on his eighty-fourth birthday on November 16, 1957, months before he died. He told her how proud he was to have received best wishes also from President Eisenhower and New York's Governor W. Averell Harriman.

She also wrote her old friend Lovie Austin the year after she had started at Goldwater. "I wish I could find words to tell you how proud I am of you," Lovie replied on May 25, 1958. "Few girls in your position would devote their lives to the sick. God will bless you and I will pray for you. Keep up the good work." She said Alberta wouldn't recognize Chicago anymore, not as they had known it together. "They're building so many skyscrapers, I have to rub my eyes to make sure it's still Chicago."

Andy Razaf wrote her on November 26, 1960, having heard from his friend Marion Cooper of Alberta's whereabouts and said, "If your nursing is half as good as your singing, you have to be tops."

Somerset Maugham, ill and ninety-two years old, wrote her on March 3, 1965, from Cap Ferrat, France, thanking her for her "charming letter" and good wishes. Pearl Bailey thanked Alberta for a get-well card. "Bless your sweet heart for writing to me while I was in the hospital," she said in a letter dated March 29, 1965.

On October 24, 1967, Alberta wrote President Lyndon B. Johnson:

> I am a loyal American Negro, and I speak for many millions of others like myself. I am writing this letter to let you know that we are praying and asking God to help you bear the burdens that are on your shoulders.
>
> We know that you have done and are doing everything you can to help us. There are some ingrates, but the majority of us understand what you are going through.
>
> We suffer when some of us do mean things. We do not approve of rioting and looting, for we know it does our cause a lot of harm.
>
> We have come a long way since you've been [in] office and we appreciate it.
>
> May God bless and keep you and your wonderful family.

In 1969 it was Alberta who was getting blessed. Bricktop wrote from Rome that she had "the most beautiful papal blessing for you" and that she would personally deliver it in a month or so when she was back in New York. It said: "Most Holy Father, Ada Smith Du Conge, most humbly presents herself before you to get Your Apostolic Blessing on her friend Alberta Hunter as a pledge of divine favour and future happiness." Alberta didn't know what to make of these words, not sounding the least bit like the torrent of cursing she was used to hearing from Bricktop.

Ivan Browning wrote in December 1972 of how happy he was to have seen Alberta on her recent vacation in California. He thanked her for her gift to him of a ten-dollar check, a handsome amount for her since she had paid six dollars a night to stay at a Salvation Army residence on her trip. "Yes, Bert, true friendship means so much in life especially as we get older," he wrote. He also told her he had heard the Jackson Five singing what he thought was her version of "You Gotta Reap What You Sow." He wanted to make sure they had received permission to use it. He also reported that Noble Sissle and Andy Razaf were seriously ill.

Over the years a few others wrote trying to lure Alberta back to the stage or the recording studios. Langston Hughes wrote on January 29, 1959, that a United Artists representative would be contacting her in the hope that she might be willing to sing some of his blues songs for an album. About the same time the Canadian Broadcasting Corporation asked her to tape some of her music for it. And Richard Pleasant, managing director of the McCarter Theater of Princeton, New Jersey, asked her on May 7 of that year to get in touch with him about some plans he had. She didn't follow up on any of these requests (although she did do a taped interview with the CBC later in 1966). She had, in fact, stopped singing. She even canceled her membership in Actors' Equity.

She wrote P. L. Prattis at the *Pittsburgh Courier* on September 12, 1961, "I get many offers to go back in show business, but I love my present profession and do not care to give it up. . . . I think it is nicer to bow out gracefully and not have people say, my Lord, is she still here?"

Her retirement from show business didn't stop her from going to Broadway shows, often taking with her as a guest a co-worker from the hospital who had never been to see a play. She also went to concerts of favorite singers like Mahalia Jackson, Lena Horne, and

Ella Fitzgerald, who recorded Alberta's "Down Hearted Blues" at the end of 1963. Alberta also went to an occasional benefit, such as the one Victoria Spivey gave in 1964 in honor of the memory of Mamie Smith, or to a fashionable party like the one Jimmy Daniels threw for Josephine Baker that same year.

Only one person managed to get Alberta singing again. That was Chris Albertson, a jazz critic who had moved to New York in 1957. One day in 1961 he looked for her name in the Manhattan telephone book and was surprised to find her listed. He called and asked her to record for Prestige Records along with two other old blues singers, Lucille Hegamin and Victoria Spivey. The name of the album was to be *Songs We Taught Your Mother*. She was flattered but told him she wasn't even humming in the bathtub anymore.

Chris put on the charm, telling her he was from Denmark and—

Well, he didn't need to say another word. Denmark. She told him how she loved the Danes more than anyone on earth. They all had been so wonderful to her. He had her in the bag.

Alberta and the other singers met at Rudy Van Gelder's studio in Englewood Cliffs, New Jersey, on August 16, 1961. They were reunited with musicians they hadn't seen for years: Buster Bailey (clarinet), J. C. Higginbotham (trombone), Gene Brooks (drums), Henry Goodwin (trumpet), Cliff Jackson (piano), Zutty Singleton (drums), Cecil Scott (clarinet), Sidney de Paris (tuba), and Willie ("The Lion") Smith (piano).

"I didn't know what to expect," Chris said. He had only heard Alberta's old recordings. "I hadn't heard Alberta sing in all those years. I was amazed at the voice I heard. Her voice had gotten deeper with age, which is normal. It happens a lot with singers."

The album included such numbers as "St. Louis Blues," sung by Lucille; "Let Him Beat Me," by Victoria; and "Got Myself a Workin' Man," by Alberta. Jimmy Rushing, a blues singer who came up from Kansas City with Count Basie's band and who accompanied the session with his friend Chris, said afterward, "Ain't that a bitch, forty years in the business and they're stronger than ever."

Chris liked working with Alberta so much that he asked her to join in another recording for Riverside in Chicago on her way to a vacation in Los Angeles. The two-record album, *Chicago: The Living Legends*, included vocalists Little Brother Montgomery, eighty-four-year-old Mama Yancey, and Blind John Davis and instrumentalists Lil Armstrong, Lovie Austin, Earl ("Fatha") Hines, Al Wynn, Banjo Ikey Robinson, Ted Butterman, Jimmy Archey, and Pops Foster. Clarinetist Darnell Howard, an old-timer, was so taken aback seeing Alberta again that he said to her, "Didn't you die?"

"No, honey," she said. She showed him and the others that she was very much alive and as professional as ever. Chris had just a few hours in between her trains to have her photographed with Lovie (in front of a dilapidated house on Chicago's South Side) for the album cover and to record Alberta singing eight songs. Nothing to it. She just got up there in front of the microphone and did it as she always had.

When it came time to do "Down Hearted Blues," Lovie, with the inevitable cigarette dangling from the corner of her mouth, looked up from the piano bench at Alberta and said, "We'll do it the way we did the last time." The last time was the first time they did it together in 1922!

"Isn't she a killer?" Alberta said.

From a technical standpoint the recording session that took place that afternoon of September 1, 1961, at the Prince Hall Masonic Temple was a "disaster," said Chris. "The mobile control unit that they sent from New York was late coming in. And the two engineers they did send had never recorded music. Not only that, they hated it. They were around the corner, so I couldn't hear the sound as it went on the tape. They kept running out of tape. Then a Chicago radio station entered on the wire. The trombone was louder than Alberta, and we had to rush because Alberta had to catch a train."

The critics didn't seem to notice the little problems. They liked what they heard. John S. Wilson said Alberta's voice was "now darker and heavier but no less apt in its phrasing" (*New York Times*, December 24, 1961, p. 16).

"Provided you are not irretrievably unnerved by the mere thought of a 65-year-old hospital nurse singing 'I'll Always Be in Love with You,' you may agree with me that the experience itself is the most rewarding to date in the continuing series of recordings on the Riverside label . . ." said Patrick Scott of the *Toronto Globe and Mail* (September 1, 1962, p. 15). He noted that her accompanists had a hard time keeping up with her.

Wilder Hobson, in "The Amen Corner" for *Saturday Review* (January 27, 1962, pp. 54–55), wrote of Alberta's singing: "This is the blues sung by a formidable spirit who conquers the disconsolate mood while she is singing about it. . . ."

One more time, in October 1971, Chris got Alberta out of her uniform to meet with Danish television producer Per Møller Hansen and be filmed for a series called *Faces in Jazz*. She received a fee of $1,150, cash, which at the time represented about two months' salary at the hospital.

Each time Chris heard Alberta sing he was astounded by the strength of her voice. "You wouldn't believe she had stopped singing," he said.

Alberta wasn't the least bit surprised. "I never abused my voice," she explained. "I've always gotten rest. I don't drink or smoke and never did. So I always preserved my health."

A few people at the hospital read reviews of her new records. Only then did they realize that Alberta had been a famous entertainer. "Every now and then a colleague would find out I had been a singer and would think I must not have been doing so well to be emptying bedpans. I'd just smile to myself. I've always kept my feet on the ground.

"They couldn't understand why I didn't mention it to them," Alberta said. "The only thing that was important to me then was that I was trying to do something to help my fellow man. Where I was concerned, it didn't mean a thing for people to say, 'Well, she's been in show business.' I was thinking whether one of my patients was uncomfortable."

If people had heard anything about Alberta, it was that she had made a lot of money in her time as a performer and had squirreled most of it away. Yet, if they asked to borrow fifty cents from her, she wrote on the back of an envelope a reminder that they owed her that amount. And she reminded them if they didn't pay up. There wasn't going to be any soft touch with her.

Alberta's reputation as a miser was nourished by scenes like that. Economical she was. Baby Doo Caston, her USO colleague, had a good explanation for her behavior: "Alberta Hunter knew, like I know and you know, that when you get a dollar in your pocket, it talks loud. You need to save for a rainy day. Because it will rain. And if you haven't made shelter, you gonna get wet. You find people who don't give away money always have it. And those that don't have it resent those that do."

Alberta did skimp on herself. She could well afford to take taxis, for instance, but would take the bus instead. But many times it was on such a bus that her little-known charity would begin.

She described one of many incidents that people like Harry Watkins often witnessed. One very cold winter day she saw a young girl with schoolbooks on the bus going up Broadway to Harlem. "She was just ragged," said Alberta. "Her clothes looked so bad, and I felt so sorry for her. So I went over to her and said, 'Miss, excuse me, but will you accept—take what I'm giving you and not get angry?' "

The girl said, "What is it?"

"I'm a nurse," Alberta replied, "and sometimes a lot of us nurses get together. We get a lot of nice things together that we don't want to throw away. We want to give them to some worthy person." (She would go out of her way not to embarrass anyone she helped.) "Would you accept some things if I get them and send them to you?" Alberta gave the girl her name so that her mother would know who she was when she called to tell her what she wanted to do. There was no phone at home, the girl said. So Alberta took down her address and sent the girl's mother a note that she would be sending some clothes and asked to call Alberta at the nurses' residence.

"When the mother called me, I knew it was all right, see," Alberta said. She asked for the daughter's size, so she could send clothes that would fit. The girl was a plump size 18. Alberta bought several nice, warm things and mailed them to the mother to give her daughter. On another occasion she asked the mother to meet her so she could give her some money to buy her daughter a Christmas present.

Alberta's good works extended to the grandchildren of her sister, La Tosca. She sent box after box of pretty new clothes to them. The mothers of the two sets of children rarely called or wrote to acknowledge the gifts. So Alberta then called them to ask if the packages arrived. "Why do you keep sending things?" Marion Cooper asked, surprised that she would do so when she received so little thanks.

"Well, I feel sorry for the children," Alberta said. Of the seven kids of June and Sam Sharp, Jr., those who were old enough to write often did to thank their aunt for her generosity.

When Rachel, the eighteen-year-old daughter, was killed in a traffic accident in Texas in 1971, it was Aunt Alberta who paid the funeral expenses. She sent her grandnephew Sam Sharp III and his fiancée five hundred dollars for their wedding present in 1975 and gave other young relatives the money they needed—as much as fifteen hundred dollars at a time—to pay off debts.

She would also send money now and then to close friends when she knew they could use it, people like Lovie Austin, Nettie Compton, Helen Phillips, and Floyd Edgerton.

And she loved to clip coupons for people who might be able to use them. Chris Albertson received many a call asking if his dog, Bessie (named after Bessie Smith, whose biography he wrote), liked Alpo or some other brand of food for which Alberta happened to have a coupon or if he liked a certain kind of cookie. He still has unopened envelopes she sent him stuffed with coupons.

Alberta never looked for much in the way of thanks from those she helped. She said she "got back many blessings" in return in other ways, such as the break Phyllis Utz and Marion Cooper had given her in allowing her to become a nurse. She felt lucky. "A lot of people do good things, but they don't get these blessings." So grateful was she that up to the time she died she would call Cooper and talk to her for forty or fifty minutes on the phone, something she did with no one else.

Alberta was always generous in thanking those who had helped her all along the way. Arthur Dickson, the pimp in Chicago, was one of them. "He was so nice to me," she said. "I've written him several times to say hello and always thanked them for the nice things they did for me when I was trying to get a start."

She also went to the bedside of Joe Glaser before he died in June

1969. Glaser, former owner of the Sunset Café in Chicago and manager of Louis Armstrong, was a close friend of Alberta's. She went so far as to say that he "might have been a gangster," but, more important to her, "If you were a lady, Joe Glaser treated you like a lady."

She added: "All those gangsters were nice fellows. In their way they might have been cruel, but they were all very kind to people. You know, they might have the ones that they wanted to get rid of or something like that, but they were big-hearted and gentlemen. I bet you those gangsters have given up more money to charity than anybody else."

Alberta donated a lot of her own money to a number of groups. In the late 1950s, when her weekly salary was no more than sixty-five dollars a week, she started sending two-, five-, or ten-dollar checks to them. She saved canceled checks to some thirty-five such institutions, from the American Bible Society to the Fresh Air Fund to the Xavier Society for the Blind.

And when others were giving nickels and dimes, if that much, to the National Association for the Advancement of Colored People, Alberta was sending checks for a hundred dollars a year. In 1976 she gave the NAACP five hundred dollars to become a life member.

Alberta also took the time and spent the money to send a telegram to the White House, as she did in 1964, signing her name and those of Harry Watkins and Marion Cooper, supporting the seating of the integrated Mississippi Freedom party representatives as the state's official delegation at the Democratic National Convention.

Her greatest and most prolonged contribution began after she had read an article in the *New York Daily News* on March 23, 1965 (p. 18). It read:

> Tyler, Ala., March 22 (Special)—As the 300 civil rights demonstrators marched past singing "Freedom, Freedom," Negro cotton picker Anson Watts and the 17 members of his family sat on their crumbling porch and waved.
>
> All 18 Wattses live in a three-room tin-top shanty, 25 feet off Highway 80 in Tyler, 12 miles from Selma.

"I just like that march fine," said Anson's daughter, Ruthie, 27, as she cuddled her 7-month-old child, Nathaniel.

LAST YEAR, NOTHING

The Wattses have been share-cropping a 12-acre cotton field for 15 years. They are paid $25 food money a month and $5 for other expenses.

"We're supposed to get a share of the crops, but last year there wasn't enough cotton so we didn't clear nothing," said Ruthie.

The family works year round, planting the cotton seeds in April, cultivating in May and harvesting from August to December.

"All of us old enough to walk are old enough to pick," Ruthie said.

A 15-foot strip of barbed wire hangs across the top of the porch. "We dry our wash on that," Ruthie explained.

Five beds are squeezed into two rooms and a hallway in the gray wooden shanty. The walls are covered with old newspapers, cardboard and sections of blue-flowered wallpaper. A picture of John F. Kennedy hangs in one room and the Crucifixion hangs in another.

A BOWL OF TURNIP GREENS

After the marchers went by little 8-month-old Margaret Anne, daughter of Anson's daughter, Hattie, was put into one of the beds close to one of two fireplaces to keep her warm. The blue sky was visible through a small hole in the ceiling.

Anson went back into the fields to chop some wood.

Two refrigerators in the kitchen in the rear of the shack were set precariously on wooden planks. The dusty ground could be seen between the planks of the floor.

"One of the refrigerators ain't working," Ruthie said, "but the other works if you plug it in and shake it a bit."

EARNS $2.50 A DAY

The refrigerator was stocked with a bowl of turnip greens, lard and globs of butter.

Mrs. Rita Davis, 56-year-old cotton-picking neighbor, came over to the Watts' shack to watch the march. "I hoe my two-acre plot alone for $2.50 a day. Been doing it for four years now," Mrs. Davis said.

"When I pick the cotton I get $2 for every 100 pounds," she said. She didn't know the price on the market.

"Do you think this demonstration will bring about a change of conditions in the Southern black belt?" your reporter asked Ruthie.

"I certainly hope it do," she said.

—John Mallon*

The article certainly made a change in Alberta's life. After clipping it, she contacted the national office of the Salvation Army in New York, sent a check, and asked it through its office in Selma, Alabama, to buy and deliver ten dollars' worth of food staples to the Watts family. The family couldn't believe it when a man drove up with a box filled with flour, meal, lard, meat, and some other items paid for and sent by an anonymous donor from New York. The receipt Alberta requested was dated July 10.

Then she asked the Salvation Army to send her the shoe and clothes sizes of each of Ruthie's children. Alberta sent the first pair of shoes some of those children ever owned. Most of the clothes she sent were purchased new at Macy's in New York. When she realized Ruthie had to walk as far as six miles into Tyler to get groceries, Alberta started sending directly to her boxes and boxes of food. She sent as many as five boxes at a time, sometimes as often as every couple of weeks. This went on for years.

Ruthie sent Alberta what little she could: pecans at Christmas or a couple of sweet potatoes from her garden. But she always sent a thank-you note. Sometimes she struggled to write it herself, but usually she had someone with more schooling do it. The notes were always sincere and heartfelt. She would say how much she, the eight children (one of whom she named Berita Ann at Alberta's suggestion), and her mother and father appreciated what Alberta had sent and how well the clothes fitted. She often said that it was terribly hot and raining or that it was freezing and raining. One of the children typically would have a bad cold or would be in the hospital. Or someone in the neighborhood had been in a fight, the police had killed a man, she was planting corn. But always she wrote that the kids were either in school, getting out of school for vacation, or going back to school. Alberta wrote Ruthie again and again, telling her she must keep those children in school, that they'd get better jobs if they had more education. She told Ruthie of her own struggle in life and eventual success as an entertainer.

"If it weren't for her, my kids wouldn't have gotten as much education as they did," Ruthie said years later.

Other things happened, too. Alberta encouraged Ruthie to start praying. "God can do things for you," Alberta told her.

"She was always talking about the Bible," Ruthie said. "She was a Christian."

Alberta also taught Ruthie to have faith in herself as well, to be more self-confident. "If you make one step, God will make two for you," Alberta told her.

One step she made Ruthie take was to the courthouse to register to vote. "You have to fight for what you want," Alberta kept telling her. Ruthie went to the courthouse nine or ten times, and nine or ten times she ended up in jail.

That was no place to be, said Ruthie. "Sometimes they didn't even put grease in the corn bread."

"Y'all can't give up," Alberta told Ruthie each time she heard that Ruthie was home from jail without her voter registration card.

Ruthie persisted because of the woman in New York who sounded like Moses on the mountain over the telephone. Finally Ruthie was allowed to register to vote. And now that she can vote and does vote, she can go in the courthouse without being arrested. She can even go in the front door of the doctor's office and be waited on in turn, rather than go in the back door and wait hours for all the white people to be helped first. Most important, "we can get better service now from the doctor. There are still places we can't go in, like restaurants," she said in 1985. "The fighting isn't over yet."

That may be so. But for Ruthie Watts there was a sweet victory.

She won her dignity. And all because of the help she got from a little old lady in New York whom she never met.

When asked why Alberta did that, Ruthie responded quietly, "She knew I needed it."

Helping those in need wasn't always a satisfying experience, Alberta discovered. She found another perfect-sounding candidate in an article of August 4, 1970, in the *New York Times*. There was a photo of a sixty-five-year-old grandmother, sitting on the sagging porch of a four-room shack, wallpapered with cardboard to keep out the cold. She and her ninety-year-old crippled husband lived in Eutaw, Greene County, Alabama, the sixth-poorest county in the nation. The total income of the twenty people living in the house was $280 a month. Those old enough to work wanted jobs but couldn't find any. The family had been evicted from a house where the rent was $10 a month because the grandmother had participated in civil rights marches.

Through the county commissioners court Alberta received an estimate of some of the children's sizes. "Since many of the . . . childrens do not ware [sic] shoes or have been unable to purchase their clothes, it has been difficult for me to arrive at sizes," wrote a court employee on September 11, 1970.

The grandmother thanked Alberta nicely for the first boxes that arrived. She got in trouble with her benefactress, however, when she started sending elaborate shopping lists to her. For herself she fancied some "nice" nightgowns to sleep in. For her four beds "four nice big spread" [sic] would do. She preferred food in cans rather than packages. Alberta sent at least one more box of the things she wanted to send. In return she got a thank-you letter repeating the request for the bedspreads.

The grandmother's next letter put the kiss of death on the relationship. She wrote that as soon as she got everything straightened out, she was going to come up "thair. But I don't wont to come whild it cold." In the meantime, she had arranged for her seventeen-year-old granddaughter Ruby Sue to go work for Alberta.

"You can send the tickey in April," she wrote, giving Alberta a month to get ready and perhaps buy another bed and bedspread for her own house. She didn't clarify if Ruby Sue would be bringing her baby along with her. Alberta concluded quickly that she was being hustled. "She thought I was a fool," she said. That was the end of that.

She had had the good sense to put the nurses' residence at the hospital as her home address since it would be obvious to any of the Alabama family who might make it to New York on their own that Alberta didn't have room for them there. She could always hide from them at her new apartment on 139th Street at Riverside Drive, which she bought in 1965 after selling the apartment she had lived in with her mother on 138th Street.

Alberta had maintained that apartment, and Harry Watkins had moved into it, at her suggestion, after her mother's death. She liked going there on her days off from the hospital to get some of his home cooking and to check any mail that might have been sent there.

However, Alberta didn't get on well with the building managers. Late in 1964 she installed an iron gate over a window leading to the fire escape, in violation of a city law, and refused to give them access to her apartment to remove it. In April 1965 their attorney threatened Alberta with legal action if she didn't comply with the law within three days. She was also asked to paint her apartment in accordance with her co-op lease. Alberta didn't like being told what to do, so she sold that apartment and bought the one at Riverside.

Now that she was seventy she figured she had a right to a little peace of mind. About the only notion Alberta had of her advancing age was that she was beginning to outlive so many people who had played an important role in her life.

One of the first to go was Willard Saxby Townsend, who died of a kidney ailment in Chicago on February 3, 1957. Before his death he became the first black on the executive council of the AFL-CIO. The *Pittsburgh Courier* gave him a fitting tribute: ". . . of the hundreds of thousands of Negro members within the rank and file of the giant CIO, none had ever approached the prominence of Mr. Townsend, both on a national and an international level" (February 16, 1957, p. 13). Willard was survived by a second wife, Consuelo, and a son, Willard, Jr., who committed suicide within a year after his father's death.

In 1967 Langston Hughes died. In October 1970 Floyd Edgerton, "Miss Florida," Alberta's accomplice in running away from Memphis, died. Alberta sent a spray of flowers to her family with a note that said, merely, "I will miss you." In 1971 Louis and Lil Armstrong died; in 1972, Lovie Austin and Mahalia Jackson; in 1976, Paul Robeson.

Alberta clipped and saved numerous articles on diets and personal health, suggesting she was trying to take good care of herself and live longer. But she preferred to continue eating what she pleased, including a lot of junk food, and to leave her mortality in the hands of God. She did make a pilgrimage to the Holy Land, possibly an attempt to get a little closer to Him, if not to satisfy an old travel urge. The group tour went to Israel as well as Greece, Cyprus, and Turkey for three weeks in the late spring of 1973. "It was the experience of a lifetime for me retracing the steps of Jesus and the apostle Paul," she said.

Alberta also took a bus trip that year to Cleveland and Memphis to see childhood friends. In Cleveland she stayed at the YWCA, but in Memphis she put on the dog to impress her friends and checked into the Sheraton Peabody.

Alberta held up fairly well during the rest of her nursing career in spite of having arthritis and osteoporosis. She broke a finger in 1970, when a sterilizer fell on her left hand. Four years later an elderly patient pushed her to the floor while she was trying to give him medication. She wasn't the least bit disturbed by the incident, even though it meant her wrist would be in a cast for a month and she would have to miss work for that period of time.

"Some nurses would have been angry with the patient," said Howard Garrison, associate director of nursing at Goldwater. "But not Alberta. She understood that he was confused and that it wasn't a deliberate act." The accident was serious enough that the state awarded her forty-five hundred dollars as compensation for the loss of her left hand for one year.

But even as Alberta neared her eightieth birthday, she was not one to give in to retirement. And she was not alone in her determination. There was Bricktop, admitting to her eighty years, and packing famous patrons into her club again, this time located in a two-story saloon called Soerabaja, located in an elegant town house in the East Sixties in Manhattan.

And Mabel Mercer celebrated her seventy-fifth birthday with four hundred friends at the St. Regis Hotel in New York. She was performing in the hotel's ground-floor bar, which had been renamed the Mabel Mercer Room. ". . . there were roses and tears and bravos so loud they could be heard over on Times Square, and it all came back, that whole lost musical age . . ." wrote Rex Reed for the *Sunday News* (February 16, 1975, p. 7).

Mabel, Alberta's contemporary, was "sitting on her throne," Reed reported, "gently waving a chiffon scarf and singing her windswept songs to a whole new generation of followers . . . listening to Mabel's songs like kids in school.

"In these baffling, bitter times of androgynous monsters in glitter bras, bizarre rock vulgarities, and screeching, dissonant nightmares passing themselves off with a jerk and a groan as musicians while they pass off their reckless, cacophonous fantasies as music, Mabel Mercer is still reminding us of the beauty and value of popular music."

Alberta felt she had to pull her own even after July 3, 1975, when she collapsed on the floor of the Dry Dock Savings Bank. She made no more of the occurrence than to write down in her notebook that it happened that day at 2:00 P.M. She stayed at home for a few days to recover.

Alberta stubbornly refused to retire or even to admit her real age. She worried when she gave a copy of one of her records to Mildred Littles at Goldwater because the cover notes mentioned her birthdate. So she swore her to secrecy. "Now don't you show this to anybody," she said, "because they put my true age on here. And if y'all knew how old I was, you'd put me out of here."

She was put at ease. "Alberta, I'm not going to touch that because that's not my business. If personnel doesn't find out, you can go on as long as you do your job."

"It didn't make any difference to me," Littles said. "So many were doing it. And why should we put a person out of work if they wanted to work and if they can do it and are enjoying it?"

But on January 11, 1977, when Alberta called her to tell her she wasn't feeling good and wouldn't be coming to work, she learned that she was to receive mandatory retirement on April 1, her birthday, because of her age. The hospital's personnel office thought she would be seventy years old on that date. The paperwork was already in process. Because of the New York City budgetary crisis, no request for an extension would be permitted.

Furthermore, Alberta was not to come to work anymore because she had enough accumulated leave to take her to April 1. She would lose it if she didn't take it.

Mildred Littles said Alberta wasn't surprised at the decision. She knew that it was hospital policy and that Littles didn't agree with it. She also knew she had remained there twelve years longer than she was supposed to.

That didn't diminish her disappointment at being forced to end a career she loved and felt herself capable of continuing. "I was really hurt," Alberta said, "because I loved nursing. I loved the thought of having to get up and go to work to serve my patients. That was my heartstring, and I had given my all. It upset me so to think that they have rules that make you leave something that you love."

"The only thing she asked," said Mildred Littles, "was that we give her her certificate of twenty years' service."

Alberta felt that she'd become nothing more than a personnel folder consigned to a musty cabinet of dead files in the hospital's basement. Ironically, Chris Albertson came along just then, asking to interview her at length about her earlier artistic career for the Smithsonian Institution. The taped interviews, conducted in March 1977, for which she was paid two thousand dollars, reveal no bitterness on Alberta's part that her past and present were subjects of historic preservation. She spoke contentedly of her past but gave no inkling of what future she might have, if any.

On April 1, 1977, her birthday, she reluctantly attended her retirement party at the hospital. Co-workers and supervisors from the afternoon shift ate cake and listened as a certificate of appreciation from the New York City Health and Hospitals Corporation was read to her. It said: "To Alberta Hunter on the occasion of retirement from the service of the City of New York in recognition of 20 years of loyalty and devotion to duty and with best wishes for a full and pleasant life."

The message on a card from 103 co-workers was warmer: "You must be very happy looking back on all you've done, the service you have given and the friendships you have won. May the things that you have thought you'd 'someday' like to do work out to make the future especially bright for you. Congratulations."

The nicest tribute to Alberta and her career as a nurse came from Marion Cooper years later as she reflected: "I've never known a more loving, kind, considerate, and tolerant human being."

But all those qualities only got Alberta a final weekly paycheck as an LPN of $220. Reeling from what she considered an injustice, she marched down to the unemployment office and signed up for initial benefits of $95 a week. To qualify for the program, she had to put in her own handwriting the following statement: "I am ready, willing and able to work, and I am actively seeking work." She added, "I would have continued working if I had not been forced to retire."

CHAPTER NINE

Coming Back and Laying It on 'Em

Late in May 1977 Alberta received an engraved invitation from Bobby Short, dapper pianist for New York's sophisticated set at the Café Carlyle. He was throwing a bon voyage party on June 5 for Mabel Mercer, who was going back to England to perform for the first time since World War II. He invited mutual friends like Geraldine Stutz, president of Henri Bendel; Ruth Ellington, Duke's sister; Eugenia Shepard, fashion columnist for the *New York Post*; George Wien, organizer of the Newport Jazz Festival, and his associate Charlie Bourgeois; and author and publisher Earl Blackwell, president of Celebrity Register Ltd. Bobby asked Mabel whom else she wanted to ask. She suggested Alberta, whom Bobby didn't know, but advised him that a little arm twisting might be necessary to get her to the party.

Bobby sent Alberta a formal reminder after the original invitation, then put Jimmy Daniels, his friend and Alberta's, in charge of getting her there.

"You're going to this one if I have to drag you," Jimmy told Alberta.

"I'm not going," she said. "And that's that."

"Get yourself together. Hot or cold, today we're going."

"I was so angry I didn't know what to do," Alberta said. She finally gave in.

It was a very glamorous affair at Bobby's fashionable apartment in the Osborne, a building kitty-corner from Carnegie Hall that has been home for decades of some of New York's top performing artists.

"Mabel thought Alberta would be amusing and funny," Bobby said. "She was none of those things. She was very quiet."

Furthermore, Alberta came in "one of her outfits," as Bobby called the simple clothes she was then in the habit of wearing. "She didn't like to dress up."

Alberta kept pretty much to herself, hanging around the baked ham that was being served, while others kept rushing back to another room to see the Tony Awards presentation on television.

Charlie Bourgeois was by the fireplace, chatting with Alec Wilder, writer of many songs, including "While We're Young." Several times Charlie noticed Alberta and glanced at her. He didn't know who she was but found her "stunning." He was especially intrigued by the enormous gold hoop earrings that later became her trademark. "The way she walked around you could tell this woman was not ordinary," he said. "She was ready to go onstage. She *was* onstage."

Alberta caught him looking at her several times. "I said to myself, 'What in the world is that man looking at me for?' " Being curious, she walked over to him. He introduced himself and presented Wilder to her as a songwriter.

"I've written a few songs, too," she said.

"Well, why don't you sing one of them?" Charlie said.

Alberta sang for the two of them a chorus of *Down Hearted Blues* as intimately and with as much style as if she were singing privately to a table of big shots at the Dreamland fifty years before.

"She had tremendous presence," said Charlie. Only then did she say she was Alberta Hunter, a name he knew as a "historical figure."

"Why aren't you singing anymore?" Charlie asked. "We need people like you."

"Who'd want an old lady like me singing?" Alberta replied, baiting him, not thinking for a minute she was too old to do anything she put her mind to.

"I know someone," Charlie said. "Barney Josephson is always looking for talent. Why don't you call him?"

"Oh, no," she said. "If Barney Josephson wants me, let him call me." She gave Charlie her telephone number.

The next morning Charlie called Barney and praised the lady he had met the night before. "Christ, don't tell me she's still around!" Barney said, who was then running The Cookery restaurant at University Place and Eighth Street in Greenwich Village. In 1970 pianist Mary Lou Williams, having a hard time finding a gig, suggested that Barney let old-timers like her perform there. He did. He invited others like Teddy Wilson, Joe Turner, Nellie Lutcher, Eddie Haywood, and Helen Humes to appear at The Cookery. Helen had quit singing in 1967, like Alberta, because her mother died. She was packing gunpowder in a munitions plant in Louisville, Kentucky, years later when she was coaxed out of "retirement" to perform at the Newport Jazz Festival and to record. Barney caught her on the rebound and put her back in the spotlight.

The Cookery looked more like a truck stop than a nightclub. Barney put a piano in the middle of the floor and presented whatever new and old talent he could get at a bargain. In his heyday in the 1940s, when he was running two Café Society clubs, he'd never thought enough of Alberta's voice or style of singing to hire her.

Charlie gave Barney Alberta's phone number. "I got very excited about it," Barney said. He called her. "Alberta, this is Barney Josephson. I must see you immediately. If you have any appointments today, cancel them all. If you're not dressed, put some clothes on and get down to The Cookery right away."

It was a little after 10:00 A.M. "Okay, I'll be down," she said. She arrived by herself exactly at noon.

"Alberta, you don't know it, my dear lady, but you're going to be singing again three weeks from tonight," Barney told her. "I didn't ask her if she wanted to or not," he said. Helen Humes was performing at The Cookery but was about to close.

"Well, you're taking an awful chance on an old lady who hasn't sung in all these twenty years," Alberta said. "I haven't even hummed a tune in my bathtub. I don't know if I can sing anymore." That was only a bit of an exaggeration since she had done the two recordings in 1961 for Chris Albertson.

Barney didn't even ask her to audition. He said all he needed to know was that she had all her teeth, as she did. He'd found that singers with dentures made a whistling sound in the mike that distracted from their performances. Alberta bragged that she didn't even have a cavity in her mouth, a miracle since all day long she drank either Coca-Cola or a glass of hot water with heaping teaspoons of sugar in it.

She said that after talking with Barney for only three minutes, she knew she was going to work for him. "I thought he was a nice man, an honest man," she said. "He's too honest to be in business. Most people in the business world would steal your eyelashes."

Barney said Alberta agreed to work for him only if he would be her manager, taking a commission on whatever engagements he lined up for her elsewhere. "I told her I would never take a penny, and I never did," he said. He told her he had managed other stars like Hazel Scott for years and never charged a commission. "I'm not starting with an old lady at eighty-two." That's the part she liked best about him. He also didn't want to tie her down with a contract.

He wanted Alberta to pull together some musicians and a show in a hurry. She agreed as long as she didn't have to have a drummer. "They just go bang, bang," she said. "I want my lyrics to be heard."

She asked Harry Watkins where she could find a good pianist. He asked a friend who suggested Gerald Cook, a former accompanist for Mae Barnes, Bricktop, and Ethel Waters, who played also on occasion for Lena Horne, Leontyne Price, Elizabeth Howell, and Johnny Hartman and had been musical director for Libby Holman from 1947 to her death in 1971.

She checked him out first and learned that he had received a master's degree in music theory at Hunter College and been a student of Nadia Boulanger at the Longy School of Music in Cambridge, Massachusetts. He was also a distinguished composer and arranger of music for theater, television, and ballet productions. Gerald was what black journalist Raoul Abdul called "quietly elegant with a sprinkle of earth."

She couldn't be in better hands with a classy fellow like that, she thought. She called him up. He didn't know who she was, but when she asked if she could come right over to talk to him about preparing for a show, he said simply, "Why not?"

She took a bus down Broadway to Chelsea and climbed the three flights of stairs to his apartment. She wanted to establish her credentials with him right away. So when she found out he was from Chicago, she told him to ask any of his older relatives about her. Little did he know that Nettie Compton, a friend of his mother's, who had given him a French Bible when he was seven, had performed with Alberta sixty years before at the Panama Café. All he could think of as a possible connection was his aunt Dell, visiting him from her home in Sag Harbor, who at the moment was in the bathtub.

"Well, I'll do just that," Gerald said. "When my aunt Dell comes out of the bathroom, I'm going to ask her about you." When his aunt emerged later, she greeted Alberta warmly and confirmed that indeed she had been very famous in Chicago.

With those reference checks out of the way, the two of them could get down to work. She agreed to pay him an hourly rate for rehearsal time. Gerald asked to see Alberta's music.

"You can't see it 'cause it all caught a rare disease in the Philippines and disintegrated," she said. So he would have to start from scratch, first writing it all down, then arranging it for a show. Gerald had his hands full as the two began meeting three times a week.

Alberta said he started off by playing what she called march music. "Oh, no, baby, don't give me any of that high class, two-two stuff," she said after hearing a few notes. "He's such a perfectionist," she explained. "He doesn't want to play anything that sounds like a nickelodeon."

He told her he was not a jazz musician and could not play like one. He told her how his grandmother had slapped his wrists when he was young anytime he tried to play blues, saying it was sinful stuff.

"Honey, you can play it because I'm going to see to it that you play it," Alberta said.

"She knew exactly what she wanted," said Gerald. He was amazed by her "zeal and enormous productivity." However, because of the

amount of work needed on her music, her opening had to be post-
poned until the fall. They worked for hours at a time. Alberta never
tired. Gerald spent many additional hours alone going back over the
tapes he made of each session, studying in his fastidious way her
tempos, phrasing, and harmony. He arranged her music in keeping
with her spontaneous style of singing but organized it to emphasize
what she did most effectively.

Gerald and Alberta practiced at The Cookery on July 12 and again
on September 6. Barney told Alberta he found Gerald's playing too
"strong" and encouraged her to do her show instead with Jimmy
Rowles, a well-known jazz pianist who had accompanied Billie Holiday. Alberta said nothing to Gerald.

Alberta began rehearsing with Rowles at her friend Chris Albertson's apartment, but she continued going to Gerald several times
a week to perfect her music. Their last session was on October 6.
George Tipton, a singer and friend of Gerald's, joined them that day
and convinced Alberta that she ought to open her show with her
own song "My Castle's Rockin'."

Even before the opening Alberta was being treated like a celebrity.
Barbara Bordnick, a New York fashion photographer, called her in
early September. She was producing a calendar of great women in
jazz for Polaroid. Not knowing whom to select, she asked Charlie
Bourgeois. His list included people like Helen Humes, Mabel Mercer,
Mary Lou Williams, Sarah Vaughan, Marian McPartland, Betty Carter,
Toshiko Akiyoshi, Anita O'Day, and Alberta Hunter.

Barbara invited Alberta to her studio for a photo session. Alberta
arrived punctually at 9:00 A.M., said Barbara, "dressed like a little
old black man" in an Eisenhower sweater, a faded plaid shirt, and
a denim skirt. Barbara admitted to Alberta that she didn't have the
vaguest idea what she did. "Do you play the piano?" she asked.

"With these fingernails, no, honey," Alberta replied showing off
her long nails flashing her favorite polish, Elizabeth Arden's Red
Door Red.

Not many photos were taken that morning. Alberta sat in a
wooden chair as big and stern as you'd expect to find in a medieval
banquet hall. For the next few hours she told the story of her life

as Barbara and her assistants sat on the floor at her feet, taking in every word.

Days later Alberta came back for a formal sitting before the cameras, wearing a black dress Barbara gave her. The pose selected for the calendar was the same one Alberta assumed naturally while waiting during long pauses between shots, her head resting in her cupped hands. The eyes sparkled as they would for the enormous audience awaiting her comeback.

Barbara, who was used to photographing the rich, famous, and talented, was bowled over by Alberta. "This woman had it," she said. "There is a quality that every great person has, that's almost tangible. Mabel had it. And Danny Kaye has it. Angela Lansbury has it. And Alberta had that quality. She had such incredible charisma. She had what to me constitutes dreams and secrets, a mystery about her. Plus she had such an innate elegance. She came from poverty, but she had a sense of style."

Alberta was different from the other women in the series in that they were history. Alberta was in her debut; she was just happening again. "She was like a young star," said Barbara. "The others had a bitterness, a bitterness that scares you, but a well-earned one."

Alberta was equally impressed by Barbara. She wrote her a note dated September 29, 1977, that read:

> Barbara darling: You are a darling if there ever was one. I have been photographed by many people, but when it comes to taking pictures you don't take any tea for the fever.
>
> I can sit for hours while you jive me and be working the devil out of me ha! ha!, but I love it cause it's a lot of fun.
>
> Thanks for all those lovely pictures. Love, love, love
>
> Alberta Hunter

Alberta called Barbara to talk about anything at all several times a day during the week before her opening on October 10. "I could tell she was nervous," Barbara said. She had her hairdresser and makeup artist get Alberta ready for the big night.

Most of Barbara's staff were in her party of twenty-three that evening at The Cookery. Nearby sat Bobby Short, Helen Humes, Charlie Bourgeois, Jimmy Daniels, Chris Albertson, Harry Watkins. Gene Shalit of NBC's *Today* show was there, as were journalists from the national media. And sprinkled throughout the audience were a bunch of nurses from Goldwater Hospital.

Barney gave one of his typical long-winded introductions, talking about all the entertainers he had helped in the past. Finally he said, "For me, ladies and gentlemen, the names I've thrown at you you may forget. If I'm remembered for anything I have ever done in this business, I want you to remember me as the man who brought Alberta Hunter back to singing again. And now, it's the greatest joy of my life, Alberta Hunter."

Both the smell of hamburgers and the clatter of plates being tossed onto the serving counter a few feet away subsided as Alberta, looking a bit weary from waiting, strolled over to the microphone. Jimmy Rowles was at the piano, Lysle Atkinson on bass. As she stepped into the spotlight, her sagging body was as magically and glamorously transformed as was Cinderella's scrubwoman appearance the moment her foot glided into her lost slipper.

Alberta told the audience how much she had loved nursing and how sorry she was she'd been tossed out when it was thought she was seventy. "I fooled them though," she said. "I lied. I'm eighty-two." The nurses, most of whom hadn't known her real age, cheered raucously. She giggled joyously at having been the one to do the jiving all those years and winked impishly at them. She was "as relaxed as a bowl of bones," said the *New Yorker* (October 24, 1977, p. 6).

Alberta thanked Charlie Bourgeois for "discovering" her. She raved briefly about Barney then decided enough talking had been done. She was raring to sing.

"This is the first song I've sung professionally in twenty years," she said. She knew people were there to see how she had held up all those years and if she could still sing.

She let loose with "My Castle's Rockin'." At first she seemed insecure with some of the high notes, but after she was about half-way through it, she was the old pro, at home onstage again. She snapped her fingers, slapped her thighs as if they were tambourines, tossed back her head of gray-black hair tightly pulled into a small bun, and beamed her chocolate-brown eyes at each face in the audience, summing them up and entrapping them in an irresistible love affair.

"My voice was so strong," she said. "My God, I sang like a horse!" Her voice had become huskier with age. It was what Jay Scott of the *Toronto Globe and Mail* later described aptly as "a contralto that wears boots" (February 9, 1978, p. 7).

The applause sounded to her "like a thunderstorm." She said to herself, "People are thinking, 'This old girl can sing a song. This old girl is here yet. This old girl, she makes me feel.' And there were tears, people wiping their eyes, happy tears, glad tears. And Barney stood there smiling as if to say, 'There she is. To think that I, after all these years, as an old man, have given an old lady a chance to come back into the business without an audition.' "

She was up and off.

"This is a song I wrote before most of you children were born. The title of the song is 'Down Hearted Blues.' Then came the world's greatest blues singer, that awful Bessie Smith. She selected this song for her first recording. And I'm still collecting the royalties.

"Men were dragging women's hearts around then, and they're still doing it." She tapped her nails on the piano and said to Jimmy, "C'mon, let's lay this one on them."

Alberta sang some sweet ballads, too: "My Blue Heaven," "Funny That Way," "Tell Me That You Love Me," and "On the Sunny Side of the Street." But interspersed with those gentle numbers she belted out the bawdy lyrics to a song she'd written entitled "Rough and Ready Man":

> *When I come home some morning*
> *all dressed up like Astor's horse,*
> *I want him to grab me and tear*
> > *off*
> *All of my clothes*
> *Just to let me know who's boss,*
> *I want a two-fisted, double-jointed*
> *rough and ready man.*

The nurses howled. They were astounded that their serious former colleague had all that in her. "When you saw Alberta walking around the halls of Goldwater starched and crisp in her uniform, you would never think that she could get up there and be so risqué and flirting," said Mildred Crisp Littles, her friend at Goldwater Hospital.

The critics in the audience were equally surprised and delighted. Gary Giddins wrote in the *Village Voice* (October 24, 1977, p. 87) that he had thought the idea of a planned comeback for Alberta was "farfetched" when he heard about it during the summer. He wrote:

> Barney Josephson, however, specializes in the farfetched and his instincts have once again been proven right by a performer who needs no apologies.
>
> Her voice quivers and moans and slurs with a projection learned during premicrophone vaudeville and she marches over the rhythm with a healthy vibrato that underscores the optimism informing all the songs. "The sun is shining and *that's* a good sign," she sings, eyes shining, finger gesticulating, and if you don't believe her, you've never believed in Santa Claus either. "The whole world smiles with you," she insists with a Jolsonesque vivacity, and what was banal yesterday and will be banal tomorrow becomes momentarily profound.

"Miss Hunter embodies all of what blues are—joyous, sly and sensual as well as sad," wrote Don Nelsen of the *New York Daily News* (October 12, 1977, p. 67). "When she sings, 'I gotta man, he's kinda old and thin. But there are plenty of good tunes left in an old violin,' [from her song 'Workin' Man'] slapping her hip to the beat, she's one of the sexiest women in the room."

Robert Palmer of the *New York Times* (October 14, 1977, p. C26) said "grown men were observed to have tears in their eyes, and a confirmed atheist [Barney Josephson] murmured, 'She can still swing, God bless her.'"

Alberta told Palmer after the first show that the applause she received "was food for a hungry person. I'm so excited I haven't been able to sleep. But the reason, really, is that I couldn't sleep for thinking how blessed I am.

"Well, it looked like I went on down the road to success," Alberta said.

To begin with, Alberta became an overnight sensation in a city where performers spend their lives trying to get noticed. *Cue* magazine (October 29, 1977, p. 6) said she was "the hottest thing in town right now. Three weeks ago, nobody knew her name."

Alberta was "simply not to be missed," raved *New York* magazine (October 31, 1977, p. 24).

Whitney Balliett wrote a beautiful, long profile article on her for the October 31, 1977, issue of the *New Yorker*.

Praise also came from special old friends. Eubie Blake, then a sprightly ninety-four years old, applauded her at The Cookery on October 19 and was easily encouraged by the adoring Alberta and her audience to accompany her on the piano. Eubie commented on her singing with him back in the 1920s: "When she sang the blues, you felt so sorry for her you would want to kill the guy she was singing about."

Dick Campbell, who had hired her for the USO, wrote her on October 31, congratulating her on her success: "I guess we'll have to say that you have your hand in God's pocket, or maybe it's because you were so good to your mother. Whatever it was, or is, you deserve all you are getting."

Gerald Cook went to see her show also. He was surprised she hadn't told him about her opening and disappointed she hadn't chosen him to accompany her. She felt awkward about the situation but wasn't going to rock the boat with Barney and risk losing her opportunity to perform again. However, within days Barney had replaced Jimmy Rowles with Claude Hopkins, who had problems accompanying Alberta. They even went to Gerald for help. He worked with them at his studio but couldn't solve their difficulties.

Barney called Gerald and asked him to start right away with Alberta. Gerald was able to begin only two weeks later because he had previous commitments, so a third pianist filled in until then. Another replacement was also made, with Al Hall joining on bass. Once Gerald and Al were in place, Alberta was in the best of hands.

The Cookery was packed every night. A line of people snaked around the corner and down the block, waiting to get into one of the three sets the trio gave six days a week. People were turned away for every show. Alberta was a smash hit. She was also a bargain inasmuch as The Cookery had no cover charge and only a $3.50 minimum for each customer per set.

As time went by, it became obvious that Alberta wasn't a passing fancy. She was back in the limelight to stay. "Once in a great while . . . the rare performer comes along who possesses the timeless ability to obscure disappointment and bitter recollections of a hundred sorrowful revivals," wrote the *Baltimore Sun* (March 23, 1978, p. B4). "Alberta Hunter, bless her soul, is one of those rare gems."

People from all over the world came to see her and ask for her to sing in their countries. Her life, comeback, longevity, and continued vitality remained good copy for newspapers from the *Peoria Journal Star* to the *New York Times*. Articles on her appeared in *People*, *Ladies Home Journal*, *Rolling Stone*, *MD*, even *Penthouse*. In March 1979 she made *Playboy*. A reader, Harold Wolff, wrote her on March 6, 1979, with a copy of the article (a review of a record album of hers) and said, "You are the only woman in the magazine who appears with her clothes on."

She was written up by the *West Australian*, *Sankei Shimbun* of Japan, *London Daily Telegraph*, *Le Monde* of Paris, *Estado de São Paulo*.

Sophisticated reporters loved her delicious, down-home explanations of her art. When Eric Shorter of the *London Daily Telegraph* (February 10, 1979, p.20) asked her if the reason the first line of early black music was often repeated was to give the singer a chance to make up the next line, Alberta set him straight, at least as far as she was concerned: "Honey, if you don't know that last line, ain't no use starting out on the first."

She was the queen of the talk shows. Gene Shalit brought her on the *Today* show for the first of many appearances on November 2, 1977. She drew the biggest mail response from viewers for any musical artist in the then twenty-five year history of the program.

A viewer in Ames, Iowa, wrote: "My whole day was enhanced listening to her—her joy of living [and] her supervoice and talent for writing encouraged me not to dread too much becoming older in this society that tends to idolize youth."

On the date of her second appearance on the *Today* show (March 23, 1978), where she was introduced as "one of the musical phenomena of our age and her age," a woman in California wrote: "Music like yours could make a Christian out of a lot of unlikely prospects."

Seeing Alberta in person was even more soul-inspiring. A letter dated April 10, 1978, said: "I must tell you my husband never clapped until he saw you perform. I mean he never clapped to a beat before in his life. After the first song he was even snapping his fingers. God, Alberta, you really know how to work it. Thank you again for a glorious evening that really changed our lives."

Another fan at The Cookery wrote, "The way you sing has done something art is supposed to do but rarely does; it has made a permanent difference to my life. When I am all through crying over how you move me, I'm going home. But I'll be back—with special friends who need your medicine."

Soon Alberta was appearing on *To Tell the Truth, Dick Cavett Show, Mike Douglas Show, Good Morning America, Merv Griffin Show, The Prime of Your Life,* and *Sixty Minutes.* She was also filmed for a thirty minute film for CBS and a tribute to Eubie Blake on PBS.

Television crews from England, Sweden, and Germany interviewed and filmed her. She turned down an offer to sing in Denmark, one of her favorite countries, because the money offered was too little. She wrote on the envelope in which the contract came, "I did not accept for the money was not even 1/3 of what I get a night."

Alberta performed at The Cookery, as agreed, until November 19, 1977. She was followed by Odetta but was booked to return on December 21 and to do a special New Year's Eve show with Helen Humes and Rose ("Chi-Chi") Murphy that was broadcast on National Public Radio.

There was no time to relax on her first break from The Cookery. On December 4 she sang "You Gotta Reap What You Sow" at the dedication of St. Peter's Church, a sanctuary that became known as New York's jazz church, located in the basement of the modernistic Citicorp Building in midtown. The message of her song didn't reach the ears of the bankers on the floors above the church, though.

Months later they sent Alberta a form letter rejecting her application for a credit card until such future time when her "circumstances" changed.

"Believe me I have been more than solvent for more than 50 years, so I don't need a 'change of circumstance' for any credit card in existence," she wrote the bank. ". . . it seems unlikely that 'who I am' could escape the notice of anyone in New York City."

People knew who she was on December 7, 1977, at Elaine's restaurant, a haunt of celebrities, when it was announced that Alberta would record her songs for the sound track of a film called *Remember My Name*, produced by Robert Altman and written and directed by Alan Rudolph. (She received twenty thousand dollars for the job.) The stars of the film were Geraldine Chaplin and Tony Perkins. When Alberta sang for the elegant crowd, according to the *New York Post* (December 8, 1977, p. 6), Joel Grey, Lillian Gish, Lauren Hutton, Robert Altman, and Geraldine Chaplin all stood on their chairs to get a better look at her and enjoy her music.

In the film that music is the backdrop for Geraldine Chaplin, playing the part of a woman recently released from prison seeking revenge against a man, played by Perkins, who walked out on her years before.

John Hammond, a friend and associate of Barney Josephson's, produced the recording of the score of *Remember My Name* for Columbia Records that December. Hammond was not new to the business of promoting talent to Columbia Records and to the earlier American Record Company, which Columbia had bought out in 1938. He was the black sheep in a wealthy New York family in the early 1930s because he often preferred the company of blacks. He asked Paul Robeson to be the godfather of his son and served for many years as a board member of the NAACP. "If the Presbyterian seminary hadn't been segregated, I'd probably have become a preacher," he said.

Hammond had promoted musicians like Fletcher Henderson, Count Basie, Teddy Wilson, and Lionel Hampton and singers like Billie Holiday and Aretha Franklin. More recently he put Bob Dylan and Bruce Springsteen on the road to fame.

The recording session with Alberta went well. Most of the songs on Alberta's album were newly arranged versions of earlier hits of hers. She did write a title song for the album that echoed an old theme in her writing, a willingness to always be a friend to a lover who strayed away. She wrote:

> *If you tried and failed at tryin'*
> *Feel you've played a losin' game*
> *If you need a friend to call on*
> *Remember my name.*
> *If you feel you're at the end of your journey*
> *Weary, worn, nothin' seems the same*
> *You're not alone, my love's eternal*
> *Remember my name.**

Altman rushed to show the film in Los Angeles before the end of the year so it could qualify for the year's Academy Awards. He thought their biggest chance to win an Oscar was for Alberta's song, "The Love I Have for You," which she led them to believe she had written just for the film. After all their effort to promote the song for an award, the Academy advised them it was disqualified because it had been recorded in 1940 by one Alberta Hunter.

"Why didn't you tell us it was an old song?" Rudolph asked her.

"I guess I just forgot," she said. "I think I found it in a trunk. But it was a real song!"

Alberta picked up fifteen thousand dollars more in January 1978, appearing in a nationally televised commercial for Final Net hairspray. In that one day on camera she made more than she earned in an entire year as a nurse.

In spite of all the fanfare she was receiving nationally, Alberta stayed at The Cookery during much of 1978, singing two sets on weeknights and three on Fridays and Saturdays. Because the restaurant had no dressing room and she didn't like going up and down the stairs to Barney's office in the basement, she sat it out between shows in a chair near the cash register by the front door, wrapped in a shawl to guard against the gusts of frigid air that swept in every

---

time someone came in. Eventually Barney relinquished a booth over by the kitchen where she could sit. He also offered to pay her taxi fare so she'd go home comfortably rather than by bus, as she said she was doing. Each night thereafter Alberta requested the taxi fare from the cashier even though Gerald continued to drive her back and forth to The Cookery in his car.

People in the audience, overwhelmed by her performances, would go to her booth to thank her, to kiss her.

"Don't get close," she'd say. "I've got a bad cold, and I don't want to give it to you." Alberta hated the physical contact of people hugging and kissing her. Harry Watkins said she was always "that way." She would give autographs at her booth and say something short and sweet to admirers, but rarely would she permit any extended conversation.

Alberta used her time in the back booth to write new songs. Two she wrote and used in her show there were "I'm Tired of Being Your Football" and "You're Welcome, Always Welcome to Come Back Home."

On April 1, 1978, her birthday, she received a visitor at The Cookery whom she was glad to talk with for hours, Eubie Blake. He told her he was living in Bedford-Stuyvesant, a rough ghetto in Brooklyn because he "was somebody" there. "If I lived on Park Avenue [in Manhattan], people might think I was just another hustler," he said.

They started a tradition of celebrating each other's birthday together. Each time one of them was blowing out candles Alberta sang for him "Memories of You," one of his greatest tunes, written with Andy Razaf for the show *Blackbirds of 1930*.

"She ain't nothing but a child," said Eubie, ninety-five, on his friend's eighty-third birthday. But then he complained, "Alberta, you haven't kissed me in forty years. Is it my breath?" She gave him a little peck on the cheek.

Several months later Eubie wrote her: "Hello Alberta, the show stopper. Please let on the old man. I've got to make a living too." He sent her the music to some of his songs that he thought she might like to sing. Among the titles were "Tan Manhattan," "Don't Make a Plaything out of My Heart," "Just Like Ham & Eggs," and "Gee I Wish I Had Someone to Rock Me in the Cradle of Love."

"I picked out what I thought you could use," he wrote. "All I ask of you is to tell your audience I'm the composer. People tell me you give me a lot of plug when you're on the stage. I thank you very, very, very much."

On the outside of the sealed envelope he wrote her another note, asking her to send him back a list of the songs he had included since he had forgotten to make one. Also, he said, he'd forgotten to include another of the songs he'd written, "You Got to Git the Gittin' While the Gittin's Good." He noted: "This is not a dirty song, but it is good for you."

All sorts of people wanted to honor Alberta that year. On March 23, 1978, the Tennessee House of Representatives passed a resolution that read in part: ". . . this body should note with a sense of pride that Alberta Hunter, a native of Memphis, has made an immense contribution to the development of an important art form, the blues, and is still very active bringing joy to all Tennesseans who are privileged to hear her fine voice. . . ."

In May Gordon's vodka gave her its "Good Gal Award." She asked that the two-hundred-dollar prize money be donated to the NAACP.

Much more important to her was her debut at Carnegie Hall on June 27, 1978. She led off the program of the twenty-fifth Newport Jazz Festival show that evening. Three days later she and Eubie Blake performed at the festival's annual concert for children, Jazz for the Young and Young at Heart, at New York University's Loeb Center. She told her young fans, "You'll have a lot of friends if you're spending your money, but when you get broke, they'll walk on the other side of the street. If you've got a dime, save five cents and give your parents a break."

She received all sorts of invitations to perform around the country, but Barney, as her manager, rejected most of them, often without telling her about them. She herself turned down the White House when a social secretary called her directly and asked her to give a concert in the Rose Garden for Washington dignitaries. Asked by incredulous friends why, she replied casually that the invitation was for her to sing on a Sunday. "It was my day off!" she said.

She did appear again on ABC's *Good Morning America* program.

The show's senior producer wrote her (September 12, 1978): "As always you are a delightful guest, and while I usually don't write thank you's to second time guests, I had to send you a special little one for all the happiness you have brought to our show and to our audience. I hope you will come on again."

The hostess on the program also wrote (August 30, 1978): "I never use soap—thanks to you." Alberta had revealed one of her secrets for looking so youthful: Her whole life long she never washed her face with anything but witch hazel. And she hung on to her teeth, Alberta said, by brushing them with baking soda.

An especially welcome tribute came her way on October 6 in Memphis during festivities for the premiere of the film *Remember My Name*. Five years earlier, when Alberta, still working as a nurse, was visiting friends in Memphis, she went entirely unnoticed by the city fathers. Now, in 1978, she received a bouquet of roses from the Chamber of Commerce and the key to the city from the mayor. "I never thought in my wildest dreams this would happen to me," she said, tears welling in her eyes. She told how as a child she wasn't even allowed to walk on the sidewalks of that city, and now here it was honoring her.

She later told reporters how happy she was to see there were no longer any COLORED ONLY signs at rest rooms and water fountains. The Civil Rights Act of 1964 and the Voting Rights Act of 1965 were beginning to reduce some of the official indignities suffered by blacks in southern cities like Memphis. But her heart was heavy that afternoon as she walked down Beale Street and saw how much of it had been torn down after years of neglect and the 1968 riots following the assassination of Martin Luther King, Jr. at the Lorraine Motel a few blocks away.

That night more than two thousand Memphians, almost all of them white, went to the gala at the Orpheum Theater, a 1920s vintage film palace. The celebrities arrived in individual silver limousines, readily available in the town that spawned Elvis Presley. When Alberta arrived, the photographers and reporters swarmed around her, making her feel as if she were in Hollywood, not a couple of blocks from the muddy Mississippi River.

Everyone expected the demure-looking little lady to say something gracious when she was asked onstage at the theater. Instead, she read them the riot act. She blasted racist attitudes that, she said, were covered up but still very apparent in the South. "Don't let this city fall in this way," she said. "People were stunned," said Alan Rudolph.

The atmosphere was lighter and less threatening at Number One Beale Street, a restaurant where Alberta gave a show later that night with Gerald and her new bassist, Jimmy Lewis. In the audience, which stood after each of her numbers to applaud her, were her invited guests, Dossie Young, her childhood friend, and several of Dossie's cousins. Dossie wrote Alberta a few days later chastising her for not coming by her house for a visit but thanking her profusely for the invitations. Her cousins, she wrote, "cannot get over that we at our young ages look so young and sexy."

Alberta especially enjoyed being with Geraldine Chaplin, who told her, she said, that she was the only person she had ever met who reminded her of her father.

Before leaving town, Alberta and the cast took a steamboat ride aboard the *Memphis Queen* on the Mississippi River. It was the first and last time Alberta was ever on the famous river.

Reviews of the film were very mixed. *Variety* (October 11, 1978, p. 31) said it "has the sheen of a beautiful film, but the hollow, empty core of an intellectual exercise."

The *Hollywood Reporter* (October 6, 1978, p. 25) called it "one of the most provocative, thematically ambitious and hauntingly memorable films of the year."

Playboy in its March 1979 issue (pp. 35–36) noted that the film "rated universal raves" for its "glorious sound track." The record by the same name, it said, "will be around for a long, long time."

John Lissner of the *New York Times* (June 3, 1979, p. D23) shared that enthusiasm for the music. He called Alberta's record "one of the most relaxed and vibrant blues/jazz sessions released in the past year."

The album also made her worthy of mention by "Ripley's Believe It or Not" (*New York News World*, March 1, 1979, p. 10A). It read:

"Alberta Hunter cannot read or write music, yet composed and performed all the songs in the film Remember My Name at the age of 83."

George Stevens, Jr., executive producer of the first of the annual Kennedy Center Honors, an awards program to recognize the lifelong achievements of performing artists, sent a letter to Alberta inviting her to attend a reception on Sunday, December 3, at the White House and to sing at a concert that evening at the opera house of the John F. Kennedy Center for the Performing Arts. The two events were to honor that year's award recipients: Marian Anderson, Fred Astaire, George Balanchine, Richard Rodgers, and Arthur Rubinstein. Also performing at the opera house would be Leonard Bernstein, Isaac Stern, and Itzhak Perlman.

"I know how difficult your schedule is performing six nights a week, and I would not propose this except that it is a very special event which will reach out to people all across the U.S.," Stevens wrote, knowing he was encroaching on her "day off." He paraphrased President Kennedy's words to underscore the importance of the awards: "I look forward to an America which will not be afraid of grace and beauty . . . which will reward achievement in the arts as we reward achievement in business and statecraft."

Kennedy had also said the United States should be remembered "not for victories or defeats in battle or in politics but for contributions to the human spirit," Stevens wrote. "I have seen you perform and I am, therefore, well aware of your contributions to the human spirit. . . . I know you will thrill this audience and it will be an historic moment in American musical history."

Alberta was equally thrilled to be able to meet President Jimmy Carter. So much so that she laid out the preposterous sum (for her) of $6,226.80 (she saved the receipt) to buy a full-length mink coat at Henri Bendel in New York to wear to Washington, the only place she ever wore it. "I didn't want no cheap one. I'd rather not have any. I bought a coat, so help me," she said. "I had to go down there looking right." (After her trip to Washington she put the coat in storage at Henri Bendel's and kept it there, for years declaring on the storage ticket that its value was only a thousand dollars so as not to attract the attention of anyone who might be motivated to swipe it had its real value been advertised. "I haven't seen the dog-gone thing since," she said.)

She was the only woman in the receiving line at the White House with a coat on. The other women had checked theirs at the door. But Alberta wanted Carter to see she had one. The president shook her hand and told her how sweet she was. "You're sweet, too," she told him.

At the reception President Carter introduced each of the honorees. Alberta remembered what he said of Marian Anderson: "Her talent was so great that racial prejudice could not stand in her way." The same could be said for Alberta.

At the opera house the audience reaction to each performer was as formal as its black-tie attire. Then Alberta walked onstage, hands on her hips, dressed in a plain pink dress with a simple frill at the neckline.

"Lay it on me," she said to Gerald Cook. She sang "My Castle's Rockin' " and "Workin' Man," swinging her hips as if she'd had ten thousand GIs out front. "C'mon, folks," she said, egging the audience to clap their hands along with her. "I'm talkin' to ya." They couldn't resist joining in. She had them almost rolling in the aisles when she sang "Workin' Man":

> *I don't want no hepster lover*
> *They've got larceny in their eyes*
> *Got a hand full of gimme*
> *And a mouth full of much obliged.*

"She stole the show from some of the world's greatest entertainers," said the *Memphis Press-Scimitar* (December 4, 1978, p. 15). She knew it, too. As she walked very slowly offstage, reluctantly so, she turned back and winked several times at the audience.

She stood in the wings, reveling in the applause. "They told me only to sing two songs," she said, sorry to have to obey.

The producer said, "Go on back out there. They're not going to stop."

Out she went, triumphantly, and sang "I Cried for You." She was the only performer to give an encore.

Her first, and only, success on Broadway (*How Come?*, in 1923) flashed before her mind as she went onstage again. Sophie Tucker wasn't in the front row as she had been in 1923, but the president and his wife were in their box, grinning like Cheshire cats.

"You gave the best performance of the evening," wrote White House Social Secretary Gretchen Poston on December 18, 1978. At the same time she invited Alberta back for a command performance at the White House on February 27, 1979.

Alberta was in Washington once again before that, also on a Sunday, January 7, 1979, for a sold-out concert at the Smithsonian Institution. The next morning the *Washington Post* (p. B-9), inspired by the Smithsonian's collection of precious jewels, called Alberta a "rare gem," the "sapphire of the blues." It added: "The warm, rich tones blazed with fiery emotions and the lustrous finish sparkled with a cool charm. . . . She grabbed the lyrics, shook them, stomped on them and then picked them up and caressed them."

None of Alberta's achievements ever matched the importance in her mind of the evening she spent at the White House on February 27. The concert marked the closing of a governors' conference.

Although the Carter White House was often described as having the ascetic qualities of the Mormon Tabernacle, that night it sounded more like the basement party room of a fraternity house. The *Washington Post* (p. B-1) described it the morning after: "For last night's black-tie audience, the raunchier the lyrics, the greater the response." Alberta's words to "My Man Ain't Handy No More" were among the most popular:

> *He threads my needle*
> *Creams my wheat*
> *Heats my heater*
> *Chops my meat*
> *My man is such a handy man.*

"Several times, Rosalynn Carter shaped her mouth into O's of amazement," the *Post* reported. "Alfred Kahn, the president's inflation adviser, sat on the edge of his chair. As Hunter tapped her black T-strap shoes, she sang about 'Get yourself a working man,' and the President roared with laughter."

"Mr. President, was that all right?" Alberta asked afterward. She said she'd wanted to put a little spice into the evening, but she didn't want to go too far.

Alberta always said her songs were just songs and the lyrics no more than "suggestive." If the listener had a dirty mind, then the songs would be dirty. Besides, she said, "Sex is only a condition of the mind. Like age. Drink some lemonade and forget it."

President Carter assured Alberta that her selection of songs was "really terrific."

The president wrote her the next day: "You continue to amaze us. Rosalynn and I loved your performance last night for the Governors following our dinner in their honor. Thank you for being with us and sharing your beautiful music."

Alberta was impressed by the "chandeliers and all those beautiful things" at the White House. But she was more taken with the fact that she had performed there. It was the most glorious moment of her long life.

"How can I describe the feeling of going to the White House, of entertaining a group of wonderful people, especially my president?" she said. "How high can you go? To think that you're at the top of the ladder after earning twenty-five cents a week [as a child]. Woo, what a feeling! How much higher? After you touch the hand of God, there's nobody else but your president."

And best of all, "they seemed to like me," she said. "They thought I was somebody."

Barney Josephson knew what it meant to her when he started introducing her at The Cookery after that night. "She started off singing in a whorehouse," he said. "That's what we had reserved for little black girls in those days. And now she's made it to the White House."

Another couple, as religious as President and Mrs. Carter, were equally impressed with Alberta in spite of her mixing in with the spiritual songs lyrics like these to "My Man Ain't Handy No More":

He shakes my ashes
Greases my griddle
Churns my butter
Strokes my fiddle
My man is such a handy man. . . . .

She received a letter from them dated March 16, 1979:

Dear Friend,
I think you are simply wonderful. Mrs. Peale and I listened to your performance last night at the Cookery with admiration and thanksgiving.
You have great talent. We were impressed that you are able to give a fine Christian witness in a public restaurant with such sincerity and loving persuasiveness.
You talked to us all like a mother to her children and everyone of us loved you. May God continue to bless you with good health and strength to entertain and to bless many, many people. With best wishes always,

Norman Vincent Peale

The Peales, editors and publishers of *Guideposts* magazine, printed an article on Alberta in the July 1979 issue and had her sing in October at the Collegiate Marble Church in New York, where Peale was the pastor.

Barney Josephson, an avowed atheist, got a kick out of being "palsy-walsy" with Peale over Alberta. The Cookery did resemble a revival tent, he admitted, the way Alberta handed out advice to youngsters in the audience "to save money, get an education, take any job, and then go after a better one, and 'There's a God, look at me, I'm an example of God's goodness,' and all that stuff.

"I don't know another entertainer in the world who can come out there and speak to the audience like you do and not be hissed off the floor," Barney told Alberta.

Alberta got away with it because she didn't come across as another authoritarian adult figure to young people. She was "the grand-mother whose cradle you've wanted to rock in all along," wrote C. A. Bustard in the Richmond *Times-Dispatch* (August 1, 1979, p. E-11). She was an even more lovable grandmother because right after giving you stern advice, she'd sock it to you with a raunchy song.

To her "children" she said, "Don't get so great that you think you're too good to reach down and help people. They don't have to be drunk. They could be in a diabetic coma or have a heart attack. Look down and put your hand down and try to pull them up."

She told them to struggle. "It's a hard road. Don't wait for somebody to hand it to you. Time waits for no one. It passes you by. It rolls on forever like the clouds in the sky. Work hard. And have a will of your own. Don't let people tell you what to do. If you know what's right, do it. Look at me. I'm happy as a lark. That's all you gotta be."

She urged them to believe in "Almighty God" but to be patient in receiving help from Him. "You may want something on a Thursday, and God knows you need it on a Friday. In His time you'll get what you want if you're patient. Hang on."

And she encouraged them to keep in touch with their parents. "If they were good parents, call them," she said. "If they were not such good parents, call them anyway. Then your conscience will be clear. Do it for Alberta. On Saturdays, Sundays, and holidays you can do it for almost nothing."

Barney was constantly amazed by Alberta's impact on young people. After each performance well-dressed young men formed a line at the pay telephone in the basement outside the men's room and waited to call their parents, as Alberta told them to do! Young people came back again to The Cookery with their parents or grandparents to hear and be inspired by Alberta's message. And they wrote her attesting to what she had done for them. "I'm not sure if even you realize how important your success is to so many people," said one man. "It's not only the great pleasure your songs and your singing bring us all, it's the encouragement you give people to hang in there and keep at it, even when things don't look too hot, because it's never too late for good things to start happening."

A young woman who had a graduate degree in architecture but was a painter "at heart" wrote: "It may perhaps seem silly to you, but at twenty-six, and with many advantages of talent and education, I feel like giving up at times. I feel as if things aren't happening fast

enough; that time is running out. Then I think of you at eighty-three
. . . you've given me renewed courage that every artist needs to get
up and make something beautiful every day."

Mrs. Lou Glasse, director of the New York State Office for the
Aging, praised her for opening the door for other older people (October 29, 1979): "There are millions of older persons in our country
who have much to contribute of their experiences, wisdom and skills.
Though there can only be one Alberta Hunter other older persons
can also significantly enrich our society. You helped to make possible
their acceptance."

Chapter Ten

Keeping Her Shoes On

Friends told Alberta she was getting too much national publicity to keep singing exclusively at The Cookery. She could earn for one appearance outside New York several times the weekly salary Barney paid her. Gerald nudged her, too, saying he didn't want to spend the rest of his life in one place.

In spite of her dedication to Barney, Alberta told him she wanted to hit the road. He told her, to no avail, that she needed to save her energy. By July 1979 she was on her way. One of the first people to book her was Hatcher Story, a resident of Courtland, Virginia, who called himself then a "nonpolitical peanut farmer." His real love was working as an impresario to bring exceptional talent to his rural area. He had already contracted the great English actor Alec McCowen to perform his one-man play *St. Mark's Gospel* soon after performing it at the White House. By coincidence Hatcher had been at The Cookery the night Alberta first opened there in 1977. She was the second White House veteran performer he charmed to the backwoods of Virginia.

"She rocked 'em. She socked 'em. She laid it on 'em good," said the *Tidewater News* (August 2, 1979, p. 2) of nearby Franklin, where the performance was held. Alberta thrived on the attention she received there as well as the southern cooking Hatcher had prepared for her. She was especially grateful that he convinced the local school board to give her an honorary high school diploma. "Alberta Hunter has more philosophy than most of the professors at the University of Virginia," he told them.

"Mmmm, I made it," Alberta said, donning a cap and gown to receive the diploma. "At eighty-four I finally made it." She told the young audience they shouldn't cheat, steal, be mean, tell lies, or use curse words. "Especially you girls," she said. "Hearing a young woman use bad words is the ugliest thing."

Barney made her get her doctor's approval to sing at the Central City Opera House in Colorado because of the high altitude (8,496 feet). He need not have worried. It was Gerald and Aaron Bell, the new bassist, who had trouble. Both gasped for breath during the performance. Alberta, hearing some commotion behind her, turned to them at one point during the show and said, "Will you two please stop that noise?"

Among other engagements, she sang at the Brooks Art Gallery in Memphis, her hometown, for a fee of seventy-five hundred dollars. "Many top singers from the Metropolitan Opera weren't getting as much," Barney said. After a concert at Vassar College Herbert Shultz, vice-president for development, wrote: "The Vassar campus is full of love and affection for you this morning. Everyone who attended your concert is talking about it. There has not been such a popular event at Vassar in many, many years."

She continued recording for CBS with an album called *Amtrak Blues*, released in May 1980. Some critics found it the best of all the albums she came to record. The *New York Daily News* (December 16, 1980, p. 37) called it "bluesy, schmoosey and wonderful."

According to Rafi Zabor in *Musician* magazine (May 1980, p. 80), "She seems to grab a song by the throat and tell it to be something; as a result, no phrase, no word goes [sic] by without standing up straight and telling you exactly what it means . . . you may feel stupid standing up in your living room and applauding this record, but if you get the urge, I say go with it."

As good as the reviews were of this and the other albums Alberta did for CBS, the records were often hard to find across the country, even in the cities where she performed. CBS was interested in rock and roll at the time and recorded Alberta only at John Hammond's insistence, according to William Krasilovsky, who became Alberta's attorney at Hammond's suggestion. Bill, a music copyright expert, organized the registration of her music and the collection of royalties from it. "He even got me some royalties from South Africa," Alberta said. "He's a knockout lawyer. And he doesn't try to rob you."

Hammond complained repeatedly to CBS that it wasn't promoting Alberta's records. In a letter dated July 30, 1981, he said he was assured "that there will be promotion, finally, this time around [for her album *The Glory of Alberta Hunter*, released in February 1982]. Although CBS has made money on her albums there has never been any promotion, and I hope this time there will really be some effort made for this 86 year old phenomenon who is at the peak of her form." The letter had little effect. The four LP records she made for CBS sold a total of fewer than two hundred thousand copies.

Many fans wrote Alberta directly to state that their local record stores didn't have her albums in stock. Time and again, as evidenced by her notations on the envelopes, she personally bought and sent copies of her albums to her fans. Some of them sent money for them; many of them didn't. It didn't matter to her. If they appreciated her as much as they said, she wanted them to have her music.

In spite of poor record sales, her importance as a singer was recognized. On November 16, 1980, she received the prestigious Handy Award as Traditional Female Blues Artist of the Year, given by the Blues Foundation of Memphis based on voting by two thousand music experts from around the world.

Alberta used The Cookery as a home base between other engagements. While there she agreed to record in November 1980 for the Voice of America a program that broadcast internationally the story of her life. But she declined an invitation to attend a farewell dinner for her friend President Carter at the White House on January 7, 1981. She preferred to pay her respects her way.

She made "Georgia on My Mind" a regular part of her repertoire and always introduced it with these words: "Ladies and gentlemen, in appreciation, honor, respect, and love for one of the finest presidents we ever had. He remembered the old people, the poor people, the helpless people, the young, everybody. He was misunderstood because he had a heart. They said he was weak. He wasn't weak. He was only being kind. And we will never forget him. I'm going to sing this song, and you'll know to whom I'm singing. A wonderful man. He has a brilliant wife, too."

Alberta insisted that the song be included on a later album (*Look for the Silver Lining*). She autographed a copy and sent it to Jimmy Carter. He wrote back on November 23, 1983: "I was honored to receive the kind words you inscribed on 'Look for the Silver Lining.' It means a great deal to me that I can call you my friend. With love and best wishes."

It was also one of the songs she sang for a German television crew that filmed her at The Cookery early in 1981. Barney, having no love for Germans, tried to discourage the effort by demanding a fee of twenty-five thousand dollars for Alberta. Eventually he accepted an offer of ten thousand dollars in cash. On the night the payment was made, he asked Alberta to take the money with her since he was afraid to leave that much in his safe. She stashed it all in her bosom. Chris Albertson, who was with her, said she should put it elsewhere lest some of it fall out. "Honey, nothing ever fell out of there unless I wanted it to," she said.

Everywhere she went, Alberta made her audiences fans for life. She stopped the show at Chicago's Kool Jazz Festival before an estimated audience of seventy-five thousand people, about the same number who had seen and been moved by Marian Anderson in front of the Lincoln Memorial in 1939.

"One need make no allowances for age because Hunter sings with an authority that would be remarkable in any artist," wrote Larry Kart in the *Chicago Tribune* (September 6, 1982, section 2, p. 10). "Blues, cabaret songs, spirituals, raunchy vaudeville tunes— Hunter enthralled the audience with everything she did."

After an equally successful performance at the Montreux Kool Jazz Festival in Detroit, Alberta packed her bags again at long last for Europe. With Gerald and Vishnu Wood, replacing Aaron Bell on bass, she sang that fall at the Third Festival de Jazz de Paris, in a concert sponsored by Radio Bremen in Germany, and back in Paris at the Grand Gala du Jazz, which also featured Claude Bolling. After Alberta had finished her set at the Gala, Liza Minnelli came over to her table to suggest she and Alberta get up on the stage and do a little spontaneous number together.

"Alberta was all smiles at Liza from across the table," said Gerald. "But when she heard what Liza wanted, she said, 'No, indeed. I'm not going to sing with her. I don't need any props. Let her get where she wants to go on her own, not on my back.' "

In Paris Alberta took Gerald on a sentimental journey to the Hôtel de Paris, where she had lived in 1927, showing him where Chez Florence—where she sang that year—had been located, the joint where she had had her hair straightened and much of it fell out, the corner dive where she had changed her money, and the place where Josephine Baker had lived.

"It was very moving," said Gerald. "She was very elegant but very emotional. She was smiling and weeping about something for herself for a change. It made her very happy."

As did the fact that the *International Herald Tribune* interviewed her and even wanted her opinion about U.S. politics. "I've been in the White House," she told the reporter (November 6–7, 1982, p. 5). "Carter, honey. Put that down in big letters. One of the finest men in the world. They didn't vote for him, now they're sorry. In all my 87 years I've never seen so much suffering. People with no place to stay, nothing to eat, little babies deprived of a hot sandwich. Every time a Republican gets elected, you might as well just pack your clothes and get ready to go to the poorhouse. Or the morgue."

Before returning to the United States, Alberta appeared in Zurich and at the Berlin Jazz Festival. Werner Burkhardt, a critic for the *Süddeutsche Zeitung*, a Munich newspaper (November 9, 1982, p. 25), wrote that she didn't want to stop singing in Berlin even at three-thirty in the morning. "She sings 'Wien, Wien, Nur Du Allein' in a strange but wonderful German. She sings it more beautifully than I have ever heard it sung since I heard Ljuba Welitsch."

A year later Alberta received an invitation to perform at the 150 Club in one of South America's most elegant hotels, the Maksoud Plaza in São Paulo, Brazil. Roberto Maksoud, son of the Lebanese family that owns the hotel as well as a large engineering company, managed the hotel efficiently and the nightclub passionately. He satisfied his love of jazz by regularly bringing performers from the

United States. Alberta agreed to appear for three weeks beginning the first week in October 1983, at $2,250 for each of three shows a week, right after the close of an engagement by Bobby Short.

Barney Josephson knew of the invitation but refused to have anything to do with it. "It'll kill you," he told her. "You're gonna come back in a box. I'm not going to sign your death warrant.

"You'll have to wear a gown for your concerts," he added. "She was coming into The Cookery at that time with a denim skirt and a cheap blouse and bedroom slippers that didn't always match."

Alberta's attorney argued with Barney. "This is the only thing that's keeping her alive," Krasilovsky said, referring to her travels. "She would have been dead long ago if you hadn't put her back to work. So if she's going to die, let her die happy in an airplane or on top of a mountain."

"I'm going to do what I want to do," Alberta said. "I'm going."

As was generally the case, it was not Alberta, but Gerald, exhausted from getting her and his affairs in order before the trip, who suffered initially. He passed out on the ten-hour flight to Brazil and broke a rib.

Brazilians were ecstatic when they saw and heard Alberta and her musicians. A naturally affectionate people, the product of centuries of mixing of the races, many of them saw their own grandmothers in Alberta. And in a country where people rarely are active beyond the age of sixty and alive beyond seventy, Alberta was a "demonstration of life."

Great music lovers, the Brazilians lavishly praised the work of her accompanists, Gerald and Vishnu. They admired Vishnu's musical technique and friendliness and said that Gerald played a duet with Alberta, framing her music, reflecting her rhythms, responding to her, egging her into a feeling.

She made sure they knew how special Gerald was to her. "He anticipates everything I do," she said. "He's a devil. He inspires me 'cause I know he knows what I'm trying to say. And he brings it out in me."

Gerald's accompaniment and presence with Alberta were always terribly discreet. That was the way he was. And that was the way she wanted it. Sometimes, she said, when she thought he was shining just a little too much, she'd turn around and look at him as if to say, "What are you doing, brother? Gonna run me off the stage?"

Alberta loved Gerald's finesse. "He's so fine," she told everyone. "You know, I love class. I cannot stand a buzzard. When I look at him, looking so lovely, I think, 'Oh, my God, how lucky I am.' "

She was fortunate that Gerald was more than an accompanist. He was also a companion and confidant. And he had patience supreme. He let her have her way to the point of letting her stir the sugar in the bottom of his glass of iced tea if she thought he had not done it enough.

"It's a rare relationship," Gerald said. "Our association is very, very close. I love Alberta the person very much. And I also love Alberta the artist very, very much. It's difficult to separate them sometimes." In working with her on music, however, he could and would make that distinction. "As much as I love you, let's try it in another way," he would say to her if he thought an arrangement was not going to work.

Brazilians were as fascinated by Alberta and her musicians as they were by this music called the blues. They wanted to know if she wrote and sang it because she had been beaten up by macho men. She quickly set them straight on that score. "Many people think a woman sings the blues only when she is in love with a man who treats her like a dog," she said to the wide-eyed young reporters who followed her every move. "I've never had the blues about no man, never in my life, honey. If a man beats me, I'll take a broomstick and beat him to death.

"But that's not the blues. We sing the blues because our hearts have been hurt. Blues is when you're hungry and you don't have money to buy food. Or you can't pay your rent at the end of the month. Blues is when you disappoint somebody else: if you owe some money to your best friend, and you know he needs it, but you don't have it to give him.

"But just plain ol' ordinary 'I don't have some money,'—that's not the blues. Most young people today don't have real needs. They just have a few worries. They have needs for things that maybe they could do without. That's not the blues."

The blues could be very therapeutic in letting a person express hurt and thinking of a way to get over it, she pointed out. "Blues is like milk to a baby."

Blues and jazz, words Alberta used interchangeably, were also important to her, she said, because they helped her gain acceptance from and communicate with people who otherwise would have ignored her. She expressed that relationship best in an interview for a book entitled *Particular Passions* by Lynn Gilbert and Gaylen Moore. It presented profiles of outstanding women like Betty Friedan, Barbara Walters, Lillian Hellman, Agnes de Mille, Margaret Mead, Billie Jean King, Elisabeth Kübler-Ross, Louise Nevelson, and Alberta Hunter, chosen because they helped shape society and opened new fields for women.

"I can touch different people that never paid any attention to me before through my jazz. Yeah, touching. It's a language. Jazz has a language all its own. Naturally it's an expression of love,"* Alberta was quoted as saying.

And love it was at first sight in São Paulo. Rarely did foreign entertainers in Brazil receive the media attention focused on Alberta. Her image and music were transmitted by television almost daily as far north as the small towns on the Amazon River. She was so moved that she even put on a dazzling blue dress, streaked with gold threads, and gold shoes to perform.

Her opening night show on October 6, 1983, received rave notices. "An unforgettable night to laugh and pray, cry and applaud a woman who brings pride to the human race," wrote Zuza Homen de Mello, critic for the *O Estado de São Paulo* (October 8, 1983, p. 14).

Alberta got so carried away singing to her Brazilian "children" that she'd turn to Gerald after what would normally be a concluding chorus of a song and say, "Don't stop me, don't stop me." And on she'd go.

The national newsweekly *VEJA* said Alberta's concerts were "the greatest and most sought-after musical event of the year" (November 2, 1983, p. 130).

Alberta could find nothing wrong with Brazilians, not even when they talked or made noise during her shows, something she wouldn't

*(New York: Clarkson N. Potter, 1981), p. 251.

tolerate with any other audience. "They make noise," she said. "But it's a happy noise. Nobody is angry."

She found them "good looking and even-minded in disposition" and attributed both to the abundance of tropical fruit they ate, especially her favorite, persimmon. She wrote down the Portuguese word for that—*caqui*—so she could impress them when she asked for it over and over.

She wrote down another word—*saudade*—a poetic word meaning a nostalgic longing for a place or person. She conquered them every time she told them that was what she was going to have when she left them.

"Those people, they know what's good," she said back home to friends who said their ears got worn out hearing about Brazil. "They remind me of southerners. They've got that warmth, that sincerity.

"This Brazil has just ruined me," she repeated endlessly. "My goodness, I tell you, I'm so happy."

"The trip was well worth the risk," said Krasilovsky. "After the White House she wanted one more great experience. It was Brazil. As soon as she got there, she sent me a postcard saying, 'This is paradise.' It made her feel that she was a young girl, that she could do it all over again. And she made a lot of money."

Barney couldn't believe his eyes or ears when Alberta returned, stronger than ever, "singing like a thrush," and acting twenty years younger.

Alberta returned to Brazil at the end of May 1984 for a month. Again she was met with adulation. She told each audience how she loved them, that Brazil was the greatest country in the world, and that she would keep coming back to be with them. "I'll be back every chance I get even if I have to pay my own way," she said. She didn't have to worry about that. Roberto Maksoud invited her to return to perform and celebrate her ninetieth birthday on April 1, 1985. She couldn't stop talking about that once she had returned to the United States.

Asked if she might buy a pretty, new dress for the occasion, she said, "Nah. But I might buy me a new pair of blue jeans." She justified her late love of sloppy clothes by saying, "I've been dressing up all my life. That's why I can't stand clothes now. I try to dress like an old lady and age gracefully. At my age it wouldn't do for me to put on a lot of sequins and try to look like a chicken."

One woman wrote Alberta and encouraged her at least to do something with her hair: "You wear it too severe. Let it loose. Put a couple of curlers in. Use a hair curler. Have it set. I'm sure that everyone watching in would agree with me."

Flo Thornley, owner of a fashionable Harlem beauty salon where Alberta had her hair "done," couldn't have agreed more. She badgered Alberta constantly to put a little style into her hairdo, but Alberta would hear nothing of it. "Wash it, pull it straight back, and tie it in a knot, honey," she ordered.

Flo had no more luck trying to alter the rest of Alberta's look. "Alberta, how can you go around looking like that?" she asked.

Alberta's typical getup then consisted of beat-up walking shoes, blue jeans and a lumberjack shirt, covered in cooler weather with a long quilted coat with the appearance of a swollen potato sack. She topped this off with a ratty knit cap pulled down low on her brow.

With shopping bags always in hand, Alberta looked like one of the destitute bag ladies who plod the streets of New York. That suited her fine and discouraged the muggers. Once Geraldine Stutz, president of exclusive Henri Bendel, gave Alberta some of the store's fashionable shopping bags, hoping to improve at least that part of her basic wardrobe. Alberta wasn't about to use them and attract attention.

It would have been one dead mugger who tried to pull anything on her. She always kept an ice pick within easy reach in one of her bags in case any poor fool dared get too close. "Anybody bother me, and they're going to get it right through the heart," she said.

The only time anyone saw her pull it out was at The Cookery one night when a giant of a man, high on drugs, stood threateningly inside the front door. Alberta sauntered over to him, flashing the ice pick below her waist not to attract the attention of any customers. He took one look at her weapon and made a hasty retreat. He was never seen near that door again. Who needed the cops for protection?

As scruffy as she looked most of the time, Alberta appeared in *Vogue* (September 1982, p. 140) with advice to its readers: "I think women should make up their minds to do something and then do it and not get scared. A woman can do anything if she's got stamina and courage. And every time a man tells you he loves you, don't believe him."

Whenever Alberta gave advice to women, she urged them to rely on themselves. "If you tell a man you love him, then you are in a bad fix. You tell him you love him, and he sees that you love him —oh, my God, is he gonna ruin you. Don't let it happen to you, honey."

Asked frequently by reporters if she didn't have suitors, she said, sure, there were plenty of "cats" telling her how "cute" she was. "I'm an old billiard drinker [not one to be fooled]," she said. "I've got a mirror as big as I am. I can see myself in it. I know how I look, so there's no need them telling me any of that. I'm too slick for that jive. They say, 'Well aren't you lonesome?'

"I say, 'Lonesome for what? I got a telephone, a radio, a television, *and* a bankbook. I ain't lonesome for nothin'.'

"Most fellows are just looking for some help, an ace in the hole. Well, I'm the wrong ace."

The *New York Post* (April 10, 1982, p. 11), proclaiming Alberta "the new kid in town" and a "national treasure," asked her secret to longevity. "Lookit, honey," she said. "I never smoked, drank, cussed, took drugs, owed nobody nothin' and never did musical exercises to warm up. All I ever did is open my mouth and sing."

The *New York Daily News* (September 25, 1983) featured her on the cover of its Sunday magazine with a story on beauty tips for the "over-70 set." Among the elegant white women who revealed their secrets was Mildred Gilbert, a former *Vogue* editor, who said, "For years I ate nothing but marvelous little lamb chops and pureed spinach."

"Oh, baby," said down-home Alberta (p. 14). "I think positive thoughts. I don't hold malice in my heart. I'm one of the happiest people in the world." Three photos of Alberta, accompanying the article, revealed the rascal in her eyes and suggested that a lifetime of "jiving" was another crucial element of her secret formula.

As casual as Alberta grew to be about her appearance, she never relaxed her demanding professional standards while performing. Critics applauded that quality. Jim Feldman of the *Village Voice* (April

20, 1982, p. 78), on the release of her album *The Glory of Alberta Hunter* and return stint at The Cookery, said: "The sheer strength of her voice, its rich, pliant timbre and lusty attack, confounds the erosive power of time. She has never sounded better or more purposeful.

"Hunter didn't simply pick up the loose ends of her musical career. She tied them in a splendid bow, displaying an audacious command of the almost-forgotten act of straight-from-the-gut, no bullshit club singing."

John Wilson of the *New York Times* (June 26, 1983, p. 44) praised a live performance, especially her rendition of an old Bessie Smith favorite, "Nobody Knows You When You're Down and Out": "The shading, the subtleties of emphasis, the thoughtful development of the song and the color and range of her voice, particularly the rich splendor of her low notes, were as moving and brilliant as anything she has done since she renewed her singing career six years ago at the Cookery. It was a masterpiece that could stand with Bessie Smith's celebrated but very different version of the song."

Peter Reilly, reviewing the album *Look for the Silver Lining* in *Stereo Review* (March 1984, p. 94), said, "Nobody—repeat, nobody—has ever sung this album's 'He's Funny That Way' or 'Somebody Loves Me' with quite the same intonations, insinuations, and mood changes as Hunter gives them. The high point here for me is Hunter's tribute to her contemporary Josephine Baker, a version of Baker's signature song 'J'ai Deux Amours.' It's the kind of performance that summons up all sort of memories and ghosts, not just of an entertainer who's no longer with us but of a whole epoch that probably ended in 1929."

On Alberta's eighty-seventh birthday, April 1, 1982, the *Daily News* (p. 91) wrote, "Alberta Hunter 87 and going on forever." ASCAP sent her a dozen roses, Jimmy and Rosalynn Carter sent their greetings, and Eubie Blake, then ninety-nine, went to play for her as usual and had his picture taken with her at The Cookery.

No one wanted to imagine she could not or would not go on and on. As Don Nelsen wrote in the *New York Daily News* (September 4, 1981, p. 19), "When you sense that Alberta Hunter is near the final song of a set, you say to yourself, 'Lord, please don't let it end.' Few performers can inspire that sentiment, and when one can—

consistently—at 86, the listener almost looks for a nimbus about the head."

Unfortunately there was a limit to the life in her, although she didn't succumb to it willingly. On June 11, 1980, the day after she had opened at George's Club on Chicago's North Side, she fell getting out of a car and fractured her wrist and hip. It was a major blow because Chicago was the first stop on a national tour that had to be canceled.

Her friend Chris Albertson called her from New York to see how she was. "I never felt better in my life," she told him. "It was as if she had broken a fingernail," he said. "Other performers in that situation would have been totally demoralized. But Alberta had an indomitable spirit that made her always look on the bright side of things."

"I should have taken a rest," she said to Chris. "But I had to be greedy and do this tour, so God said, 'I got to stop this woman,' and that's exactly what He did."

Alberta went home to New York after that first accident, telling all the journalists who asked about her, "This old jalopy's got a lot of mileage on her yet."

One of the first calls she received at home was from her old friend Mae Barnes, who told her that her fall was a warning that it was time for her to stop. "Bertie, why do you have to keep working like this? For what? You can go to an uncharted island and just rest yourself."

"I like show business" was Alberta's response. Actually she was consumed by it because she had nothing else in life. She couldn't let go. She was afraid to let go.

"Without show business she couldn't do nothing," said Mae.

"A lot of girls that I have worked with have told me that the worst thing they ever did was to retire," Alberta said to justify her decision to keep working. To her people who stopped working were weak-minded or lazy. Worse were those who accepted mandatory retirement, which she called "an imposition on a person's right to live."

"Just keep working" was her message to older people. "If they say you're too old to do this kind of work, get another kind of work. Just keep busy.

"You're never too old. What is old? What is age but something on a calendar. As long as you've got a mind, as long as you're willing to think, as long as you're willing to work, help yourself and help others. There's no age limit. You have to be strong, have a mind of your own. Don't quit.

"America is ruining a lot of people," she said, referring to mandatory retirement practices. "They're killing the spirit of a lot of people. They make them lazy, make them go on welfare. Some of them commit suicide because they think they're too old.

"We older people are much younger in mind than a lot of the youngsters that are saying those things. I'm eighty-nine, happy as a lark, eatin' like a pig, and extremely happy, and I'm going to keep going. There's no such thing as retirement for me. When I retire, it's because God Almighty has said, 'Come home.' "

Sure, she was taking risks with her health. But as she said, "If you don't take a chance, what's the use of living?" And Alberta intended to live every moment of life. "Time means so much to me," she said. "I don't throw one golden second away."

Alberta inspired others around her to live life to the fullest, said Barbara Bordnick. "Alberta taught us that you don't grow old and then die. You live and then die, which is a big difference."

Alberta better explained her love of, if not need for, work in a song she wrote in 1949 (originally entitled "I'm Having a Gay Time") and sang frequently in her last years:

> *I'm having a good time,*
> *Please don't blame me,*
> *I'm knocking myself out*
> *Don't try to tame me*
> *Let me have my fun,*
> *I've got to have my fling,*
> *Some folks say I'm blowing my top*
> *Talk don't mean a thing,*
> *I'm playing it cool while I'm living*
> *'Cause tomorrow I may die*

That's why I'm having a ball today
And I ain't passing nothin' by
So, if I make my bed hard
That's my problem
Let me lay
I'm having a good time living my life today.

Alberta fell again while singing at The Cookery on February 17, 1981, and fractured her left leg. On that hospital visit she had a pacemaker implanted, an instrument she vehemently denied having two years later to even as close a friend as Harry Watkins. She went home after two weeks but was back in the hospital for a week in mid-April for everything from a "changing mental status," nausea, and diarrhea to irritability, confusion, and dyspnea (painful or difficult breathing).

But back she went to The Cookery in early May as if nothing had happened and nothing more could happen to her. "I feel like a million dollars," she said to anybody who looked worried and inquired about her.

The top brass at IBM were so impressed by Alberta's spirit and determination that they commissioned a ten-minute film from producer Stuart A. Goldman to use as a motivational tool in a meeting of its sales force from around the world.

President Ronald Reagan invited Alberta to sing at the White House on December 4, 1982. But the night before, she checked into St. Vincent's Hospital for what turned out to be a two-month stay. Alberta was suffering from internal bleeding but wouldn't authorize the doctor to do exploratory surgery on her. "Look, I've been around doctors for years," she said. "I know you guys. All you want to do is use the knife. You treat me medically."

"We're either going in, or she'll be dead tomorrow," her physician told Gerald, who authorized the surgery. Alberta had a gangrenous small intestine and right colon. Her small bowel and part of her large bowel were removed.

When she awakened after the operation, Gerald gave her a copy of an article in *Time* magazine (December 13, 1982, p. 82) to distract her. Its kind words were better for her than any get-well card. It likened her to a line from her song "Workin' Man": "There's plenty of good tunes, honey, left in an old violin." It said: "Particularly in this rare and indestructible Stradivarius; there is no one else alive who can sing like Hunter."

Her hospital stay kept her from appearing in a show Bobby Short had planned to do with her on January 7, 1983, at Carnegie Hall. She also missed the celebration of Eubie Blake's hundredth birthday at the Shubert Theater, days before he died.

Alberta's pace was less hectic that spring. She began to receive awards from groups that probably thought she was on her way out. On May 3, 1983, she received New York City's Mayor's Award of Honor for Arts and Culture. Other recipients were John Ashbery, Merce Cunningham, Rudolf Serkin, Maureen Stapleton, and Saul Steinberg.

She was given a Certificate of Appreciation by the citizens of Shelby County (which included Memphis). And in June 1983 B'nai B'rith at its nineteenth Annual Award Dinner Dance in New York gave Alberta its humanitarian award.

The acknowledgment she coveted most came on June 22, when she returned to her devoted fans at The Cookery for the first time since her surgery. In early August she was back at St. Vincent's Hospital for treatment of tachycardia. She returned to The Cookery at the end of the month. In September she fell again and received a steroid injection in her right knee. But that didn't stop her from taking the ten-hour flight to São Paulo for her first engagement there.

On her return to New York she tried to keep working at The Cookery, still feeling indebted to Barney. At that point she could no longer get to and from the bathroom downstairs on her own. She rejected Barney's suggestion that he and Gerald carry her up and down the stairs or take her back and forth to his apartment, nearby, every time she wanted to use the bathroom. He offered to install a portable toilet in the dishwashing area of the kitchen on the ground floor.

"That was so undignified a solution for so dignified a lady," said her attorney, Bill Krasilovsky. Gerald asked Krasilovsky to insist that she not return to The Cookery.

Alberta agreed reluctantly. She made it clear she held no grudges against Barney. "I will always think of Barney as a fine man, a good friend, as a man who gave me a chance when I was eighty-two years old, whereas the average owner of one of the clubs would have said, 'A what? A woman that age? Why, no.' "

Barney didn't take the news well, Alberta said. "He was so hurt he turned it [The Cookery] into a barbecue stand."

The Cookery without Alberta couldn't make it. Barney sold it and went to work part-time for the new owner, who did turn it into a barbecue restaurant. Alberta became irritated with Barney months later only when, as if to justify his actions, he told people she was retiring from show business. "I never intend to retire," she said. "When I die, I'll die with my shoes on. I might loosen the strings a little, but I'll be on my feet with my shoes on."

The strings were never loosened. Even when Bricktop died on February 1, 1984 (two months before Mabel Mercer died), Alberta wouldn't admit that she might be next. She told Jean Claude Baker, Josephine Baker's "adopted" son, triumphantly, "Oh, my God. There she is, and here I am."

She saved her strength for her second trip to Brazil. That summer several people close to her died. Dearest was Jimmy Daniels, who collapsed in June shortly after participating in a concert at Carnegie Hall.

The two of them had had their quarrels. Jimmy moved to a larger, more expensive apartment in 1977 so that Alberta could live there while she was performing nearby at The Cookery. She told Krasilovsky she was living with Jimmy because he was a good cook, "not because of sex," lest her attorney doubt her intentions. She agreed to pay part of the rent. Jimmy waited on her hand and foot, cooked all her meals, and cleaned up after her.

When she returned from her first trip to Brazil, she didn't want to pay him for the time she had been away in spite of the fact that he'd had to pay the higher rent anyway to keep the place available to her. Jimmy was ticked off but didn't have the nerve to tell her to move out. She said she was "sick of his fancy food." He was tired of going all over town at her command to buy certain food items at specific stores because they were on sale for a few pennies less. She decided she was not made for communal living at any price and moved back to her Roosevelt Island apartment, which she had maintained all along. But she kept most of her things stored in Jimmy's apartment so he couldn't rent what had been her room to anyone else.

Nevertheless, his death hurt her. She missed him. "If Jimmy were here, I could talk to him about something that's on my mind that nobody will understand like he would. I know he's here listening, but still he's missing. He's with me, but he's not with me. That's the blues.

"A lot of people say, 'Oh, so-and-so has died, I've got to get some flowers.' Don't take any money and buy flowers. Buy someone a sandwich."

Alberta grew more and more suspicious of strangers and cranky with her few friends. People would call her and say, "Well, I'd like to see you for about an hour."

"I'd think, oh, my God, no!" said Alberta. She told them not to come, that she wasn't up to it. She wouldn't even let a grandnephew studying near her come visit.

She treated Gerald, who had already dedicated more than five years of his life almost exclusively to her, like an errand boy. "No child could love and do for a parent more than Gerald did for her," said Barney Josephson. "He was at her beck and call."

She wanted him to pay her bills, to bring her mail, to take her to the doctor, to take her to a half dozen of her banks once a week, to keep her well rehearsed for their performances. She never offered to pay for his gas, tolls, parking fees, or the traffic fines he received on her account. When his car was being repaired, as occurred often, she complained that he couldn't take her somewhere at that instant.

"Don't go giving me that jive all the time," she would say to him. "Go buy a new car. That car is in the shop more than I am." Often he did hire a car, sometimes with a driver, to take her on her rounds.

She also complained when she had to talk to Gerald's telephone answering machine. She couldn't stand not having him immediately available to her; she suspected he was indeed at home when she called and simply used the machine to keep her at a distance. "I hate that machine worse than the devil hates a Christian," she said.

Pauline Reed, a longtime friend in Chicago, explained Alberta's increasing cantankerousness. "Getting old is hell," she said. "When you try to hang on to your sanity and your objectivity, your personality can change."

Alberta created a nasty scene with Gerald after an outdoor performance she gave on July 4, 1984, at New York's South Street Seaport. She came to the pier with Harry Watkins in a chauffeur-driven car. After the show Gerald asked her to return in the car with Harry, with whom she was going to stay that night in their Riverside Drive apartment. Gerald wanted to go out to dinner with a woman friend who was waiting for him. Alberta took one look at the woman and told Gerald, loud enough for his friend to hear, that he was not to "go around with other women" while he was with her.

"I'm a jealous woman," she said weeks after the incident. "That's just my nature."

Gerald's patience lasted only to the door of Alberta's apartment, where he left her, having agreed to meet his friend later. Then he exploded. "Alberta, you're selfish, and you're rude," he said to her. "You must never do this again to a friend of mine."

"He read it to me, honey," Alberta said later. "And then he even put a period at the end of it."

The two of them made up with each other to the point where they could continue to travel and perform together. But Alberta tested Gerald's wits by refusing to give interviews that were necessary to help promote ticket sales.

During the summer of 1984 they were at the Baltimore Arts Festival, at Detroit's Music Hall, and in Denver, where she had to tell the audience she couldn't get through the show. She sang a few songs, the last she was ever to sing before a live audience.

Alberta's entertainment days were coming to an end, although she still didn't want to admit it. It was a traumatic realization for a woman who felt, as Gerald said, that "her performing was even more important than life to her."

Her nephew Sam Sharpe, Jr., tried to get backstage after the show in Denver to see her but was stopped by a guard who had orders to let no one near her. The telephone operator at her hotel wouldn't connect him to her room. She left town without answering his messages.

All she could think about was getting back home. But as soon as she got there, her health failed quickly. Since moving back into her own apartment on Roosevelt Island the year before, she had refused to let anyone come in to cook for her. She depended on Brother Harry, Thelma Keith, a friend of Gerald's, or a neighbor to bring her an occasional plate of food. She also refused to take most of the medicines her doctor prescribed for her. Gerald became infuriated with her again and told her attorney he simply could do nothing more with Alberta.

She went to stay with Harry Watkins but drove him to distraction with her demands and complaints. Krasilovsky picked her up there and forced her to go to St. Vincent's Hospital for intravenous feeding.

Engagements across the country were canceled. At least that saved her from singing for the Republicans at their national convention in Dallas. She rejected their first offer, saying she would only perform for much more money, seventy-five hundred dollars. "Ronald Reagan knows that he's starving a lot of poor people," she said. "That's not right. And then I end up singing for him."

However, once the Republicans had agreed to pay her price, she accepted. She did some fast rationalizing. "There are Republicans who've been good to me," she said. "There're a few people who don't treat me right. A few Democrats don't treat me right. So that's that. I'm going down there, and I'm going to sing my head off."

Her hospital stay resolved all that, as angry as it made her. She was angry at the weakening of her body and took her frustration out on everyone around her. She said that she was on nine thousand medications and that she wasn't going to take any of them. "If I die, I'm gonna die anyhow. I'm not gonna die till God's ready for me."

She laid it on the doctors. "Doctors have a lot on their minds. They got to hustle. They got to keep their wives well. They got to keep their sweethearts happy. I'm no fool."

And she railed against all the hospital staff because they didn't serve her Coca-Cola. She said she paid to be on Medicare and thus had a right to receive the benefits she wanted, including the soft drink of her preference.

They told her they didn't have any Coke at the hospital and didn't have anyone to go and get it.

"Well, call up and tell 'em to send it over," she said. "I'm not paying for whatever they call that other stuff." (Krasilovsky for months had added a rider to all her contracts for performances stipulating that Coca-Cola would have to be made available in her dressing room.)

In spite of Alberta's irascibility, she wasn't an unreasonable patient, said Mary Phillips, a Jamaican working there as a nurse's aide. "She never rang unless she really needed something. She just knew what she wanted, and she knew what her rights were."

Gerald, who had cleaned up Alberta's apartment and put some pictures on her barren walls to make it look more cheerful, couldn't believe the junk she made him take back home from the hospital for her. He carried two big plastic garbage bags containing: three six-packs of Coca-Cola; countless empty plastic beverage bottles; old newspapers; boxes of spaghetti; four big bottles of dill pickles; four bottles of witch hazel (at least one of which had leaked out over everything else); little bags and envelopes of sugar, saccharin, and Sanka coffee (she never drank any kind of coffee); dried fruits; and a bag of plastic spoons, forks, knives, and cups, which she insisted she was saving to give to kids in her building for "their little parties."

"Alberta, I wouldn't give this crap to my worst enemy," Gerald said. "I've been waiting for the children to pick up your empty bottles for years."

"I'm a sick woman," she said. "How can you do this to me?"

They didn't talk to each other for another week after that.

Alberta was down to eighty-five pounds. She grew weaker. She took only some of her many prescribed medications, and those she took irregularly. Notes on little scraps around her apartment said, for example, "September 7: I took heart medicine Sunday."

A visiting nurse came to see her that day. She asked him to tell her if her breath was bad. "I want to keep my mouth lovely," she told him. "Lots of people don't want to tell you, but I want to know."

Krasilovsky called her the same day. Asked how she was, she responded in a husky voice as if she were Mount Rushmore, "I'll be around till Judgment Day."

He asked her if she would like to do a joint concert with jazz singer Betty Carter.

"I don't need any buildup, anyone to lean on," she said haughtily. "All these years I've worked alone. She didn't think about me when I was struggling. If Betty Carter's concerts are slacking, let her build them back up. No, I'm not interested, and that's all there is to that. Good-bye."

Then she turned to the handsome young male nurse, still waiting to take her blood pressure, raised her voice an octave, and shifted gears into charm, full speed ahead.

"I'm a female Marco Polo," she told him, batting her eyelashes at him. "I've traveled all over this earth."

Now Alberta's traveling days were over. It was all she could do to get into her jeans, brown flannel shirt, baggy jacket, and bedroom slippers on September 10 to appear briefly on the *Good Morning America* show. That was her last television appearance, and it was a very feeble one at that. Her memory failed her several times while she was singing.

For several weeks Alberta propped herself up in bed to retell the story of her life for this book. She cackled as she remembered the good times. She cried when she told how much it meant to her to be able to work as a practical nurse at Goldwater. She praised God and cursed the Internal Revenue Service.

She was eternally optimistic. Even days before she died, when she was obviously having great physical difficulties, Alberta kept saying, "How anybody can be called sick and feel like I do, I don't know. I feel like a million dollars."

She doubled her long fingers a hundred times a day to keep them in shape. She stubbornly tried to cook, so as to leave no obstacle undefeated in her life. As she always said, "I don't know anything I haven't done, except maybe learn how to cook." She would fill a pan with black-eyed peas and cook them all day long. "I'm gonna eat like a dog," she'd say, relishing her intended accomplishment. The next day she'd admit that she'd almost burned up the kitchen and had to throw out the charred beans.

She did a lot of thinking. "I'm gonna be bald-headed when I grow old because I use it so much," she said. "Think, think, think." Sometimes she thought about how fortunate she had been in life and felt sorry for those who weren't. They didn't have a Gerald to look after them, she said. "There are so many girls and fellows that are good at heart but don't have someone to think about them like I do. They're alone by themselves. So when I sit and cry sometimes, I'm crying for the other fellow."

She criticized many modern black singers for not enunciating their words. "I would enjoy them so much more if I could understand what they're saying," she said. "That's why on a lot of records nowadays they print the lyrics."

Alberta was equally critical of college-educated black women whose grammar was still bad. "Read newspapers" was her advice for them to learn to speak correctly.

She thought about racial prejudice and how sad it was that it still existed. "All's not right yet. Some places you go right now, you're not as welcome. You're not treated as politely and as kindly as you would be in some other city. There's still much prejudice, a lot of it!" Parents were passing it to their children, and they to their friends, she said. "Some of the white children do things they did years ago because . . . they're still taught that hatred where color is concerned. Many of them don't want to do it. They want to be kind. But they don't have minds of their own. They're led by the bad ones."

She asked God to help her forgive those who had discriminated against her all her life. "I ask God to help me get that bitterness out of my heart," she said.

Alberta slept facing the window so she could see the sun rise. "This is what I asked for years ago when I wrote the words to a song: "The sun is going to shine in my door someday."

Even on dark, rainy nights Alberta looked out her window and "picked out some kind of beauty. I can look over there and out of the clear blue sky I can see a face or a picture," she said. "Sometimes it's a face I remember and want hard to remember. Sometimes it's somebody I wish I could remember and can't."

The person she thought of most during those days and nights was her grandmother. "She was such a sweet thing," Alberta said. "She had a heart. She was sympathetic, understanding, kind. My grandmother was a lovely woman. I wish I could call her and say, 'Granny, come to me and lay your head on my shoulder, and let me touch you a little while and thank you for the lovely things you did for me when I was growing up, thank you for the good thoughts that you gave me, and thank you for my God, who was so good to me. Thank you for telling me about Him so I understand now that I'm a grown woman. Thank you for giving me all the good things. And as bad as things may appear to be, maybe compared to somebody else, they could be worse.' "

Alberta felt very close to God. In fact, she was His messenger, she said. Asked how she knew that, she said, "Because I'm different. I'm out here by myself. I'm extremely happy. I feel inside that God is talking to me, and I'm listening. There are others that He's talking to, too, but they're not listening. He's telling me, 'Never lose faith, keep my hand in your hand, and you can't go wrong. And I will always see that you will be happy, never lonesome.' "

She felt she did the Lord's work first by nursing bodies for twenty years and then by nursing the spirits of all those who saw or heard her perform. As her nephew Sam Sharpe said, "Going to see her was like going to an old-time faith healer. People go in with aches and pains and come out feeling like jumping up and hopping down the street all the way home."

Alberta closed many a show by saying to the audience, "If you came in with a troubled mind or heart and I have erased some of it, then I feel that my living has not been in vain."

Alberta said she spread God's message by buying a meal for a hungry person or encouraging others to love Him. "If a man looks like he has doubt in his mind, doesn't believe in God, I'll say, 'You're thinking the wrong way. I'm an example of God's goodness. I'm eighty-nine years old. Take me as an example of one of God's people. Keep me in mind. See me in your mind's eye wherever you go. And remember, it's God, not me. That's right.' "

God had made her free from cares, Alberta said.

"Except for the income tax," she said. "They're gonna get me, or I'm gonna get them. But I won't go to the poorhouse."

They got her. In her last weeks she paid the IRS more than sixty thousand dollars in back taxes, although she protested loudly, said Krasilovsky. He was amazed that a woman who "loved God so much and had such a high sense of morality was such a tax cheat." In her mind, he said, she thought paying seven thousand dollars a year in taxes was as much as she ought ever to have to pay.

"If I wanted to, I could stop work right now instead of paying the income tax people and go on relief," she said. "Instead, I go on and work, trying to earn my money with an honest living, and the income tax people worry me to death. They nearly drive me crazy.

"They don't think how little an elderly person has to live on because they're so busy trying to take it away from them. They don't pay any attention to all the old people out in the streets with no place to stay.

"Now, the government wants to look at my books. Just because I'm making fifteen cents. Millionaires go years and years and never pay a dime and get away with it. It's disgraceful."

"Alberta didn't disclose her assets to anyone, and she didn't want to pay taxes on interest-bearing accounts," said Krasilovsky. He discovered she had them only when the IRS knocked on her door. "She talked about taxes like a Hollywood tough guy," he said.

"They're not going to put an old lady like me in jail," she said. "I just refuse to pay. You just tell them they can come and take me away anytime at all."

The only thing that bothered her more was the possibility that she might have to go back to the hospital. To any of the few people she would let come to see her, she pleaded, "Don't let them put me in the hospital. I want to stay right here. I'm as happy as I can be."

She had her way again. She was at home at the end. On October 17 Carol Wright-Vaughan of Pacemaker Testing of New York phoned Alberta because she was overdue for her monthly testing. "That wasn't like her," she said. Because she repeatedly got a busy signal, she called the other number she had for the apartment Alberta shared with Harry Watkins on Riverside Drive.

Harry then tried for some time to call Alberta. He knew Alberta didn't like to be on the phone for more than a few minutes. He called Gerald, who then went to the apartment and found Alberta in her green hospital pajamas and bedroom slippers, sitting in an armchair on the other side of the room from her bed, her head propped on an arm, dead.

Frank E. Campbell, a prominent undertaker in Manhattan, picked up the body. When that evening the undertaker advised her attorney, Bill Krasilovsky, of a sizable minimum fee for their services, he told them Alberta had stipulated that no more than seven hundred dollars was to be spent on her burial and that she wanted to be cremated. She had always said she would be happy to be buried "in a paper bag or a corrugated box."

Campbell's told Krasilovsky he was free to remove Alberta's body with no charge whatsoever for its services to that point. "We stole the body," said Bill. He and Gerald looked in the yellow pages of the telephone book and found a firm on Staten Island that would pick up the body and cremate it. Alberta would have been delighted with the bargain price.

She was buried in the plot she bought at the time of her mother's death at Ferncliff Cemetery in Hartsdale, New York.

Alberta's feelings about her death were similar to those of Lady Mendl, as reported in an article Alberta had clipped and saved from the *Montreal Herald* (July 26, 1950): ". . . no funeral, no flowers, please and above all no exhibition even for the most loving friends. I want their memories of me to be in their hearts. If I have been of any help to any living being, let them think of that the day they hear I am dead. Amen."

"And let them know I am finally free," Alberta said in a song she wrote in 1949, "When I Go Home":

> *My way seems dark on every hand*
> *Sometime I just can't understand*
> *Just why fate is so against me*
> *Against my every wish or plan*
> *I'm gonna keep on aiming high*
> *Guess I'll have to struggle 'till I die*
> *But I can lay down all my burdens*
> *When I go home*
>
> *When I go home, when I go home*
> *I'm gonna lay down all my trouble*
> *When I go home*

I do my best in every way
To spread good cheer from day to day
I always try to help each person
That I see falling by the way
And when this race on earth is run
I seek no praise for what I've done
'Cause I can lay down all my burdens
When I go home.

Discography

Alberta Hunter

Abbreviations for Recording Companies

ARC - American Record Company
BB - Bluebird
BS - Black Swan
BV - Prestige/Bluesville
CO - Columbia
De - Decca
DRG - DRG
GE - Gennett

HMV - His Master's Voice
JB - Juke Box
OK - OKeh
Pm - Paramount
RLP - Riverside
ST - Stash
Vi - Victor
W - Wheeler

Titles of LPs

ST 123	-	*Young Alberta Hunter: The Twenties*
ST 115	-	*Classic Alberta Hunter: The Thirties*
DRG 5195	-	*The Legendary Alberta Hunter: The London Sessions—1934*
BV 1052	-	*Songs We Taught Your Mother* (sung by Alberta Hunter, Lucille Hegamin, and Victoria Spivey)
RLP 418	-	*Alberta Hunter with Lovie Austin's Blues Serenaders*
JS 35553	-	*Remember My Name* (original sound track recording)
Columbia JC 36430	-	*Amtrak Blues*
FC 37691	-	*The Glory of Alberta Hunter*
FC 38970	-	*Look for the Silver Lining*

Abbreviations for Instruments

alt - alto sax	org - organ
bbs - bass	pno - piano
bjo - banjo	sop - soprano sax
clt - clarinet	tbm - tambourine
cor - cornet	tbn - trombone
dms - drums	tpt - trumpet
flt - flute	ts - tenor sax
gtr - guitar	tb - tuba
ob - oboe	vln - violin

(This discography lists original release as well as performances re-issued on LPs.)

Uncertain if accompanied (acc) by Ray's Dreamland Orchestra or Henderson's Novelty Orchestra, but musicians are thought to be Howard Scott, tpt; Chink Johnson, tbn/clt/ts; Fletcher Henderson, pno/bbs

(PLACE AND DATE OF RECORDING)
New York, c. May 1921

MATRIX #	SONG TITLE	CATALOG #
P-120-1,-2	He's a Darned Good Man (to Have Hanging Round)	BS 2019
P-121-2,-3	How Long, Sweet Daddy, How Long	BS 2008, ST 123

Accompanied (acc) by either Henderson's Novelty Orchestra or Ray's Dreamland Orchestra, with unknown tpt; tbn; clt; ts; Fletcher Henderson, pno

New York, c. May 1921

P-124-2,-3	Bring Back the Joys	BS 2008
P-125-3	Some Day Sweetheart	BS 2019

Acc by unknown tpt, tbn, two clts, alt, pno, and bbs

New York, July 1922

1105-1,-2,-3	Down Hearted Blues	Pm 12005, ST 123
1106-1	Why Did You Pick Me Up When I Was Down, Why Didn't You Let Me Lay	Pm 12004
1107-2,-3	Gonna Have You, Ain't Gonna Leave You Alone	Pm 12005, ST 123
1108-1,-2	Daddy Blues	Pm 12001
1109-1,-2	Don't Pan Me	Pm 12001
1110-2,-3	After All These Years	Pm 12004

Acc by Eubie Blake, pno

New York, July 1922

1111-1,-2,-3	I'm Going Away Just to Wear You Off My Mind	Pm 12006
1112-1,-4	Jazzin' Baby Blues	Pm 12006

Acc perhaps by Sam Wooding's Orchestra with unknown tpt, tbn, clt, alt, pno, bbs

New York, September 1922

1179-1,-2	You Can't Have It All	Pm 12008
1181-1,-2	Lonesome Monday Morning Blues	Pm 12007

Acc by Henderson's Novelty Orchestra, probably with Elmer Chambers, tpt; George Brashear, tbn; Don Redman, clt; Ernest Elliott, alt; Fletcher Henderson, pno; and Charlie Dixon, bjo

New York, February 1923

1316-1,-2	Come On Home	Pm 12013
1317-1,-2	You Shall Reap Just What You Sow	Pm 12021

Acc by the Original Memphis Five: Phil Napoleon, tpt; Charlie Panelli, tbn; Jimmy Lytell, clt; Frank Signorelli, pno; Jack Roth, dms

New York, February 1923

1318-1,-2	'Tain't Nobody's Biz-ness If I Do	Pm 12016
1319-1,-2	If You Want to Keep Your Daddy Home	Pm 12016

Acc by Fletcher Henderson's Orchestra

New York, February 1923

1320-1,-2	Bleeding Hearted Blues	Pm 12021
1321-1,-2	Chirpin' the Blues	Pm 12017, ST 115
1322-1,-1	Someone Else Will Take Your Place	Pm 12017
1323-2	Vamping Brown	Pm 12020
1324-2	You Can Have My Man If He Comes to See You Too	Pm 12018, ST 123

Acc by Original Memphis Five

New York, February 1923

1325-1,-2	Aggravatin' Papa	Pm 12013

Acc by Henderson's Dance Orchestra; with Elmer Chambers, cor; unknown tbn and clt; Fletcher Henderson, pno

New York, February 1923

1326-2	I'm Going Away to Wear You Off My Mind	Pm 12019

1327-2	Loveless Love	Pm 12019
1328-2	You Can Take My Man but You Can't Keep Him Long	Pm 12020
1329-2	Bring It With You When You Come	Pm 12018, ST 123

Acc by Fletcher Henderson, pno (* with Joe Smith, cor)

New York, May 1923

1420-2	Mistreated Blues	Pm 12043
1425-2,*-4	Michigan Water Blues	Pm 12036
1426-1,*-2*	Down South Blues	Pm 12036
1426-4	Down South Blues	Pm 12036

Acc by Fats Waller, pno

New York, c. May–June 1923

1455-2	Stingeree Blues	Pm 12049
1456-1	You Can't Do What My Last Man Did	Pm 12043

Note: The Paramount Records catalogue of releases up through January 1924 wrongly credits 1456 to Anna Jones.

Vocal acc by her Paramount Boys with Tommy Ladnier, cor; Jimmy O'Bryant, clt; and Lovie Austin or J. Glover Compton, pno

Chicago, October 1923

1528-1	Experience Blues	Pm 12065
1529-1,-2	Sad 'n' Lonely Blues	Pm 12065

Acc by Lovie Austin, pno (*with John O'Brigant, clt)

Chicago, October 1923

1530-1,-2	Miss Anna Brown	Pm 12066
1531-1,-2	Maybe Someday*	Pm 12066

Acc vocally by the Elkins-Payne Jubilee Quartette and by unknown pno

New York, February 1924

1666-1,-3	Old-Fashioned Love	Pm 12093
1667-1,-2	If the Rest of the World Don't Want You (Go Back to Your Mother and Dad)	Pm 12093

Acc by the Red Onion Jazz Babies with Louis Armstrong, cor; Aaron Thompson, tbn; Buster Bailey, clt; Lil Armstrong, pno; Buddy Christian, bjo

New York, November 6, 1924

9167	Everybody Loves My Baby	Ge 5594

New York, November 8, 1924

9176-A	Texas Moaner Blues	Ge 5594

Note: Both recordings issued as Josephine Beatty

Acc by the Red Onion Jazz Babies with Louis Armstrong, cor; Charlie Irvis, tbn; Sidney Bechet, clt/sop; Lil Armstrong, pno; Buddy Christian, bjo; Clarence Todd, vocal on *

New York, December 22, 1924

9246	Nobody Knows the Way I Feel Dis Mornin'	Ge 5626, ST 123
9247-A	Early Every Morn	Ge 5626, ST 123
9248-A	Cake Walking Babies (from Home)*	Ge 5627

Note: all three recorded as Josephine Beatty

Acc by Perry Bradford's Mean Four: probably Bubber Miley, cor; Charlie Green, tbn; Don Redman, alt; Perry Bradford, pno

New York, December 11, 1925

73830-B	Your Jelly Roll Is Good	OK 8268, ST 123
73831-B	Take That Thing Away	OK 8268, ST 123

Acc by Perry Bradford's Mean Four: unknown tpt,* tbn, clt; presumably Perry Bradford, pno

New York, January 8, 1926

73903-B	Everybody Does It Now	OK 8278
73904-B	A Master Man With a Master Mind*	OK 8278
73905-B	Don't Want It All	OK 8315

Note: Alberta confirmed this recording date but called 73905-B "Gimme Some of What You're Sitting On." This may be a substitute title or the most memorable line from the song.

Acc by unknown cor; clt/alt; pno

New York, January 14, 1926

73919-B	I'm Hard to Satisfy	OK 8294, ST 123
73920-B	Empty Cellar Blues	OK 8315
73921-B	Double Crossin' Papa	OK 8294, ST 123

Acc by Clarence Williams, pno

New York, August 16, 1926

74252-A	If You Can't Hold the Man You Love (Don't Cry When He's Gone)	OK 8365, ST 123
74253-A	You for Me, Me for You	OK 8365

Acc by Jimmy Wade, cor; "Gus" (last name not listed by Alberta), pno

New York, August 26, 1926

74322-B	I'm Tired Blues	OK 8409
74323-B	Wasn't It Nice?	OK 8393
74324-A	I Didn't Come to Steal Nobody's Man	OK 8393
74325-B	Everybody Mess Around	OK 8383

Acc by Luckeyth Roberts, pno

New York, August 27, 1926

Baby Mine	OK Unissued
Sweet Papa Makes All Hard Roads Easy	OK Unissued

Acc by Perry Bradford's Mean Four; Jimmy Wade, cor; unknown tbn, clt and bjo

New York, September 1, 1926

74333-A	Don't Forget to Mess Around	OK 8409
74334-B	Heebie Jeebies	OK 8383

Alberta Hunter is said to have recorded at least three sides for Vocalion (presumably in Chicago) late in 1926. The first two titles were accompanied by King Oliver, cor, and Lil Armstrong, pno, and the third by a group that included Johnny Dodds, clt. These sides were apparently never issued:

Dead Man Blues
Someday, Sweetheart
Don't Pan Me When I'm Gone

Vocal acc by Mike Jackson, pno

Camden, N.J., February 26, 1927

37688-2	I'll Forgive You 'Cause I Love You (but the Wrongs You've Done I Can't Forgive)	Vi 20497
37689-2	I'm Gonna Lose Myself 'Way Down in Louisville	Vi 20497
37690-2	My Old Daddy's Got a Brand-New Way to Love	Vi 20651
37691-2	I'm Down Right Now but I Won't Be Down Always	Vi 20651

Acc by Fats Waller, pipe organ

Camden, N.J., May 20, 1927

m 38045-2	Sugar	Vi 20771

| m 38046-2 | Beale Street Blues | Vi 20771 |
| 38048-2 | I'm Going to See My Ma | Vi 21539, ST 123 |

Acc by unknown pno; gtr

New York, July 18, 1929

| 148822-2 | Gimme All the Love You Got | Co 14450-D, ST 123 |
| 148823-3 | My Particular Man | Co 14450-D |

The next twelve sides were all recorded in London in the fall of 1934 with Jack Jackson's Orchestra at the Dorchester Hotel. Acc by Jack Jackson, Harry Macfarlane, Freddy Mann, tpts; Eric Tann, Tony Thorpe, tbns; Dave Esher, Colly Eisner, vlns; E. O. Pogson, clt/alt/flt; Noel ("Chappie") D'Amato, alt/gtr; Stan Andrews, alt/vln; Allan Warner, clt/ts/ob; Harry Rubens, pno; Tiny Stock, bbs; and Percy Hampton, dms.

September 24, 1934

| OEA 618-2 | Two Cigarettes in the Dark | HMV 6525, DRG 5195 |
| OEA 619-2 | Miss Otis Regrets (She's Unable to Lunch Today) | HMV 6525, DRG 5195 |

October 12, 1934

| OEA 641-2 | Soon | HMV 6530, DRG 5195 |
| OEA 642 | Where the Mountains Meet the Sea | HMV 6529, DRG 5195 |

October 22, 1934

OEA 649-2	A Lonely Singing Fool	HMV 6536, DRG 5195
OEA 650-2	Have A Little Dream on Me	HMV 6537
OEA 651-2	What Shall I Do?	HMV 6536, DRG 5195

October 25, 1934

| OEA 654-2 | I Travel Alone | HMV 6535, DRG 5195 |

October 31, 1934

OEA 662-2	Two Little Flies on a Lump of Sugar	HMV 6541, DRG 5195
OEA 663-1	Stars Fell on Alabama	HMV 6542, DRG 5195
OEA 664-2	Long May We Love	HMV 6542, DRG 5195

November 2, 1934

| OEA 666-3 | Be Still My Heart | HMV 6546, DRG 5195 |

Acc by unknown pno, gtr

New York, March 20, 1935

TO-1526-1	Driftin' Tide	ARC unissued
TO-1527-1	You Can't Tell the Difference After Dark	ARC unissued, STASH 115
TO-1528-1	Second Hand Man	ARC unissued, STASH 115
TO-1529-1	Send Me a Man	ARC unissued, STASH 115

Acc by Charlie Shavers, tpt; Buster Bailey, clt; Lil Armstrong, pno; Wellman Braud, bbs

New York, August 15, 1939

66104-A	Chirpin' the Blues	De 7644
66105-A	Down Hearted Blues	De 7727, ST 115
66106-A	I'll See You Go	De 7644, ST 115
66107-A	Fine and Mellow	De 7633, ST 115
66108-A	Yelpin' the Blues	De 7633, ST 115
66109-A	Someday, Sweetheart	De 7727, ST 115

Note: Some copies of De 7633 are labeled "Yelping Blues."

Acc by Eddie Heywood, Jr., pno

New York, June 3, 1940

051210-1	The Love I Have for You	BB B8539, ST 115
051211-1	My Castle's Rockin'	BB B8539, ST 115
051212-1	Boogie-Woogie Swing	BB B8485, ST 115
051213-1	I Won't Let You Down	BB B8485, ST 115

Acc by Leroy Jones, clt; Sam Clanton, pno; Al Casey, gtr; Al Matthews, bbs

New York, August 26, 1946

. . . . .	Take Your Big Hands Off	JB-510, ST 115
. . . . .	He's Got a Punch Like Joe Louis	ST 115
. . . . .	Don't Want No Man That's Lazy	JB-511
. . . . .	Your Bread May Be Good, but It Ain't as Good as Mine	

Acc by Budd Johnson, ts; Howard Biggs, pno; Al Casey, gtr; Thomas Barney, bbs; Bud Johnson, ts; Gene Brooks, dms

Linden, N.J., January 11, 1950

1158	Midnight Blues	Regal 3252
. . . . .	The Man I Love Is Gone	Regal 3276
. . . . .	Reckless Blues	Regal 3276
1160	I Got a Mind to Ramble	Regal 3252

Unknown acc

New York, March 26, 1952

. . . . . .	I Want to Thank You Lord	W-4207
. . . . . .	You Got to Reap Just What You Sow	W-4208

Acc by Buster Bailey, clt; J.C. Higginbotham, tbn; Cliff Jackson, pno; Sidney De Paris, tb; Zutty Singleton, dms

Chicago, August 16, 1961

308	I Got a Mind to Ramble	BV 1052

309	I Got Myself a Workin' Man	BV 1052
310	Chirpin' the Blues	BV 1052
311	You Gotta Reap Just What You Sow	BV 1052

Acc by Lovie Austin's Blues Serenaders: Jimmy Archey, tbn; Darnell Howard, clt; Pops Foster, bbs; Jasper Taylor, dms; Lovie Austin, pno

Chicago, September 1, 1961

312	Down Hearted Blues	RLP 418
313	Moanin' Low	RLP 418
314	You Better Change	RLP 418
315	Now I'm Satisfied	RLP 418
316	I Will Always Be in Love with You	RLP 418
317	Streets Paved with Gold	RLP 418
318	St. Louis Blues	RLP 418

Acc by Al Hall, bbs; Connie Kay, dms; Jackie Williams, dms on "Chirpin' the Blues" and "I Begged and Begged You"; Wally Richardson, gtr; Vic Dickenson, tbn; Doc Cheatham, tpt; Budd Johnson, ts/clt; Gerald Cook, pno

New York, December 27, 1977

AL 35553-1D	Workin' Man (a/k/a I Got Myself a Working Man)	(Columbia) JS 35553
AL 35553-1D	You Reap Just What You Sow	JS 35553
AL 35553-1D	The Love I Have for You	JS 35553
AL 35553-1D	I've Got a Mind to Ramble	JS 35553
AL 35553-1D	Remember My Name	JS 35553
BL 35553-1A	My Castle's Rockin'	JS 35553
BL 35553-1A	Down Hearted Blues	JS 35553
BL 35553-1A	Some Sweet Day	JS 35553
BL 35553-1A	Chirpin' the Blues	JS 35553
BL 35553-1A	I Begged and Begged You	JS 35553

Acc by Aaron Bell, bbs; Billy Butler, gtr; Jackie Williams, dms; Vic Dickenson, tbn; Doc Cheatham, tpt (first session only); Frank Wess, ts/flt (second session only); Norris Turney, ts; Gerald Cook, pno

New York, December 17, 1979

(Columbia)

AL-36430	Nobody Knows You When You're Down and Out	JC 36430
AL-36430	Always	JC 36430
AL-36430	My Handy Man Ain't Handy No More	JC 36430
BL-36430	Old Fashioned Love	JC 36430
BL-36430	Sweet Georgia Brown	JC 36430

New York, January 8, 1980

AL-36430	I'm Having a Good Time	JC 36430

AL-36430	The Darktown Strutters' Ball	JC 36430
BL-36430	Amtrak Blues	JC 36430
BL-36430	A Good Man Is Hard to Find	JC 36430
BL-36430	I've Got a Mind to Ramble	JC 36430

Acc by Jimmy Lewis, bbs; Billy Butler, gtr; Butch Miles, dms; Vic Dickenson, tbn; Doc Cheatham, tpt; Budd Johnson, ts; Gerald Cook, pno

New York, July 28, 1981

(Columbia)

AL 37691-1A	Ezekiel Saw the Wheel	FC 37691
AL 37691-1A	I've Had Enough	FC 37691
AL 37691-1A	Wrap Your Troubles in Dreams	FC 37691
AL 37691-1A	Some of These Days	FC 37691
AL 37691-1A	The Glory of Love	FC 37691
BL 37691-1A	You Can't Tell the Difference After Dark	FC 37691
BL 37691-1A	I Love You Much Too Much (Ich Hob Dich Tzufil Lieb)	FC 37691
BL 37691-1A	I Cried for You	FC 37691
BL 37691-1A	The Love I Have for You	FC 37691
BL 37691-1A	Sometimes I'm Happy	FC 37691
BL 37691-1A	Give Me That Old Time Religion	FC 37691

Acc by Vishnu Wood, bbs; Billy Butler, gtr; Butch Miles, dms; Vic Dickenson, tbn; Dock Cheatham and Jonah Jones, tpts; Gerald Cook, pno; Jimmy Lewis, bbs in "Without Rhythm"; Frank Anderson, org, and Lincoln Clapp, tbm, in "Now I'm Satisfied"

New York, June 13, 1983

(Columbia)

AL-38970	Without Rhythm	FC 38970
AL-38970	Look for the Silver Lining	FC 38970
AL-38970	Now I'm Satisfied	FC 38970
BL-38970	He's Funny That Way	FC 38970

New York, June 17, 1983

AL-38970	Georgia on My Mind	FC 38970
BL-38970	Black Man	FC 38970
BL-38970	On the Sunny Side of the Street	FC 38970
BL-38970	Somebody Told Me So	FC 38970

New York, June 24, 1983

| BL-38970 | Somebody Loves Me | FC 38970 |

New York, 1983

| Al-38970 | J'ai Deux Amours | FC 38970 |

This discography is based on information found in Alberta Hunter's archives and in the following sources: (1) *Blues and Gospel Records 1902–1943* compiled by

Robert M. Dixon and John Godrich, 3d ed. (Chigwell, Essex, England: Storyville Publications and Co., 1982); (2) *Jazz Records 1897–1942*, compiled by Brian Rust (London: Storyville Publications and Co., 1969); (3) *Jazz Records 1897–1942*, compiled by Brian Rust, 4th rev. ed., 1978 (New Rochelle, N.Y.: Arlington House Publishers, 1978); (4) *Jazz Records 1942–1967*, edited by Jorgen Grunnet Jepsen (Copenhagen: Karl Emil Knudsen, 1969).

VIDEOGRAPHY

===== // =====

Alberta Hunter

Alberta Hunter: Jazz at the Smithsonian
  (A Video LP release of the Sony Corporation—catalogue # Jo065,
copyright 1982)
Acc by Jimmy Lewis, bbs; Gerald Cook, pno

> *My Castle's Rockin'*
> *Down Hearted Blues*
> *Handy Man*
> *When You're Smiling*
> *Nobody Knows You When You're Down and Out*
> *Without Rhythm*
> *Without a Song*
> *Darktown Strutters Ball*
> *Rough and Ready Man*
> *Time Waits for No One*
> *Black Man*
> *You Can't Tell the Difference After Dark*
> *Remember My Name*

INDEX